Americanism"[3], represent the second approach (not just Donald Trump but also *de facto* Bernie Sanders). It may be that the first wall the new president will build will be one dividing the Atlantic. President Obama's visit to the UK in spring 2016 and his desire to conclude the US trade agreement with the EU as a whole, rather than the bloc without UK, seems to be a positive indicator. It is also a kind of support for European integration in its present form. At the same time, the price of the UK remaining in the EU can be weakening of the union, and it is hard to believe that a weak partner will manage to get significant concessions from the Americans. In the 20th century, the United States in defending its own and universal values also defended Europe against the threat of totalitarianism, against which Europe was unable to defend itself. At the same time, the United States did not use the post-Cold War "peace dividend" to the extent that the EU has. "Old Europe" still wants to enjoy the highest level of security without paying for it while constantly reviving resentment about Europe's standing in the world and the way it achieves its objectives by seeking the independence of Europe and a distancing from the United States. On the other hand, Europe's buying and exchanging dollars co-financed a "stupid war"—the American intervention in Vietnam and bore the costs of American ineptitude east of Aden. The EU and the US resemble an old married couple. It is easy to point out the growing differences between the partners, which are derived from a variety of conditions in which they live. It is equally easy to point to potential, attractive new partners or new alliances. For the US it has become the "pivot to Asia" while for the EU there is the never-ending story of the hope for Russia's Europeanisation. However, it seems that what speaks for bracing and deepening transatlantic relations is that despite some achievements and a yearning, new alliances are a mirage. The hopes and fears of the TTIP's economic effects form a mirror. Supporters see the expected benefits. After all, free trade has been and remains a source of wealth for countries and societies. The opposition talks about the dangers that the TTIP carries. They fear that not only will they not see the benefits of the TTIP, but also that they may lose their sense of "ownership". Paradoxically, it can be concluded that if the TTIP enters into force, both predictions will prove correct. In recent years, on both sides of the Atlantic, there is increasing social stratification. Even if income in absolute numbers is not reduced (or even, as in the CEEC, if it grows significantly), the relative differences in income, education, health, life expectancy projections, participation in culture, policy impact, etc. will increase. These changes are in conflict with traditional society and traditional social divisions.

3 For more on the "Jacksonian tradition", see: Mead (2009, pp. 3–29).

President Obama can be (and is for some among the masses of highly educated new Americans – descendants of immigrants)[4] illustration and proof of the American dream, for those "(constantly) losing". This includes workers who fell victim to job relocations, and farmers – victims of progress in agricultural production and processing techniques, who believe the adage "once a loser, always a loser." The enthusiasm in Europe that accompanied the candidacy and the beginnings of the Obama presidency and the fact that American society has never been as divided as it is today shows the essence of the phenomenon. On the one hand, the virtual Atlantic bridge is the axiological community of values—a "(political) gentlemen's club"—but on the other, the divergence of the public over transatlantic progress is swaying its foundations. Supporters of the Atlantic community can only hope that it will survive the test of the deepening economic dimension, i.e., the result of the TTIP negotiations will not diminish the allies in case of failure, or that the agreement on implementation would transform EU-US transatlantic relations in a one-way street.

The diversity and complexity of all the above problems is reflected in this book. Its dominant part is prepared in the framework of the project funded by National Science Centre of Poland based on decision DEC-2013/09/B/HS4/01488. The book consists of eighteen chapters, each concerning a different aspect of the TTIP. Chapters 1–5 can be regarded as the first part of the book, focused on the general aspects of the TTIP while the next thirteen chapters (6–18) are devoted to very specific areas. Among them are four chapters dealing with the effects of the TTIP on Poland's trade in goods and services (each taking into account different aspects and methods).

Chapter 1 (*The Transatlantic Trade and Investment Partnership and International Security System*, written by Elżbieta Czarny and Jerzy Menkes) provides an analysis of the possible impact of TTIP on the international security system. The authors reach the conclusion that closer economic cooperation between the EU and the US would supplement their political alliance. Moreover, it would allow both parties to increase their impact on the global economic order, including non-discriminatory liberalisation of economic cooperation within the framework of WTO.

4 This is illustrated by the biographies of two of the senators who were presidential candidates as well as other public figures. Ted Cruz is the son of a political dissident who left communist Cuba and is also a graduate of Harvard Law School. Marco Rubio, too, is a descendent of Cuban immigrants and a law school graduate. Jerry Yang came from Taipei and Sergey Brin is from Russia. They are co-creators of Yahoo and Google and are now billionaires.

Chapter 2 (*Regional Trade Agreements of the EU and the US—what is the Common Ground,* by Magdalena Słok-Wódkowska) is a comparison of RTAs concluded by the EU and the US. The content and legal enforceability of such trade agreements is analysed in detail in order to find the differences in philosophies of concluding RTAs by both parties of the TTIP. It allows for formulating some predictions concerning the future of the TTIP.

The importance of regulatory differences is also reflected in Chapter 3 (*Regulatory Cooperation Under the TTIP. If You Can Read This, You're Too Close,* by Marcin Menkes) which concentrates on regulatory actions within the TTIP framework.

Chapter 4 (*Geographical Indications in the US-EU TTIP Negotiations,* by Dominika Bochańczyk-Kupka) is devoted to geographical indications. This is an area that so far has turned out to be a difficult one in which to reach consensus. There are many reasons for this difficulty, such as the differences in the European and American legal systems for protecting GIs, the historical background of such protection, and differences between the public and private approaches towards this protection. Such analysis provides an explanation of where the negotiation positions of both parties come from and allows some predictions about finding a common position.

A discussion on the rights of foreign investors in disputes with states (and vice versa) is found in Chapter 5 (*ISDS and the TTIP—A Polish Perspective,* by Jerzy Menkes and Magdalena Słok-Wódkowska), which presents the Polish and other Central and Eastern European states' point of view on this issue. The authors describe problems that seem to be caused by ISDS as well as possible ways of solving them.

In Chapter 6 (*Will Polish Exports Be Affected by Trade Diversion Resulting from the Transatlantic Trade and Investment Partnership?,* by Elżbieta Czarny, Paweł Folfas and Katarzyna Śledziewska) offers an analysis of the potential impact of the TTIP on Poland's position on the EU market and its potential losses in favour of American goods. The authors claim that the trade diversion effect will be limited to a few groups of commodities, as the structures of the Polish and American exports to the EU differs significantly.

An evaluation of tariff and non-tariff barriers in the bilateral trade of the EU member states and the United States is carried out in Chapter 7 (*Trade Barriers in Services and Merchandise Trade in the Context of the TTIP: Poland, EU and the United States,* by Jan Hagemejer and Katarzyna Śledziewska). The authors use a gravity framework and find out that in merchandise trade, the tariff equivalent of non-tariff barriers is at least twice the level of the tariffs. Moreover, non-tariff

barriers in services trade tend to be higher than those in merchandise trade. Sectoral and country differences are pointed out as well.

Chapter 8 (*Liberalization of Trade Flows under the TTIP from a Small Country Perspective. The Case of Poland*, by Jan Hagemejer) provides a comprehensive evaluation of possible TTIP effects on the Polish economy using a computable general equilibrium model. The results of empirical *ex ante* evaluations suggest a large heterogeneity of the TTIP impact on individual countries. In the case of Poland, simultaneous trade liberalisation with a third partner is not expected to bring sizeable gains to its economy. The authors also observe that the US-EU-15 trade expansion is crowding out some trade in a few important Polish trading sectors.

Chapter 9 (*How Can the TTIP Affect the Polish economy. A Study Based on Input-Output Tables*, by Michał Przybyliński) assesses the possible effects of a reduction of non-tariff barriers to trade between the EU and the US resulting from the TTIP on changes in production and the number of employees in Poland. The input-output table is used to supplement estimates delivered in an earlier paper based on the GTAP model.

Chapter 10 (*The Potential Effects of the TTIP on Polish Exports to the United States*, by Bożena Pera) discusses changes that may occur in the structure of Polish exports to the US, compared with selected countries of Central and Eastern Europe. Using several methods (e.g., agglomerative clustering, the Canberra metric), the author compares the structure of CEE exports and US imports and concludes with the statement that the future free-trade zone between the European Union and the United States will not contribute to major changes in the export structure of Poland and other analysed countries.

The sensitivity of talks in the energy sector is underlined in the following two chapters. Chapter 11 (*The Potential Impact of Transatlantic Trade and Investment Partnership on Crude Oil and Distillates' Trade between the US and the EU, with Implications for Poland*, by Andrzej P. Sikora, Stanisław Cios, Marcin Krupa, Adam Szurlej and Rafał Jarosz) focuses on the oil sector and particularly on the dynamics of this sector in the US and the possible influence on the future trade pattern with the EU. Some other aspects related to the oil trade, such as refined products, are discussed in this chapter as well.

The next part, Chapter 12 (*Energy in the Transatlantic Trade and Investment Partnership—the Domestic Perspective*, by Honorata Nyga-Łukaszewska), presents the situation with the Polish energy market in 2014. In order to see exactly where the TTIP's potential lies, the author takes a closer look at the country's primary energy balance, broken down by the different fuel types (coal, oil, gas and renewables production/consumption).

The next three chapters deal with specific issues such as research and development, ICT, and public health, from the perspective of cooperation between the US and the EU. Anna Odrobina, the author of Chapter 13, entitled *The European Union as the United States' Partner in Research and Development Cooperation*, confirms that the US and the EU are still the most important mutual partners in terms of R&D cooperation but that they both are more actively involved in projects in other parts of the world. As a result, the EU's position as the US's main partner in this field is weakening.

Chapter 14 (*Trade in ICT Services Between the EU and The US in the Context of the TTIP*, by Sylwia Talar) concentrates on ICT services. The EU has a deficit in trade with the US in this sector, but widespread usage of ICT can bring positive effects in terms of economic development.

The third specific area, analysed in Chapter 15 (*Concerns Over TTIP Regarding Public Health*, by Katarzyna Byszek) is public health. Controversies over TTIP negotiations in this field are presented, especially those related to regulatory differences between the parties and the accusations of a lack of transparency during the consultation process.

The last three chapters give a more general overview of TTIP as they discuss regions of the EU, US trade deals and development-policy issues.

Chapter 16 (*Regions in the United States and the European Union in 21st Century—Wealth of Citizens, Convergence Processes and Spatial Dependencies*, by Paweł Folfas) aims to find out whether absolute income beta-convergence exists in the case of regions of the United States and of the EU-28 during the period 2000–2011. The research is based on econometric models (the spatial lagged model, or SLM, spatial error model, or SEM, and the Durbin spatial model).

Chapter 17 (*Trade Deals with the US. What Can We Learn from the Aussie Case?*, by Bartosz Michalski) uses the case of the free trade agreement concluded between the United States and Australia (AUSFTA) in order to point out some possible trade effects and political controversies during the currently negotiated US-EU agreement. Some practical aspects for Polish stakeholders are also identified.

The last part, Chapter 18 (*The TTIP and Banana Trade from the Aspect of Policy Coherence for Development*, by Julianna Pontet and Beata Udvari), is devoted to the development impacts of the TTIP, i.e. the effects of the agreement on developing countries. Here, the banana trade is investigated. The main conclusion is that the European Union should pay special attention to making TTIP development friendly to avoid endangering the interests of the ACP countries.

We hope that this book contributes to a better understanding of various aspects of the TTIP and, more broadly, the transatlantic ties and their global context.

References:

Kagan R., 2003, *Of Paradise and Power: America and Europe in the New Order*, Alfred A. Knopf, New York

Mead W. R., 2009, *Special Providence: American Foreign Policy and How It Changed the World* Routledge, New York

Elżbieta Czarny, Jerzy Menkes (Warsaw School of Economics)

Chapter 1. The Transatlantic Trade and Investment Partnership and the International Security System

This chapter[1] presents an analysis of the specificity of the Transatlantic Trade and Investment Partnership (TTIP) as a discriminatory liberalisation agreement (after WTO, such agreements are called RTAs, Regional Trading Agreements) between the EU and the US. We stress that the importance of the TTIP goes beyond the economy, affecting the internal social and political systems of its signatories as well as the global agenda. We contrast the TTIP with another agreement, the Trans-Pacific Partnership (TPP), which the US negotiated with Asian countries. We analyse feedback on the TTIP negotiations concerning the regional and universal dimensions of security. We are of the opinion that closer economic cooperation between the EU and the US rationally complements their political and defence alliance. Such cooperation is currently in particular demand given the situation of an international security gap as revealed by Russia's expansionist policy, the European migration crisis, and general instability in the world.

1. US policy towards Europe and Asia after WWII

After WWII, the US pursued national interest defined by a declared ideology[2] and applied with various methods to its politics (Hass 1995, p. 50). In particular, US leadership and neo-internationalism were applied[3]. The method of choice was voluntary and reactive to violence and the lack of respect for law in the world. The choice resulted also from a cost-benefit estimate as wells as the possibilities and

---

1 The project is funded by the National Science Centre of Poland based on decision No. DEC-2013/09/B/HS4/01488.

2 See: Mauk, Oakland (1999). Earlier, in 1970, R. Williams formulated the catalogue of fundamental American values, listing them as: "Equal Opportunity, Achievement and Success, Material Comfort, Activity and Work, Practicality and Efficiency, Progress, Science, Democracy and Enterprise, Freedom" (after Macionis 2005, p. 66).

3 For more, see: Apodaca (2006, p. 149). A policy of neo-internationalism does not exclude either unilateralism or leadership, or their combinations in individual cases.

needs shaped significantly by both current developments and the international order, but not those solely influenced by the US.

The applied politics had also been determined by the US's perceived values and its concept of international relations. Its approach to international institutions was specifically ideological so that active American participation in their operations as well as in their use was a tool of US politics (for more on institutional liberalism, see: Keohane 1989, p. 4). US political preferences, starting with the choice not to accede to the League of Nations, through the imposition of a non-ultimate character to Article 5 of the Washington Treaty, to its cautious approach to humanitarian intervention and responsibility to protect (R2P), echo Old English moderation with permanent alliances. The US, and in particular its legislative branch, is reluctant to adopt *in blanco* commitments. It definitely prefers cooperation based on a case-by-case[4] assessment. This is a serious challenge for both the US and the rest of the world when options and prospects for operations of international institutions have been related to the US's choice of neo-internationalism. This strategy allows using any organisation or institutionalised form of international cooperation co-created by the US as needs arise to implement values identified with the 'purpose and principles' of the UN Charter. Concurrently, the strategy adopted by the US[5] means that the hyperpower[6] may selectively use the complete range of policy-making instruments[7]. As part of leadership policy, the US heads alliances and organisations as well as informal coalitions. In policy execution, the

4 PM Lord Palmerston expressed that clearly in his House of Commons speech (1 March 1848): "We have no eternal allies, and we have no perpetual enemies. Our interests are eternal and perpetual, and those interests it is our duty to follow", see: Hansard's Parliamentary Debates, August 1891, 3 series, vol. 97, col. 122. These preferences underlined Great Britain's non-inclusion to institutionalized cooperation during the Congress of Vienna.

5 The US resorted to similar methods as a superpower in the bipolar world.

6 A hyperpower is "a country that is dominant or predominant in all categories … this domination of attitudes, concepts, language and modes of life"—the definition was coined by the French Minister of Foreign Affairs Hubert Vedrine in his speech to the Association France-Ameriques in February 1999 (quoted from: "The New York Times", 1999.02.05). Hyperpower status means a complete range of dominance, which distinguishes it from the USSR and the US, one attributed to their military potential during the Cold War period.

7 Among the positive practices of the American neo-internationalism, implementation policy is, among others, the ability of many international organizations to effect operations, such as the UN Security Council's actions regarding Haiti or the UN and NATO's actions regarding Bosnia and Herzegovina, as well as the response of, for example,

The TTIP presents both an opportunity and a challenge. For the negotiating parties, it is a chance to improve their position in the world economy and in politics as well as in international organisations. It can give impulse to accelerate non-discriminatory liberalisation negotiations. It can create new standards in regional trading agreements (RTAs) and, more generally, in international economic relations. For Europe, facing many problems (migration, the possibility of Brexit and Grexit, contradictions among the euro-area members as well as between them and the rest of the EU, economic inefficiency, overregulation and bureaucracy), the TTIP can be a chance to push the EU economy forward. For the least efficient industries, or even entire national economies, the TTIP, however, can represent the threat of losing the game. These threats are present especially among the new member states (NMS) from Central and Eastern Europe. Most of them are post-communist countries starting their way toward democracy and market economy as late as in 1990. They are lagging behind in terms of technology, and their economies still have relatively traditional structures based (at least partly) on agriculture and food processing.

From the very beginning of the TTIP negotiations, the political consensus during treaty-making (*pacta de contrahendo*) seemed obvious. Threats were expected in the details. The reality painfully verified these predictions. On all specific issues, the negotiators seem to work out compromises and real differences appear to be smaller than their perception. However, with regard to the fundamental question, which is, either acceptance or rejection of the fact that there exists a transatlantic economic space, it is difficult to predict the decisions of either the EU or the US. It cannot also be stated *ex ante* to what extent the two negotiating sides are willing to compromise or, rather, believe they can persuade the partner towards their views and proposals. However, with the TTIP negotiations started, it is very difficult to return empty-handed and continue the previous relationship as if nothing has happened. The possible loss of image would be very costly. It is logical that failure would weaken the transatlantic link. It seems also that the threats to the TTIP are not transatlantic but specifically European and American. In Europe, this concerns the previously mentioned problems, but the most important one is the controversy, among others, with the new member states about European values. All of the problems, though, shake the very foundations of the European project. It may be that we will not be participants in the process of deepening integration (as in the TEU, "This Treaty marks a new stage in the process of creating an ever closer union among the peoples of Europe") but in its demise. The candidates in the US presidential election (with the exception of Hillary Clinton), in an internal dispute between "Wilsonian internationalism" and "Jacksonian

Elżbieta Czarny, Andżelika Kuźnar, Jerzy Menkes

Introduction

"Men are from Mars, Women are from Venus[1]"—this sentence, when taken for granted, points to the supposed fundamental nature and essence of the differences between the sexes. At the same time, it indicates that the source and core of these differences lies in the culture, because the natural differences are recognized as *la petite différence*. What makes women and men destined for each other is nature, and it is nature that forces relationships. "Americans are from Mars, Europeans are from Venus"[2]—here as well, the essence of the differences lies in culture. But nature does not force a relationship between these different "species". The Atlantic is a reality and, regardless of universal cohesion and globalisation, Americans and Europeans are not "doomed" by nature to form a relationship. The size of the socio-politico-economic gap between them depends solely on their political decisions. The *security community*—NATO—was to make (and has made) war between Germany and the rest of the West impossible. At the same time, this *community* was not meant to create anything new inside the old West, that is, among the Allies of World War I and II. The aim was to maintain ties and to prevent neo-isolationism.

The 21st century has resulted in an unprecedented expansion of the transatlantic space to include new countries. There was significant multi-dimensional convergence within both Europe and the framework of the transatlantic community. At the same time, these processes have been accompanied by a deepening division between "the West" and "the Rest". It seems logical to give the Transatlantic Trade and Investment Partnership (TTIP) a try to eliminate the different depths of the transatlantic bonds and bring the relations within the sphere of the economy to such a level of advancement as is present in the areas of policy and security.

The TTIP is not the first approach to a cooperation agreement between the EU and the US. For example, in the first decade of the 21st century, there was the "Merkel's Plan". At the same time, economic relations between the EU and the US are, with or without the TTIP, very intensive.

---

1 The title of a popular family therapy handbook by J. Gray.

2 This statement is the starting point of Kagan's concept of different routes, followed (from at least a quarter of a century) by the US and EU (see: Kagan 2003).

Bożena Pera
Chapter 10. The Potential Effects of the TTIP on Polish and other CEEC Exports to the United States 153

Andrzej P. Sikora, Stanisław Cios, Marcin Krupa, Adam Szurlej, Rafał Jarosz
Chapter 11. The potential impact of the Transatlantic Trade and Investment Partnership on crude oil and distillates' trade between the US and the EU, with implications for Poland 169

Honorata Nyga-Łukaszewska
Chapter 12. Energy in the Transatlantic Trade and Investment Partnership – the Domestic Perspective 183

Anna Odrobina
Chapter 13. The European Union as the United States' Partner in Research and Development Cooperation 195

Sylwia Talar
Chapter 14. Trade in ICT Services Between the EU and the US in the Context of the TTIP 209

Katarzyna Byszek
Chapter 15. Concerns over the TTIP Regarding Public Health 221

Paweł Folfas
Chapter 16. Regions in the United States and European Union in the 21st Century – Wealth of Citizens, Convergence Processes and Spatial Dependencies 233

Bartosz Michalski
Chapter 17. Trade Deals with the US. What Can We Learn from the Aussie Case? 243

Julianna Pontet, Beata Udvari
Chapter 18. The TTIP and Banana Trade from the Aspect of Policy Coherence for Development 257

Elżbieta Czarny, Andżelika Kuźnar, Jerzy Menkes
Instead of conclusions 267

Table of Contents

Elżbieta Czarny, Andżelika Kuźnar, Jerzy Menkes
Introduction 7

Elżbieta Czarny, Jerzy Menkes
Chapter 1. The Transatlantic Trade and Investment Partnership and the International Security System 15

Magdalena Słok-Wódkowska
Chapter 2. Regional Trade Agreements of the EU and the US — What Is the Common Ground? 33

Marcin Menkes
Chapter 3. Regulatory Cooperation Under the TTIP. If You Can Read This, You're Too Close 55

Dominika Bochańczyk-Kupka
Chapter 4. Geographical Indications in the US-EU TTIP negotiations 65

Jerzy Menkes, Magdalena Słok-Wódkowska
Chapter 5. ISDS and the TTIP—A Polish Perspective 77

Elżbieta Czarny, Paweł Folfas, Katarzyna Śledziewska
Chapter 6. Will Polish Exports Be Affected by Trade Diversion Resulting from the Transatlantic Trade and Investment Partnership? 89

Jan Hagemejer, Katarzyna Śledziewska
Chapter 7. Trade Barriers in Services and Merchandise Trade in the Context of the TTIP: Poland, the EU and the United States 101

Jan Hagemejer
Chapter 8. Liberalization of trade flows under the TTIP from a small country perspective. The case of Poland 117

Michał Przybyliński
Chapter 9. How Can the TTIP Affect the Polish Economy. A Study Based on Input-Output Tables 143

Bibliographic Information published by the Deutsche Nationalbibliothek
The Deutsche Nationalbibliothek lists this publication in the Deutsche Nationalbibliografie; detailed bibliographic data is available in the internet at http://dnb.d-nb.de.

Library of Congress Cataloging-in-Publication Data
Names: Czarny, Elżbieta, editor. | Kuźnar, Andżelika, editor. | Menkes, Jerzy, editor.
Title: The impact of the Transatlantic Trade and Investment Partnership on international cooperation / Elżbieta Czarny, Andżelika Kuźnar, Jerzy Menkes (eds.).
Description: Frankfurt am Main ; New York : Peter Lang, [2017] | Series: Polish studies in economics, ISSN 2191-8848 ; Vol. 8
Identifiers: LCCN 2016052509 | ISBN 9783631678558
Subjects: LCSH: Transatlantic Trade and Investment Partnership. | United States—Foreign economic relations—European Union countries. | European Union countries—Foreign economic relations—United States. | United States—Foreign relations. | European Union countries—Foreign relations. | International trade—Political aspects.
Classification: LCC HF1456.5.E8 I49 2017 | DDC 382.0973/04—dc23
LC record available at https://lccn.loc.gov/2016052509

This project is funded by National Science Centre of Poland
on the basis of the decision Nr DEC-2013/09/B/HS4/01488.

NATIONAL SCIENCE CENTRE
POLAND

ISSN 2191-8848
ISBN 978-3-631-67855-8 (Print)
E-ISBN 978-3-653-06972-3 (E-PDF)
E-ISBN 978-3-631-70262-8 (EPUB)
E-ISBN 978-3-631-70263-5 (MOBI)
DOI 10.3726/978-3-653-06972-3

PL Academic Research is an Imprint of Peter Lang GmbH.

Peter Lang – Frankfurt am Main · Bern · Bruxelles · New York ·
Oxford · Warszawa · Wien

This publication has been peer reviewed.

www.peterlang.com

Elżbieta Czarny / Andżelika Kuźnar / Jerzy Menkes (eds.)

The Impact of the Transatlantic Trade and Investment Partnership on International Cooperation

PL ACADEMIC RESEARCH

Polish Studies in Economics

Edited by Ryszard Kokoszczyński

Volume 8

PL ACADEMIC RESEARCH

The Impact of the Transatlantic Trade and Investment Partnership on International Cooperation

US not only shares with its partners the obligations and costs of actions but also preliminarily accepts their policy and neutralises opponents. The positive balance of American leadership practice includes both economic (e.g., NAFTA) as well as social and political activities (e.g., the US role in German reunification, peaceful resolution of the Northern Ireland conflict, operations within the 'Partnership for Peace' programme, as well as proceedings with Warsaw Pact member states, in particular the institutionalisation of cooperation after the bloc's breakup, that is, with Central and Eastern European states). The Korean Peninsula and the Middle East are the areas of implementation of leadership policy. American leadership is accomplished by activities promoting peaceful elimination of threats to international peace in South-East Asia and the Persian Gulf. Still, American leadership politics were first and foremost carried out during the Cold War.

After WWII, the US contributed to establishing the security community in Europe, having its stake in laying the foundations of European political and economic integrity and participating in building a system based on respect for fundamental human rights and freedoms, democracy, rule of law and a market economy. The system was supposed to be (and actually was) a strong counterbalance and, in substance, an antithesis to the Eastern Bloc marked by its members' dependency on the Soviet Union, political and economic centralism, and the lack of individual freedom.

The US inspired and supported cooperation among Western European countries and promoted institutionalisation of it. It was not incidental that Winston Churchill appealed for construction of the 'United States of Europe', neither that BENELUX, the first post-WWII European political and economic grouping, merged the closest US allies (Belgium and the Netherlands), while the OEEC[8], being the foundation of European reconstruction, was the implementation regime for the Marshall Plan. The US also set forth the concept of anchoring a free and democratic Germany in a free and democratic Europe, which for Germany became a security guardian and for Europe a warrant for the re-education of German society. This situation lasted until the end of the Cold War and the crumbling of the eastern bloc, at which time the US advocated the transformation of the Central and Eastern Europe countries and supported their desire to join the European and

organizations (such as NATO or the UN) and state-participants in the "Partnership for Peace" response to the terrorist attacks of 11 September 2001.

8 The OEEC (*Organisation for European Economic Co-operation*) was established in April 1948 in Paris to facilitate European economic reconstruction and cooperation with the US. Its successor, the OECD (*Organization for Economic Co-operation and Development*), commenced activity at the end of September 1961.

transatlantic institutions. The US also promoted the idea of the reunification of Germany, part of which had already been an important member of the West. Just Americans formulated the *consensus* under which the regime of the reunification of Germany was completed.

The European Communities' 'Founding Fathers' followed the desire to build a united Europe of a federational nature. This desire, however, did not stem from idealism and thinking in pan-European terms, but rather from a pragmatic desire to safeguard the continent against another war. Convinced that war is the effect of the simultaneous occurrence of nationalism and the economic marginalisation of European countries, in institutionalised cooperation they saw the only effective barrier to a self-propelling mechanism leading to war. They believed that cooperation and the geographic proximity of nations not separated by state boundaries would eradicate oppression and pave the way for unity. This European dream was clearly expressed by EEC Commission President Walter Halstein, when he said that the European Economic Community made war in Western Europe impossible (for more, see: Müller 2012, p. 2).

The European communities' construction was solely a tactical manoeuvre. Anticipating a political climate for creating a federation, the communities had to establish an economic foundation for its construction. States' integration which was focused on a sphere in which these States had a very limited presence was paradoxical. In a regular market economy, the state has the only regulatory power. So, the creation of the communities necessitated the formal development of a common market separated from the countries themselves. Political considerations enhanced this economically rational conduct. Political concerns devitalized the arguments of cooperation opponents. The choice of an institutionalized model of integration was pragmatic and, besides internal determinants, was taken with regard to geopolitical concerns.

US relations with states in Asia were much more complex. The atomic bombing of Hiroshima and Nagasaki in August 1945 left a mark for many years on US policy towards Japan as well as the Japanese perception of the US. Furthermore, until the outbreak of the Korean War in 1950, when the US unequivocally supported one party over the others, the US did not define its political strategy within Asia. At that time, the US implemented only global policy, under which there was a reference to Asia.

The lack of a US strategy for Asia did not change the presence of China among the major powers after WWII, as understood by the US. China's presence was *de facto* formal. The Great Powers wanted both to keep and demonstrate unity. For the second purpose, the presence of China as one of four co-chairs of the

UN-establishment conference was solely because of its importance in US policy during WWII[9].

Still, a uniform US policy to Asia was difficult to see, in contrast to Europe. Asia is a continent that is politically, culturally and religiously diverse. Its states differ economically, in particular with respect to their economic potential and development in terms of their inhabitants, which translated into a certain attractiveness as partners in international cooperation and their potential to participate in it. Whether there is a feedback loop between Europe's uniting and strengthening the transatlantic links, then the profound differences and conflicts dividing the Asian states did not allow for a similar community of interest to develop with the US.

The distinction in US policy towards Europe and Asia is influenced by the diversity of the European and Asian societies and is decisive when it comes to their involvement in international cooperation. We consider individualism in the transatlantic society and collectivism in Asia to be the most important difference. Thus, the social wisdom of a society developed by individuals with personal property and relative rights and freedoms is different from the patterns of authoritarian societies with depersonalised property. Furthermore, societies living in Europe and Asia have a dramatically different past and memory.

The lack of Asian cooperation institutions similar to those in the transatlantic area is not a coincidence. In this case, the institutionalization of Asian cooperation results predominantly from imitation, such as the legal and constitutional solutions dominant in the region. European models are willingly adopted, which may result from the multiplicity of experience across Europe and their selective adoption by Asian states.

The existing disparity in international relations favouring the US does not enhance the openness of Asian societies. Consequently, an imperial international order is constructed that does not prevent the appointment of Asian states or their participation in the establishment of organizations within the framework of American policy. The cooperation of Asian states and their participation in international cooperation, limited by political concerns, replicate cooperation methods and forms in fairly loosely affiliated international organizations of the forum type. However, the potential to build the institution into an actor in international relations is relatively low, as it requires a profound level of integration to which Asian countries have not consented or agreed.

9 At President Roosevelt's initiative, since 1942 the allied coalition included China, Great Britain and the USSR. This story continues also to China's permanent membership of the UN Security Council.

An important limitation of Asian state participation in cooperation (regional, trans-regional and global) is the disparity between a state's military coverage, even if global, and its economic and political impacts (*global reach* versus *global grasp*). The relatively small political impact of Asian countries results from significant fragmentation on the continent manifested by suspicion and animosity. It even prevents closer cooperation of states in the same hemisphere (for example, Japan and South Korea).

This situation, however, does not mean there are no Asian models of cooperation. At least two examples confirm they exist. The first is the Shanghai Cooperation Organization, a regional organization in the meaning of Chapter VIII of the UN Charter. It has existed under this name since 2001, when Uzbekistan joined the Shanghai Five, i.e., Russia[10], China, Kyrgyzstan, Kazakhstan and Tajikistan. The Shanghai Cooperation Organization was established to settle local disputes, that is, implementing political objectives, namely peaceful ends to frontier disputes. Another aspect of the organization's cooperation is visible as well—the desire to defend an authority considered legitimate, that is, the manifestation of eastern-style (post-communist) legitimacy.

Another example is the Economic Cooperation Organisation (ECO), established in 1985 by Turkey[11], Iran and Pakistan (and expanded since 1992 to include Afghanistan, Azerbaijan, Kazakhstan, Kyrgyzstan, Tajikistan, Turkmenistan and Uzbekistan). ECO's inclusion in membership of otherwise antagonist states may indicate Asian countries' ability to cooperate pragmatically (for more, see: Czarny 2013, Ch. 4).

The relative underdevelopment of multilateral integration organizations can be due both to political and economic reasons. The first ones we considered in the context of this analysis were the Asian states mutual relations in terms of connecting and dividing. The main economic reason is the orientation of many

10 Asian states' prevalence in this organization results in our considering it Asian, bearing in mind that part of Russia geographically is in Europe.

11 The regional location of Turkey on the basis of political, economic and cultural criteria seems difficult. Already in the 19th century, Turkey was the first non-Christian country that was a rightful member of the (Christian) international community. Currently, as a NATO member, it belongs to the transatlantic space and the western hemisphere; adding to that its ongoing EU accession proceedings, it confirms its European aims. Turkey on the one hand and NATO and the EU on the other are interested in the Turkish role as an Asian local economic power and its impact on transforming local societies and states into free market economies. Thus, despite Turkey's membership, we consider ECO in the context of integration in Asia.

states in the region towards export to industrialized countries, predominantly those off continent. For the region, investments from industrialized countries are important, as inflows support economic development in Asia. Capital-rich, industrialized states are potential donors of the direct capital necessary for boosting the Asian economies. That, additionally, discourages economic contacts within the continent and encourages those seeking such capital to look outside it. This explains the Asian states' tendency to enter bilateral agreements on discriminatory liberalization of economic cooperation (including with states from other continents), and thus explains the relatively low range of integration on the continent.

2. The US political dilemma: orientation towards Asia or Europe?

The modern international order is determined by two factors of crucial importance and conflicting impact. The first is the stability paradigm as a determinant of operational methods and political values, in particular in US political strategy. The other is organic turbulence in the world. The instability determinant is the lack of an effective regime of control over different actors' activities (non-state, states, or groups of states). In the unipolar order in which the US is a hyperpower, there is both a place and a need for regional and supra-regional economic and political powers like the EU. There is also the will and desire not to limit international relations to common values and the unity of civilizations. Still, the position of states and regions[12] varies in American foreign policy.

The current US policy towards Asian countries determines mid- and long-range world policy. The US promotes the institutionalization of economic and political cooperation in the transatlantic formula in its "pivot to Asia". The economic component of this is the Trans-Pacific Partnership treaty, being a free-trade treaty[13] aimed at connecting the American partners (the NAFTA countries, Chile,

12 The region is conventionally isolated, relatively homogenous, and distinguished from adjacent areas by natural or acquired traits. There are physiographic (e.g., climate, soil) and economic (e.g., agricultural, industrial) or economic and administrative regions that are objects of planning and management (*Encyklopedia Geografii* 2002, p. 531). Because the region is described not only by natural but also acquired features, the same term refers to common values and not only to areas of geographical vicinity (Czarny, Menkes, Śledziewska 2010).

13 *The Trans-Pacific Partnership* is to be a liberally discriminating agreement of international cooperation significantly broader than solely free trade. It provides for lowering

Peru) with Asian ones (Brunei, Japan, Malaysia, Vietnam, Singapore) and those from Australia and New Zealand[14]. Currently, the economies of the TPP states account for 40% of world GDP (for more on the TPP states' economic significance, see: Fuller 2014).

The US "pivot" is influenced by Asian, European and global factors. Assigning Asia a greater role in US policy is a nod to such economic factors as its bigger role in the world economy and US-China bilateral relations, diminishing cultural and civilisational differences between their societies, as well as convergence and political issues. In particular, in recognizing the territories of NATO countries as inviolable in military conflicts and attempts to move military confrontation to the periphery, the latter becomes crucial for security issues.

The "pivot" concept is also influenced by the fact that the US assumes Europe will not be the main source of instability in the future. Outside Europe and at the point of turbulence, the US has very limited power to initiate and control the process of social, economic and political change. To increase its influence in these areas, the US has attributed greater importance to Asia. It is hard not to notice the defensive—from the US perspective—character of the TPP. For a long time, but in the last two decades in particular, the EU and the US have competed for access to developing markets, including those especially important to the other. So, the EU has concluded agreements on discriminatory liberalisation of economic cooperation with Mexico and Chile, and with Asian states (South Korea and Singapore). To improve its position on discriminatory liberalization, the US altered the character of its agreements with ACP[15] (the Cotonou Partnership), under which the unilateral EU concessions have been supplemented with bilateral agreements, which results in giving EU companies easier access to a signatory's market. Expansion of discriminatory liberalization agreements with

tariffs and other trade barriers and introduces protection of intellectual property rights as well as rules for private investor dispute settlement with host states (ISDS). Better standards for employees and environmental protection are included. The TPP negotiations were closed in autumn 2015.

14 The US accepts and promotes Asian (and European) orientation toward Australia and New Zealand. On the one hand, these states more frequently accept the fact they are part of the Asian region rather than a separated European segment, while on the other hand, they are a geographically natural US bridge to Asia.

15 The EU-ACP regime includes EEC (currently EU) special trade relations with the African, Caribbean and Pacific region (ACP), and the former colonies of EEC states united pursuant to the Georgetown agreement of 1975 for coordinating policy with the EEC (EU).

the EU has been so large that the US considered their proliferation dangerous to their own interests[16] and started to retrieve their position centring similar contracts, including TPP.

There are many reasons for the relative mutual distancing of Europe and the US. They are particularly visible in periods of stabilization and prosperity. Among them are the significant discrepancies between their social and cultural models as well as the European conviction that its security is assured at little to no cost. Many Western European countries continue to benefit from the post-Cold War peace dividend, consequently ignoring the political changes affecting their security. Europe rejects the use of power, and has lost the will and ability to defend freedom and democracy against threats to its values. In Europe, even during the Cold War, the idea of German unification in the formula of Finlandization gained popularity, exactly as the concept to impede both of the then-dominant powers. Thus, the economic and social problems in the US have been, and for many still are just compensation for their hyperpower frustration (symptoms that include US standing towards France in carrying on with the wars in Indochina and Algeria, and the Suez Canal conflict[17]) and the rationale behind grounding European security using its own force. Even the Russian aggression in Ukraine did not lead to the end of the group of "Russia's friends", which plays a significant role in policy and the economy of Europe.

Even if one acknowledges the EU and US have shared the belief in Russia's transformation, its withdrawal from aggressive stances and destabilizing the international order, implementation of a counter-policy of the former USSR system, and driving towards a partnership based on respect for law and common values, the consequences of this belief are different in US and European policy. The US, secure thanks to its geopolitical and military position, still feels responsible for international security. For Europe, rapprochement with Russia can result in political and military dependency (political power, energy and other resources, military conflict near the EU-borders).

---

16 See e.g. "US companies, workers and farmers are being surrounded by preferential trade and investment agreements negotiated by their foreign competitors' governments. Time is running out for the United States to get back into the game." In: The Case for US Trade Leadership: The United States is Falling Behind, 2001, http://web.archive.org/web/20021030045704/http://www.brtable.org/pdf/498.pdf.

17 It is worth noting that discrepancies between the US and Western Europe occurred during the Cold War period, i.e., at a time when both parties shared a common paramount objective of limiting the possibilities of the Soviet Union's expansion.

On security issues, there are increasingly numerous opinions in analyses heralding a return to the pre-WWI situation[18] in international relations. China seems to be the successor of an anti-hero, the Germany of the Kaiser. One of the US reactions, preceding the threat, has been its joining the geopolitical region of the Pacific and constructing the architecture of Asian security as an insider rather than an outsider. The concept comprises the belief that although history repeats itself, a subsequent iteration can exploit the experience.

3. The TTIP's importance for the transatlantic region

The TTIP would strengthen and intensify the bilateral economic relations between its parties. Future cooperation can be perceived as a consolidation of the Atlantic bridge and an upgrade of economic cooperation to a level comparable to a political, defence and cultural alliance. The TTIP negotiations and (potentially if ratified) its implementation would verify the approach of the transatlantic region's societies to two paradigms (instrumental and axiological).

The first paradigm makes representation the form of executing power in a democracy. This paradigm has recently been challenged in its rejection by grassroots anti-ACTA[19] groups and verified by the US society's approach to the TTIP and TPP, Canada's to the CETA[20], and the Europe's to the CETA and TTIP. Providing that the occasional common opinion stems from herd instinct rather than a response to information about current developments (for more, see Hall and

18 See the opinions of Nouriel Roubini (K. Moodley, *Roubini's New Doom Scenario*. Jan. 23, 2014 http://www.businessinsider.com/roubinis-new-doom-scenario-2014–1), Abe Raises – Japan's PM (G. Mezzofiore, *1914 All Over Again? Japan's PM Abe Raises Ghost of WWI with China*, January 23, 2014 http://www.ibtimes.co.uk/1914-all-over-again-japans-pm-abe-raises-ghost-wwi-china-1433530) and H. Summers, former Secretary of the Treasury for President Clinton and Director of the National Economic Council for President Obama (2014 CIC Globalist of the Year Gala. https://www.youtube.com/watch?v=Yp3rxxuQUfY&feature=youtu.be).

19 The ACTA (*Anti-Counterfeiting Trade Agreement*) was a regime to counter intellectual property rights infringement. It was initiated in 2006 by Japan, the US, Canada, the EU and Switzerland. The agreement was signed, i.a., by 22 EU Member States (including Poland), the US, Canada, Australia, Japan and South Korea. In 2012, the European Parliament refused to accept the agreement. Its opponents objected to the agreement as a threat to freedom of speech, software with open-source development, as well as access to generic drugs.

20 The CETA (*Comprehensive Economic and Trade Agreement*) was in negotiations since 2008 and is a free trade agreement between the EU and Canada. Its text was officially presented on 25.09.2014, but its ratification will take at least two years.

Nelson, 2004, 92–103, on NAFTA perception), still, in democratic states they cannot be ignored.

The second paradigm acknowledges, following from Adam Smith, that the source of wealth is the international division of labour (Smith 1954). This paradigm sets as a foundation the UN Charter and European integration, considering free and fair trade a tool for social and economic development. The conviction held by opponents of the TTIP, TPP and CETA that free trade means pauperization, has led to a rethinking of Smith's idea. Its critics imply that autarky brings development. However, this statement is not supported by any argument of a successful modern autarky.

The TTIP can change the transatlantic order. In the inter-state area resulting from the Marshall Plan's implementation, order stemmed from the poles, which were policy and security, and source of energy to sustain it derived from common values[21]. This order can be transformed into a perfect triangle: politics, security and economy. However, for this to happen, it is necessary to gain confirmation from institutions as part of a democratic system with the functional ability to meet its statutory competences (negotiating and entering into agreements and gaining the public's acceptance) and the desired normative regulations. Still, strengthening the economic interest community, difficult in a situation where there is competition for access to local markets, is necessary.

Thus, the EU's efforts to develop relations with the US should not be ignored. The EU, and wider Western Europe, must fear the effects of a possible US turn towards the Pacific and reduction of American presence in Europe. That would create a security vacuum, particularly dangerous in the face of Russia's return to the aggressive and expansionist policy of the former USSR. However, there is a basic difference between the USSR and today's Russia: Putin's Russia is unpredictable but rational, whereas the USSR was arational. In its confrontation with Ukraine, Russia not only reinforces the desire to enlarge its territory at the expense of its neighbours and destabilize adjacent states but also uses economic tools to subordinate other states (e.g., by differentiating natural gas prices; for more, see: Czarny, Menkes, Toporowski 2009).

Economic interests force the EU and the US to cooperate. This is due to the massive flood of commodities, services and capital between them (although analysis of this is not within the scope of this chapter; for more see e.g. Czarny,

21 That does not mean that the cooperation has always been harmonious. Even during the Cold War, tensions were raised, e.g., during the Suez Canal crisis in 1956 and later in the Vietnam War. Examples of economic disputes were considered separately in this chapter.

Folfas 2016, pp. 31–46). The parties are natural allies in international organizations.

Economic interests can also prompt the US to remain an EU ally. It should not be expected that any other partner would have been such a good partner in combating such threats as international terrorism. The shared values system makes Europe a more natural partner for the US than the culturally, politically and religiously diverse Asian states that are becoming the main candidates for economic cooperation.

Despite intensive economic and political cooperation, the transatlantic partners are not bereft of economic conflict, which does not foster intense cooperation. The most spectacular case was the US suit over privileged access to the common banana market of the EU and ACP producers. In 2001, the WTO ceded to the American rationale. On the other hand, in 2001 the US groundlessly levied taxes on steelworks (suspended after the WTO had granted the EU the right of retorting in the form of its own customs duties). Some conflicts between the US and the EU have turned quite ideological. Such is the case of beef containing hormones or genetically modified food and animal feed (GMOs, Genetically Modified Organisms)[22].

4. The TTIP's global significance

The TTIP's importance is derived from the global roles of the parties to it. The US role as the only hyperpower is not questioned. Still, the integration of Europe has not always gone undisputed, nor European Communities have always been viewed as a world (or even regional, i.e. European) power[23].

---

22 Prestowitz, the president of the Economic Strategy Institute (ESI), summarized the EU objections in the following manner: "So if you had a cancer-curing GM corn, I don't think you would have any problems selling it in Europe" (www.econstrat.org/news/cprestowitz_cnnmoney_02162003.htm after Mann 2007, pp. 208–209.

23 The main external barrier we consider is the USSR's undertakings aimed at preventing European unity and promoting internal divisions in Western Europe (the "salami" strategy). As far as internal barriers are concerned, we consider moderation of the European integration process in cooperation concerns driven by differences in states' foreign policy strategies and their respective national interests. On one end of the scale was France, perceiving in European integration a tool to reconstruct its power status and safeguard its security. Great Britain took the other, hesitant as it was about its geopolitical standing and torn between the choice of ties with the US rather than with continental Europe.

The EU's creation came in successive stages, despite facing barriers both external and internal (Menkes 2005, pp. 189–201). Currently, Europe's ability to create and implement foreign and security policy is seldom doubted[24]. Making use of US military potential in political and military operations is part of the independent position of Europe, which is not duplicating the US (and NATO) potential, using subsidiarity and the compatibility of both partners. However, with time, we increasingly share the opinion of Kagan (2002), who wrote: "The 1990s witnessed not the rise of a European superpower but the decline of Europe into relative weakness. The Balkans conflict at the beginning of the decade revealed European military incapacity and political disarray; the Kosovo conflict at decade's end exposed a transatlantic gap in military technology [...] Europeans could provide peacekeeping forces in Bosnia and Kosovo. But they lacked the wherewithal to introduce and sustain a fighting force in potentially hostile territory, even in Europe."

Europe has proven its ability to successfully function in the sphere of global international relations. Among the examples are both its persuading Iran to initial cooperation in the area of non-proliferation and in defining and implementing policy towards the so-called Arab Spring. The EU is confronted with the consequences of the instability challenge in post-totalitarian countries and those where dictatorships have collapsed. Syria provides evidence that falling dictatorships defend the status quo at any price (often brutally), and that their collapse as a result of social pressure neither results in immediate nor in automatic establishment of democracy, rule of law, and respect for law and freedom. That the collapse of an undemocratic regime creates (in a non-existent civil society) a power vacuum, it triggers internal conflicts in which nobody protects the people and neither is there a state nor law. One of the effects of state collapse is people fleeing, or massive migration.

Still, the EU has constantly been confronted with challenges that seem to require deeper integration to meet them. Such a challenge is evident in Greece, where the inflow of hundreds of thousands of refugees and migrants has overwhelmed the existing society. Some see as a remedy more unity in Europe, while others opt for withdrawal from integration and a return to only an economic dimension, releasing states from limits on their national interests.

In the geopolitical dimension, the TTIP should allow Europe and the US to maintain dominance in the world economy and increase the stability of the global economic system. It may also encourage states blocking the current WTO round

24 For the modern context, see, e.g.: Sobczyk (2012).

on non-discriminatory trade liberalization to increase their inclination to cooperate. That assumption seems to be manifested by, for example, the decision at the Davos Summit (January 2014) to resume negotiations on trade and pro-environment services, which although covered by the Doha mandate are stalled by discussions of merit. Otherwise, the threat that the WTO negotiations may be downgraded significantly or replaced by numerous non-transparent bilateral or multilateral RTAs may become real. That would be detrimental to world economy, composed as might be of separate groups of trade partners. Not only would the process of development of the worldwide economic system based on the non-discrimination principle be stopped, but it could also be replaced by a number of agreements. Such a situation could force the world economy to retreat to the pre-war period when the world was divided by numerous protectionist and discriminatory economic agreements (for more, see: Czarny 2013, Ch. 1).

The TTIP, assuming it is concluded, will probably be the model for subsequent arrangements on non-discriminatory liberalization of economic cooperation. The agreement may alter the multilateral, pending WTO negotiations, either by providing ready-made solutions or at least initiating discussion. TTIP-adopted solutions will undoubtedly be used in other RTAs.

Conclusions

The conclusion of the TTIP negotiations is pending. Current analysis and assessment of their status is not feasible. That is due to two paradoxically contradictory reasons. On one side, it is the effect of a lack of information on the parties' initial positions, and all the more on their fall-back positions and paths to consensus. On the other side, the negotiations' merit, volume, and transparency prevent tracking. Only after potential ratification, when we gain access to the agreement, its official interpretation, statements by its negotiators, etc., will a comprehensive analysis of both the TTIP and its creation process be possible.

Thus, we can for now consider only partially the issues in the agreement. Still, what seems important for the entire agreement and what can be stated is the fact that the negotiations are carried out on the grounds of a commitment to conclusion of the contract (*pactum de contrahendo*). The parties seem to be convinced that failure is impossible, given the political necessity to enter into the agreement. Next to numerous other factors, including the already indicated benefits (profit) it brings, there are costs to failure. The EU and the US could prevent or even develop existing relations in all the dimensions and in all the spheres without deciding to conclude the TTIP. But a failure in the work on the agreement would surely result in crises and a setback in mutual relations, which given the current complex and unstable international situation, would go beyond the price of unmet goals.

The US has just concluded the TPP negotiations and is negotiating the TTIP. An important signal from the US administration was the signing by President Obama in June 2015 of *Trade Promotion Authority*, the first since 2002, and the *Trade Preferences Extension Act*. That means that the TPP and TTIP will be voted on in their entirety, with no amendments[25].

It is positive that the world political and economic situation seems to strengthen and consolidate US-EU cooperation. Decisive in this were errors on the part of both parties. The US wasted the intellectual heritage of Kissinger by allowing Chinese and Russian options to prevail when there was potential in mutual contacts within the framework of a US-Russia-China triangle. Europe, in turn, acknowledged that Russia had adopted Western patterns, becoming more Europe-like, and that President Putin would not stop disguising enforcement units in suits, but also that Russia would be a member of the Council of Europe, which meant that it should recognize and respect European values. It is hard to overestimate the scale of these mistakes. A chance comes with a return to cooperation and making the Atlantic an inner lake of the community of democracy, security and economic prosperity.

The importance attributed in this analysis to Russia seems well grounded. It is justified by the role of Russia as perceived in the context of US, Europe and Asia relations. This is the case regardless of developments, whether Russia chooses the path of development or if it falls. The optimistic scenario provides for a more stable and safe world thanks to multilateral cooperation, while the pessimistic version assumes that multipolarity can ease the costs of instability and security threats.

References

Apodaca C., 2006, Understanding US human rights policy. A paradoxical legacy, New York.

Churchill W., 1943, Post-War Councils on World Problems. A four year plan for England (Broadcast from London over BBC, March 21) "Vital Speeches of the Day", No. IX.

Czarny E., 2013, Regionalne ugrupowania integracyjne w gospodarce światowej, PWE, Warszawa.

25 https://www.whitehouse.gov/blog/2015/06/29/trade-here-s-what-president-signed-law, access date: 31.05.2015

Czarny E., P. Folfas, 2016, Unia Europejska i Stany Zjednoczone w globalnej produkcji i międzynarodowej współpracy gospodarczej a TTIP, in: Partnerstwo Transatlantyckie. Wnioski dla Polski, E. Czarny, M. Słok-Wódkowska (eds.), PWE, Warszawa, pp. 31–46.

Czarny E., J. Menkes, K. Śledziewska, 2010, Gravity Model and OECD in territorial division of the World, "Argumenta Oeconomica", No. 2(25).

Czarny E., J. Menkes, P. Toporowski, 2009, Gazprom – threat to Europe?, Poznań University of Economics Review, No. 1.

Encyklopedia Geografii, 2002,Warszawa.

Fuller J., 2014, Why almost everyone hates the trade deal Obama's negotiating in Japan, "Washington Post" 23.04.

Hall H. K., D. Nelson, 2004, The Peculiar Political Economy of NAFTA: Complexity, Uncertainty and Footloose Policy Preferences, in: Political Economy of Trade, Aid and Foreign Investment Policies, pp. 91–109.

Hansard's Parliamentary Debates, August 1891, 3 series, vol. 97, col. 122.

Hass R. N., Paradigm lost, 1995, "Foreign Affairs", No. 74(1).

Kagan R., 2002, Power and Weakness, Policy Review, No. 113, June/July 2002, www.policyreview.org/JUN02/kagan.htm/

Keohane R. O., 1989, International Institutions and State Power: Essays in International Relations Theory, Boulder.

Macionis J. J., 2005, Sociology, New Jersey.

Mann G. H., 2007, Transatlantische Freihandelszone, Peter Lang, International Verlag der Wissenschaften, Frankfurt a. M.

Mauk D., J. Oakland, 1999, Cywilizacja amerykańska, Astrum, Wrocław.

Menkes J., 2005, European Security Policy and the Challenge of the New World Peace Order, in: Europe and Complex Security Issues, K. Żukrowska (ed.), SGH, Warsaw.

Müller H., 2012, The Point of No Return Walter Hallstein and the EEC Commission between Institutional Ambitions and Political Constraints, "Les Cahiers Europeens de Sciences", No. 3.

Rawls J., 2010, Wykłady z historii filozofii polityki, Wydawnictwa Akademickie i Profesjonalne, Warszawa.

Smith A., 1954, Badania nad naturą i przyczynami bogactwa narodów, Państwowe Wydawnictwo Naukowe, Warszawa.

Sobczyk M., 2012, Europe Still Seeks Voice, Kissinger Says, "The Wall Street Journal", no. 27.06.2012. "The New York Times", 1999.02.05.

e-sources:

Henry Kissinger, http://en.wikiquote.org/wiki/Talk:Henry_Kissinger, access date 15.03.2014.

The European Parliament resolution including recommendations on TTIP negotiations, http://www.europarl.europa.eu/sides/getDoc.do?pubRef=-//EP//TEXT+REPORT+A8-2015–0175+0+DOC+XML+V0//PL, access date 31.05.2015.

The Case For US Trade Leadership: The United States Is Falling Behind, 2001, http://web.archive.org/web/20021030045704/http://www.brtable.org/pdf/498.pdf, access date 31.05.2015.

The White House portal, https://www.whitehouse.gov/blog/2015/06/29/trade-here-s-what-president-signed-law, access date 31.05.2015.

Magdalena Słok-Wódkowska (University of Warsaw)

Chapter 2. Regional Trade Agreements of the EU and the US — What Is the Common Ground?

The European Union (EU) and the United States (US) are among the most important economies of the world and they are crucial trading partners for each other and for others. Moreover, they are key forces shaping global trade law, mainly within the framework of the World Trade Organization (WTO). On the other hand, they are also hubs of regional trade agreements (RTAs), concluded mainly with smaller and/or less-developed partners.

Therefore, the Transatlantic Trade and Investment Partnership (TTIP), which has been negotiated since July 2013, is perceived as one of the most important RTAs ever. Negotiations were supposed to be easy and concluded by the end of 2014. The reality proved otherwise and the differences have proved to be deeper. The main aim of this chapter is to address that issue and compare the RTAs of the EU and the US.

According to the WTO database, the European Union is party to more than 40 RTAs notified to the WTO, while the United States has issued notice of 14. This difference results from a completely different attitude towards regional, extra-WTO integration. It is probably also because the aims of the EU and the US in terms of their RTAs are different. Moreover, the degree of integration in the RTAs concluded by both parties varies by region and when they were concluded.

In my research[1], I analyse the content and legal enforceability of the EU and the US trade agreements. In the first part I divide them and characterize particular groups of agreements concluded by both sides (although a landscape of the EU RTAs is much more complicated than the US RTAs). In the second part, I examine which areas are covered by a certain agreement with a given partner, dividing the areas into those covered by WTO law and those not covered by it. The analysis includes all agreements that form free-trade agreements (FTAs), customs unions (CUs) or economic integration agreements (EIAs) that are in force. I also refer

1 The project is funded by the National Science Centre of Poland based on decision No. DEC-2013/09/B/HS4/01488.

briefly to some agreements that have been signed but which are not yet in force, such as the one recently negotiated between the EU and Canada—the Comprehensive Economic and Trade Agreement (CETA), which is very often referred to in the context of the TTIP. The methodology of the research is based on the work of Horn, Mavroidis and Sapir.

The analysis will lead to comparisons of the EU and US philosophies for concluding an RTA, which, in my view, are very different. It will also enable the formulation of some predictions concerning the TTIP.

1. Characteristics of the EU and US regional trade agreements

The European Union itself is a regional trade agreement in the meaning of WTO law Article XXIV of the General Agreement on Tariffs and Trade (GATT), as it is a customs union, and Article V of the General Agreement on Trade in Services (GATS) and required notification under Article XXIV of GATT after conclusion of the treaty establishing the European Economic Community. Beside this, the EU and its predecessors, the European Economic Community (EEC) and the European Community (EC), had always been great proponents of regional integration and have a long history of establishing free-trade areas.

This is the first significant difference between the EU's and the US's attitude towards RTAs. The US has been quite reluctant to engage in economic integration outside the WTO framework. Its first RTA was concluded in 1985 with Israel and then the next one in 1987 with Canada (replaced in 1992 by the North American Free Trade Agreement, or NAFTA). Obviously, the attitude of the US towards regional integration as an addition to GATT was rather negative.

It is also quite clear that the US reversed its practice after 2000. Between 2000 and 2007, the US concluded 12 regional trade agreements. All of them are called "free-trade agreements", but besides liberalisation of trade in goods they also cover trade in services and chapters related to intellectual property or public procurement. They were all notified as FTA or FTA & EIA to the WTO. The US's RTAs are listed in Table 1.

Table 1. US RTAs

Signatory	Type of agreement	Signed	WTO notification
CAFTA – DR[2]	FTA	2004	FTA& EIA
Israel	FTA	1985	FTA
NAFTA	FTA	1992	FTA& EIA
Jordan	FTA	2000	FTA& EIA
Chile	FTA	2003	FTA& EIA
Singapore	FTA	2003	FTA& EIA
Australia	FTA	2004	FTA& EIA
Morocco	FTA	2004	FTA& EIA
Bahrain	FTA	2005	FTA& EIA
Colombia	FTA	2006	FTA& EIA
Oman	FTA	2006	FTA& EIA
Peru	FTA	2006	FTA& EIA
Panama	FTA	2007	FTA& EIA
South Korea	FTA	2007	FTA& EIA

Source: http://www.ustr.gov/trade-agreements/free-tradeagreements

It is also worth noting that all of the US RTAs except the one with Canada are currently in force. Recently, the United States signed the Trans-Pacific Partnership (TPP) with Australia, Brunei Darussalam, Canada, Chile, Malaysia, Mexico, New Zealand, Peru, Singapore, and Vietnam (six of them are currently parties to free-trade agreements with the US). Though quite controversial, the TPP seems to be the most important trade agreement signed by the US next to NAFTA. The other major trade partnership is the Transatlantic Trade and Investment Partnership between the EU and the US, very often treated as a counterpart of the TPP.

The EU and the US attitude towards RTAs has been entirely different not only because of the total number of agreements but also because the EU concludes different types of agreements than the US. All of the EU's trade agreements vary significantly in their times of conclusion and scopes, and above all, in the degree of integration proposed by the Union. Most of them have been concluded as Association Agreements. These are a special kind of international treaty concluded

2 Dominican Republic–Central America–United States Free Trade Agreement.

by the European Union (and previously by the EEC and EC) with particularly close partners. It has a specially designed legal basis, currently it is Article 217 of the Treaty on the Functioning of the European Union (TFEU). As the European Court of Justice explained in the *Demirel* judgement, Association Agreements create "special, privileged links with a non-member country which must, at least to a certain extent, take part in the Community system"[3].

This statement is crucial for a better understanding of EU RTAs. If an RTA is an Association Agreement, it is obvious that although the creation of a free-trade area is always an important part of an RTA, it also will include some political provisions adjusting the partner to the maximum extent possible to the EU legal framework. Association Agreements cover a very broad range of issues and always have a trade part that includes not only the creation of an FTA but also usually covers trade in services and other trade-related issues and might be qualified as WTO+[4]. As a consequence, Association Agreements also can be economic integration agreements (EIA) within the meaning of the WTO law.

EU Association Agreements may be divided into five major groups. The most advanced seem to be Stabilisation and Association Agreements (SAA), concluded with future candidate states, currently those from the Western Balkans. Their aim is to prepare these countries for future membership. They are always[5] EIAs and they entail liberalisation of a very broad range of service sectors. They also require a certain level of harmonisation of legislation (implementation of EU law by a partner state).

The second group are Euro-Mediterranean agreements (Euromed), which are concluded with states from North Africa. Usually these are former EU member state colonies or their close neighbours. They are also covered by European Neighbourhood Policy. All of these Euromed agreements were concluded before 2002 and were notified only as FTAs to the WTO, although they all consist of some provisions for liberalisation of trade in services. As all of these agreements having been concluded more than 10 years ago, the EU has started negotiations of new Association Agreements, including so-called Deep and Comprehensive FTAs (DCFTAs).

The new negotiated Euromed agreements are likely to be similar in some ways to agreements concluded in 2014 with the Eastern Partnership states—Ukraine,

3 Meryem Demirel p… Stadt Schwäbisch Gmünd, (12/86) [1987] ECR I-3719, par. 9.

4 For a list of the WTO+ and WTO-X areas, see: Horn, Mavroidis, Sapir (2009).

5 The only exception is Bosnia and Herzegovina, which signed an SAA in 2008. Its entry into force is blocked by some political controversy. An interim agreement, which covers only trade in goods, has been operational since 2008.

Moldova and Georgia. All three of these agreements include a DCFTA. They liberalise trade in services and were notified as both FTAs and EIAs. A characteristic of these agreements is that they directly oblige the partner states to implement enumerated EU legislation. It is unclear whether their aim is to integrate the Eastern Partnership more closely with the EU within the general framework of European Neighbourhood Policy or to prepare them for full membership in the (distant) future.

Another group of RTAs are Economic Partnership Agreements (EPAs), negotiated and concluded with the group of ACP (Africa, Caribbean, Pacific) states. All of these states are linked with the EU by one common Association Agreement—the Cotonou Agreement, concluded in 2000 and amended in 2005 and 2010. Cotonou provides a framework for cooperation, political dialogue and, above all, development aid, although trade with the ACP states is liberalized under EPAs. Interim EPAs cover only trade in goods, while full EPAs cover trade in services, too.

The EU concluded two other Association Agreements that do not suit any of the above groups—ones with Chile and Central America. The agreement with Chile was signed in 2000, while the other was signed in 2013.

Only a few FTAs that were notified to the WTO by the EU are not Association Agreements. Their aim is therefore purely economic and they are much narrower. They are also much more like the FTAs concluded by the US. One has been concluded with Peru and Colombia (and has been provisionally operational since 2013). The most important FTA economically is the one concluded with South Korea. It is the first of a new type of EU RTA, that is, one that has been concluded with a developed economy and with a purely economic objective. The agreement entered into force in 2011, and at the same time was the first agreement concluded with an Asian state. In September 2013, another DCFTA was initialled after the EU completed negotiations with Singapore. The EU also finalized negotiations with Canada, although the agreement has not been signed yet. These three agreements (with South Korea, Singapore and Canada), classified in this chapter as EU new-type agreements, are probably the best benchmarks of what we can expect from the EU during its negotiations with the US. All three of these agreement types should be better indicators of what can be expected from the TTIP than previous EU RTAs. However, we also need to take into account the TPP as a litmus test of what the US is aiming for. Therefore, an analysis restricted to agreements that are already in force may not be sufficient in the case of the TTIP and will be supplemented by this separate analysis of the three EU new-type agreements and the TPP.

Table 2 shows the 27 agreements in force that are taken into account in this study. I excluded from it those RTAs notified to the WTO that have been concluded with non-independent countries. I also excluded member states of the European Free Trade Agreement (Iceland, Norway, and Switzerland). These states are linked with the EU through very special ties, which include much deeper integration and cover a majority of EU economic legislation.

Table 2. EU RTAs covered in the research

RTA Name	Type of agreement (Group)	Signed	WTO Notification
EU – Albania	SAA	2006	FTA& EIA
EU – Algeria	Euromed	2002	FTA
EU – Bosnia and Herzegovina	SAA (Interim)	2008	FTA
EU – Cameroon	ACP	2009	FTA
EU – CARIFORUM States	ACP/EPA	2008	FTA& EIA
EU – Central America	Association	2012	FTA& EIA
EU – Chile	Association	2002	FTA& EIA
EU – Colombia and Peru	FTA	2012	FTA& EIA
EU – Côte d'Ivoire	ACP/EPA (Interim)	2009	FTA
EU – Eastern and Southern Africa States Interim EPA	ACP/EPA (Interim)	2009	FTA
EU – Egypt	Euromed	2001	FTA
EU – Former Yugoslav Republic of Macedonia	SAA	2000	FTA& EIA
EU – Georgia	AA DCFTA	2014	FTA& EIA
EU – Israel	Euromed	1995	FTA
EU – Jordan	Euromed	1997	FTA
EU – South Korea	FTA	2010	FTA& EIA
EU – Lebanon	Euromed	2002	FTA
EU – Mexico	Partnership Agreement	2000	FTA& EIA
EU – Moldova	AA DCFTA	2014	FTA& EIA
EU – Montenegro	SAA	2010	FTA& EIA
EU – Morocco	Euromed	1996	FTA

RTA Name	Type of agreement (Group)	Signed	WTO Notification
EU – Pacific countries	ACP/EPA (Interim)	2009	FTA
EU – Serbia	SAA	2008	FTA& EIA
EU – South Africa	ACP	1999	FTA
EU – Tunisia	Euromed	1995	FTA
EU – Turkey	Association	1996	CU
EU – Ukraine	AA DCFTA	2014	FTA& EIA

*agreements cover services but are not notified as EIA.
**notified to the WTO only as an early announcement.
Source: own research based on: http://ec.europa.eu/trade/policy/countries-and-regions/

The agreements negotiated and signed by the EU and the US vary significantly. The world of the EU RTAs is far more complex while the US RTAs are very similar to one another. They are all free trade agreements. Because of its specificity, the EU concludes deeper partnerships in the form of Association Agreements, which also differ mainly because of the different goals they are meant to achieve.

Beside these differences, the US and the EU have similar FTA partners. Among the 20 states that have established an FTA with the US, 15 also have a free-trade area in force with the EU. But FTAs with eight of them (the agreement with Central America as well as with Colombia and Peru) entered into force only in 2013. Two more countries—Canada and Singapore—are about to sign RTAs. There are also two Gulf region states—Bahrain and Oman—with whom the EU had started negotiations on an EU-GCC (Gulf Cooperation Council) Free Trade Agreement and then suspended them due political tension. Only Australia has an agreement with the US but not with the EU and is not negotiating one either, although there are plans to start negotiations in the near future[6].

6 Such a plan was expressed by the Commission in its strategy "Trade for All, Towards a more responsible trade and investment policy", 2015, http://trade.ec.europa.eu/doclib/docs/2015/october/tradoc_153846.pdf, p. 32.

2. Methodology of the analysis

The starting point of my analysis is the work of Horn, Mavroidis and Sapir, as presented in 2010[7]. They divided all of the areas mentioned in a given agreement into those covered by WTO law (marked as WTO+) and those not covered by it (marked as WTO-X). They discovered that in the EU RTAs there are twice as many WTO-X provisions than in comparable agreements concluded by the US. The WTO-X agreements might be further divided into two categories: areas related to trade and economy, such as economic cooperation or the environment, and areas not related to the economy at all, such as cooperation in criminal matters.

Horn, Mavroidis and Sapir pointed out that the various provisions of the EU RTAs may be of a very different nature. Some of them are concrete and related to specific obligations while others are more general or vague. They concern cooperation between partners rather than provide them with rights and obligations. They cannot be used as a basis for dispute settlement or arbitration. Therefore, they can be classified as nonenforceable.

The analysis by Horn, Mavroidis and Sapir covered 14 of the EU RTAs in force in 2009, both relatively new RTAs as well as the oldest EU RTAs, such as the EU–Turkey Association Agreement, under which a customs union has been formed, and the Agreement on the European Economic Area. Nonetheless, the analysis can be qualified as obsolete as in the past few years a number of significant new RTAs have been negotiated by the EU. Among them are the EU–South Korea comprehensive free-trade agreement and several major agreements with South American countries. Also, the number of Economic Partnership Agreements concluded on the completion of the Cotonou Agreement with the ACP states has recently increased.

At the same time, the number of US agreements taken into account by Horn, Mavroidis and Sapir did not change at all during the past few years. Therefore, in this part of the chapter I mainly refer to their research with only necessary adjustments to categories defined in the further analysis. Moreover, the US agreements, as stated above, generally do not vary between each other and there are only slight differences. The majority of them cannot be included in this kind of research as it does not take into account sectors covered by liberalisation. As mentioned above, I supplemented the analysis of the US RTAs with TPP, even though this agreement is not yet in force, but presented it separately.

7 See, for example, World Trade Report 2011, http://www.wto.org/english/res_e/booksp_e/anrep_e/world_trade_report11_e.pdf.

All of the agreements[8] concluded by the EU and the US were surveyed in order to define the areas they cover. Following Horn, Mavroidis and Sapir, I divided these areas into two groups—WTO+ and WTO-X—but then I also divided the WTO-X group into two subcategories—those related to the economy and those not related to it. WTO+ is the areas covered by the WTO (Table 3).

Table 3. WTO+ areas

FTA industrial goods (FTA ind.)	Tariff liberalisation; elimination of non-tariff measures.
FTA agricultural goods (FTA agr.)	Tariff liberalisation; elimination of non-tariff measures.
Public procurement	Progressive liberalisation; national treatment and/or non-discrimination principle; publication of laws and regulations on the internet; specification of public-procurement regime.
Trade-related intellectual property rights (TRIPs)	Harmonisation of standards; enforcement; national treatment, most-favoured nation treatment.
Movement of workers	National treatment for legal workforce, right to employment for families of the legally employed, right to transfer key personnel or trainees in case of commercial presence.
Commercial presence	Right to establish a company in a partner country, related to mode 3 of the GATS.
Supply of services	Services delivered within the territory of one party, from the territory of another (mode 1 of the GATS) and consumption of services abroad – services delivered outside the territory of one party in the territory of another one, to a service consumer of another party (mode 2).

Source: Slok-Wódkowska, Sledziewska, Anatomy of the EU Regional Trade Agreements – What really influences economic integration?, 2015, http://www.delab.uw.edu.pl/wp-content/uploads/2015/12/trade_working_paper_Delab.pdf

8 All information about the EU agreements is based on texts from the European Commission website and the Official Journal of the EU.

Focusing mainly on other WTO+ issues, I did not analyse in detail various aspects of the trade in goods, such as technical barriers to trade (TBT) or sanitary and phytosanitary measures (SPS). They are almost always present in the EU and US RTAs. In the majority of cases, there is a reference to the WTO legal framework and confirmation of its acceptance. In both cases (the EU and the US) trade chapters usually also cover countervailing measures as well as subsidies.

I have excluded trade-related measures on investments. In the majority of the EU agreements, investments are not directly involved and they only briefly mention investments, promotion and protection of them. On the other hand, they are always present in the US agreements. The US usually combines RTAs with bilateral trade agreements. The most significant example of such a combination is NAFTA. In the EU trade agreements, investment chapters are present in only two recently negotiated but not yet signed agreements with Singapore and Canada (for more, see: Słok-Wódkowska, Śledziewska 2014).

Usually, in the EU RTAs there are no special provisions on trade-related aspects of investments covered by the TRIM Agreement. They are treated as part of investment provisions. A similar situation is related to state aid. It is part of competition policy, which is broader than only rules of state aid. Therefore, provisions related to that were qualified as a part of competition policy, together with rules related to companies directly.

Except for a few areas covered by WTO law, there are many areas related to or strengthening WTO rules. They are all related to the economy in a broad sense. Particular areas are discussed in Table 4.

Table 4. WTO-X areas related to the economy

Agriculture	Technical assistance to conduct modernization projects; exchange of information.
Competition policy	Maintenance of measures to proscribe anticompetitive business conduct; harmonisation of competition laws; establishment or maintenance of an independent competition authority, agreement on implementation of EU competition rules, rules on state aid.
Consumer protection	Harmonisation of consumer protection laws, including exchange of information and experts; training.
Data protection	Exchange of information and experts; joint projects, implementation of EU data protection principles.
Development aid	Financial aid from the EU to a partner country, development aid.

Economic cooperation	Assistance in economic development, all kinds.
Environmental laws	Development of environmental standards; enforcement of national environmental laws; establishment of sanctions for violation of environmental laws; publications of laws and regulations.
Financial cooperation	Assistance in reinforcing of financial institutions and system.
Industrial cooperation	Assistance in conducting modernisation projects; facilitation and access to credit to finance.
Investment protection and promotion	Obligation to promote and protect foreign investments, provisions related to standards of protection.
Movement of capital	Liberalisation of capital movement; prohibition of new restrictions, both to finance direct and indirect investments.
Working conditions	Regulation of the national labour market; affirmation of International Labour. Organization (ILO) commitments; enforcement, adoption of certain standards.

Source: Słok-Wódkowska, Śledziewska 2015, Anatomy of the EU Regional Trade Agreements—What really influences economic integration?, http://www.delab.uw.edu.pl/wp-content/uploads/2015/12/trade_working_paper_Delab.pdf

Most of the areas in the EU RTAs are not related to the economy. They are various areas, some of them rather general, others narrow and precise. Description of areas not related either to WTO law or to other economic or trade-related issues is presented in Table 5.

Table 5. WTO-X areas not related to the economy

Political dialogue	**Convergence of the parties' positions on international issues.**
Approximation of legislation	Application of the EU legislation in national legislation.
Border control cooperation	Exchange of information; drafting legislation; training on visas and asylum; conclusion of re-admission agreements in the future, prevention and control of illegal immigration.
Corruption	Regulations concerning criminal offence measures in matters affecting international trade and investment.
Cultural and audio-visual cooperation	Promotion of joint initiatives and local culture, promotion of the audio-visual industry; encouragement of co-production.

Political dialogue	**Convergence of the parties' positions on international issues.**
Disarmament	Obligation to disarmament, to adjust to international instruments related to disarmament.
Education and training	Measures to improve the general level of education.
Energy and mining	Exchange of information and experience; development of joint initiatives.
Gender	Promotion of gender equality.
Health	Monitoring of diseases; development of health information systems; exchange of information.
Human rights	Respect for human rights.
Illicit drugs	Treatment and rehabilitation of drug addicts; joint projects on prevention of consumption; reduction of drug supply; information exchange.
Indigenous people	Promotion of rights and culture of indigenous people.
Information society	Exchange of information; dissemination of new technologies; training.
Money laundering	Harmonisation of standards; technical and administrative assistance.
Organised crime	Harmonisation of standards; technical and administrative assistance.
Public administration	Technical assistance; exchange of information; joint projects; training.
Racism and xenophobia	Obligation to fight racism and xenophobia, cooperation and assistance.
Regional cooperation	Provisions related to cooperation, promotion of regional cooperation; technical assistance programs.
Regional development	Assistance in regional development, cohesion.
Research and technology	Joint research projects; exchange of researchers; development of public-private partnership.
Rule of law	Enforcement of law, cooperation and assistance on rule of law mainly from the EU sight.
Small and medium enterprise	Technical assistance; facilitation of the access to finance.
Social development	Assistance in building social society, cooperation in raising living conditions.

Political dialogue	**Convergence of the parties' positions on international issues.**
Social security	Coordination of social security systems; non-discrimination regarding working conditions.
Statistics	Harmonisation and/or development of statistical methods; training.
Taxation	Assistance in conducting fiscal system reforms.
Terrorism	Exchange of information and experience; joint research and studies.
Tourism	Cooperation in strengthening tourism infrastructure and market.
Transport	Cooperation in building and maintenance of transport infrastructure.

Source: Słok-Wódkowska, Śledziewska 2015, Anatomy of the EU Regional Trade Agreements—What really influences economic integration?, http://www.delab.uw.edu.pl/wp-content/uploads/2015/12/trade_working_paper_Delab.pdf

In the second stage of the research, after dividing the RTAs into various areas covered by them, I verified whether they are enforceable. By enforceable I mean the provisions which are precise enough to be challenged in a formal dispute are not explicitly excluded from such disputes.

3. Areas covered by the WTO law

Trade-related measures are probably the most important and concrete parts of the RTAs concluded by the EU. They are also key parts of US trade agreements. First of all, every analysed agreement covers trade in goods. Moreover, in the case of all RTAs, the provisions on trade in goods and abolishment of tariffs are fully enforceable. They usually refer directly to trade in industrial goods and separately to the agricultural goods and fisheries. Only in two of the EU RTAs are there no specific provisions related to trade in agricultural goods. Enforceable provisions on trade in agricultural goods do not necessary equal their full liberalisation. It simply means that in all cases there is a certain degree of liberalisation or facilitation of trade in agricultural goods.

The majority of agreements also cover SPS and TBT provisions as well as others related to countervailing measures and subsidies. Among the US RTAs, there were only two exceptions—agreements with a much narrower scope related to trade in goods were signed with Israel and Jordan. In the case of Israel, it might be explained by the fact that it is the only agreement signed before the Uruguay Round even started.

The situation with trade in services is much more complicated, especially in the case of the EU. First of all, only 13 out of 24 agreements have been notified as EIAs to the WTO. All of these agreements cover all aspects of trade in services except mode 4 of GATS. They refer to the right to establishment and cross-border supply of services. The majority refer directly to modes 1 and 2 and mention also use of services abroad. There are some (e.g., all of the SAAs) that refer simply to cross-border supply of services, leaving it unclear whether they also cover mode 2 of GATS, although it is quite clear from other provisions of these agreements that use of services is also allowed. Although only 13 agreements are official EIAs, an additional nine cover the right to establishment and two include enforceable obligations within these fields (the ones with Jordan and Algeria). These agreements are all Euromed agreements as well as EU-South Africa and EU-Turkey. Only those countries that have concluded interim agreements did not refer to the right to establishment in any form. Eighteen agreements (13 EIAs and five others) refer to supply of services. Fourteen of these provisions are enforceable (the EIAs and EU-Algeria). The situation with the US trade agreements is far more simple. All of the EIAs cover trade in services. They refer to all modes of services supply.

Among other issues covered by WTO law, intellectual property rights are referred to in some form in 20 of the EU agreements. Only 13 of the provisions are enforceable, though. For example, the Association Agreement with Central America does cover that topic, but it is not enforceable. The interim EPA with Cameroon and interim SAA with Bosnia and Herzegovina also refer to intellectual property. At the same time, all of the US agreements (including the US-Israel agreement concluded before TRIPS negotiations have been started) refer to intellectual property rights covered by TRIPS, and all of these provisions are enforceable. Moreover, all agreements except US-Israel relate more generally to intellectual property rights.

A very similar situation is present in public procurement. Twenty of the EU RTAs cover this area but only 12 are enforceable. The government procurement provision in the EU-Korea agreement is not enforceable, but one should take into account that both South Korea and the EU are parties to the WTO Government Procurement Agreement (GPA) with its concrete rules and concessions. Among the US RTAs, provisions on public procurement are always present. They are usually enforceable, except the one with Jordan.

Provisions on the movement of workers can be found in only 11 EU RTAs, but in nine of them they are concrete enough to be enforceable. These provisions vary in the level of liberalisation. For the majority of agreements, they only supplement provisions on the right of establishment. They refer only to direct investments and enable investors to hire key personnel and some highly qualified specialists. In some cases, the free movement of trainees is allowed. However, in the US RTAs, any preferences on the movement of workers related to investments are explicitly excluded.

All of the WTO areas covered by WTO law are also covered by the new-type EU RTAs, as well as by TPP. All of these agreements cover liberalisation of trade in goods and services as well as protection of intellectual property. They also cover public procurement (except EU-South Korea, where it is non-enforceable), even though all of the parties to EU new-type agreements are also parties to the Government Procurement Agreement of the WTO. Therefore, the coverage of public procurement in the TPP might be of greater importance, as not all of the TPP parties are parties to the GPA.

4. Economic and trade-related measures not covered by WTO

The most "popular" area to cover with an RTA for both the EU and US is environmental protection. Many RTAs have provisions related to environmental protection among all areas qualified as trade- and economy-related. They also sometimes include provisions related to climate change and/or sustainable development. Environment-related provisions are present in all of the US RTAs that are EIAs, and they are always enforceable. In the EU RTAs, only in two cases (EU-Colombia and Peru, and EU-CARIFORUM) are these provisions in fact enforceable. In the majority of cases they simply refer to future cooperation and assistance. Besides being far vaguer then the US RTAs, there is broad variety among the EU provisions related to the environment. At the same time, the US RTAs are very similar and contain obligations related to possible environmental regulations conflicting with trade-related measures, the relationship between an RTA and multilateral trade agreements, or consultations between the parties.

For the EU, there are two areas in which almost all of the provisions present in its various RTAs are enforceable. These are competition policy and movement of capital. Provisions on free movement of capital are almost always limited to direct investments, while portfolio investments are excluded. In this case, the provisions in the US RTAs are similar and always enforceable as well. This coincidence might be explained by the fact that these provisions are strongly related to investments and cross-border supply of services. In fact, provisions that enable the transfer of capital related to foreign direct investments are an inevitable part of the liberalisation of services. In contrast, competition provisions in the US RTAs are never enforceable. In the EU RTAs, they usually mirror exactly relevant provisions of the TFEU (current Articles 101 and 102 as well as 108 in relation to state aid). They simply expand the scope of EU competition policy to include its partners.

Areas such as industrial, economic and agricultural cooperation are present only in the EU Association Agreements and are never enforceable. They are always parts of chapters related to broad cooperation with partners. Their aim is clearly the creation of a framework for assistance projects for the EU partner states.

Data protection provisions can be found in a relatively small number of 13 agreements. Only eight of these are enforceable, namely in the SAAs with Serbia, Montenegro and Albania, as well as the EPAs with CARIFORUM, Cameroon and the Eastern Partnership states. They can be enforced only because they require a partner state to accept and adopt a set of EU rules concerning data protection. They are never present in the US trade agreements.

The US trade agreements, even though they never enable movement of workers, always contain provisions related to working conditions (chapters on labour). They are always enforceable. Their main goal is to exclude possible conflicts between labour law and free movement of goods or services. Provisions related to the same topic in the EU RTAs are of a very different nature. Their aim is very often to export EU standards to less-developed states with less-developed standards or systems. Coverage and enforceability of the provisions in all categories is presented in Table 5.

Table 5. Coverage and enforceability of the provisions in areas not covered by WTO

Area Covered	EU		US	
	Number of provisions	Enforceable provisions	Number of provisions	Enforceable provisions
Agriculture	18 (0*)	1 (0)	0 (0)	0 (0)
Competition policy	21 (3)	17 (3)	7 (1)	0 (1)
Consumer protection	13 (0)	1 (0)	2 (0)	0 (0)
Data protection	13 (0)	8 (0)	0 (0)	0 (0)
Development aid	13 (0)	4 (0)	0 (0)	0 (0)
Economic cooperation	19 (0)	0 (0)	0 (0)	0 (0)
Environmental laws	24 (3)	5 (0)	13 (1)	13 (1)
Financial cooperation	16 (0)	1 (0)	0 (0)	0 (0)
Industrial cooperation	19 (0)	0 (0)	0 (0)	0 (0)
Investment protection and promotion	15 (2)	0 (2)	11 (1)	11 (1)

Area Covered	EU		US	
	Number of provisions	Enforceable provisions	Number of provisions	Enforceable provisions
Movement of capital	22 (2)	19 (2)	12 (1)	12 (1)
Working conditions	10 (3)	4 (3)	13 (1)	13 (1)

* brackets indicate areas covered by the three "new-type RTAs" for the EU, and TPP for the US.
Source: own analysis.

The development aid coverage listed in Table 5 might be misleading. Although 13 countries have in their RTAs some provisions on potential financial aid from the EU, only a few of them (4) are concrete. This is mainly because an RTA cannot be the legal basis for concrete financial aid, only a full SAA. All ACP countries get financial aid from the European Development Fund, based on EU internal legislation as well as the Cotonou Agreement.

If we compare areas covered by the EU and the US RTAs here, the differences are significant. The only areas that seem to be common ground are environmental protection and working conditions, although they are much more often enforceable in the US RTAs. Nevertheless, when we compare only the new-type EU RTAs, their scope is much more similar to the US RTA model than the EU's usual model (for concluding political agreements with less-developed states). Moreover, if we take into account the example of competition policy, we might see that its presence in TTIP looks possible—competition policy is covered by all three of the new-type EU RTAs and by TPP.

One of the most controversial parts of TTIP is going to be investments. It is obvious from the negotiation mandate for TTIP that they are going to be included. The EU made it clear in a Communication from the European Commission (COM(2012) 343, p. 6) that it intends to include investment chapters in its RTAs, and it is covered by the two newest agreements. Investment chapters are always present in the US agreements, as well as in the TPP.

5. Areas not covered by the WTO law

Although there is a broad range of various areas not related to trade and economy covered by RTAs concluded by the EU, only a few are enforceable. In fact, the vast majority are standard clauses used in EU Association Agreements. Each has a part concerning what is broadly understood as cooperation. In these chapters, one can find a great variety of issues mentioned. They usually lack any details, setting mainly goals for mutual cooperation. Therefore, as shown in Table 6, the majority of areas mentioned here are not enforceable.

It is quite the opposite in the case of the US RTAs. They concentrate on trade- and economy-related measures and their scope is much narrower. Among the areas listed below, there is only one area that frequently appears in the US trade agreements—anti-corruption measures. This might be obviously explained by the fact that corruption strongly interferes with investment. Fighting corruption can be treated here as a part of US efforts to protect foreign direct investment.

Table 6. WTO-X areas not related to economy

Area Covered	EU		US	
	Number of provisions	Enforceable provisions	Number of provisions	Enforceable provisions
Human rights	3	0	0	0
Approximation of legislation	15	3	0	0
Border control cooperation	13	2	0	0
Corruption	6	0	10	8
Culture and audio-visual cooperation	18	0	0	0
Disarmament	2	0	0	0
Education and training	16	0	0	0
Energy and mining	19	0	1	1
Gender	2	0	0	0
Health	6	1	0	0
Illicit drugs	18	0	0	0
Indigenous people	1	0	0	0
Information society	20	0	0	0
Money laundering	16	0	0	0
Organised crime	10	0	0	0
Political dialogue	18	0	0	0
Public administration	6	0	0	0
Racism and xenophobia	1	0	0	0
Regional cooperation	21	2	0	0
Regional development	5	0	0	0

Area Covered	EU		US	
	Number of provisions	Enforceable provisions	Number of provisions	Enforceable provisions
Research and technology	19	0	0	0
Rule of law	10	0	0	0
Small and medium enterprise	9	0	0	0
Social development	14	0	0	0
Social security	9	2	0	0
Statistics	17	0	0	0
Taxation	6	0	0	0
Terrorism	9	0	0	0
Tourism	19	0	0	0
Transport	19	3	0	0

Source: own analysis.

All areas covered in these "cooperation" chapters of the EU Association Agreements might be divided into two or three groups. The first consists of standard areas usually included into any agreement, such as transport, tourism, and statistics. Each Association Agreement touches on problems of criminal justice and cooperation within this field, but only two areas are covered by the majority of them—illicit drugs (usually both trade and production) and money laundering.

The second type are those areas that can be found only in one or two agreements. A special provision on fighting racism and xenophobia was placed only in the EU-Algeria agreement. Disarmament was mentioned only in the EU-Central America agreement. Gender issues are explicitly present only in two agreements, ones concluded with Central America and Chile. This is especially surprising if we take into account that the first mentioned RTA is one of the newest whereas the other was concluded over 10 years ago. These special areas probably mirror some special needs of the given partner country. A case in point may be indigenous people, which is an area mentioned only in the EU-Central America agreement.

A third group would be provisions mentioned only in a particular type of agreement. A great number of issues, absent elsewhere, can be found in SAAs, especially areas related to strengthening the rule of law and civil society or quality of life. This can be explained by the special aim of these agreements, which are concluded to prepare third states for future full EU membership.

It is worth mentioning that none of these non-economy related areas were included into the EU's new-type agreements. We should expect, though, that among these issues, only corruption (covered by the majority of the US RTAs as well as TPP) will be included.

Conclusions

There are no doubts that there are huge differences between the EU and US trade agreements. An analysis of all of the RTAs already concluded by both parties proves that they vary in nature, scope and the enforceability of provisions. The most important factor here is probably a difference in philosophy regarding RTAs. For years, the US concluded purely free-trade agreements extended to include liberalisation of services. The aim was economic. There were only a few partners, usually already closely linked with the US economically or politically. Simultaneously, the EU concluded agreements in which trade-related provisions and the establishment of a free trade area was only part of broader association. Their aim was not just economic but mainly political. It is also clear that the EU's philosophy has recently changed. Since 2011, the Union has started concluding more economic-oriented agreements and with stronger partners. On the other hand, the US seems now to be more open to RTAs, as well.

Taking into account only the scope and enforceability of the agreements, these differences seem to be even more significant. The majority of the discrepancies, however, concern non-economy related areas of WTO-X. This difference is not significant for the future of the TTIP, as the majority of these areas are not included in its negotiating mandate. The TTIP will probably be similar to agreements with South Korea, Canada and Singapore (EU new-type agreements), which do not include a majority of provisions typical of the older EU RTAs, such as co-operation in non-economy related fields, political dialogue or development aid. They are usually part of Association Agreements. Therefore, when we compare only the EU new-type agreements with the US RTAs and TPP, the differences are much smaller.

The differences in core areas—WTO+ or WTO-X—as related to the economy are not overly significant. There are always enforceable provisions related to liberalisation of trade in goods and services, as well as references to core WTO agreements, such as TBT or SPS. Beside liberalisation of tariffs, I suppose that they mainly confirm the WTO obligations of parties. In the TTIP, we should also expect provisions on environment and competition policy, although the potential enforceability of these provisions is rather doubtful.

References

Horn H., P. Mavroidis, A. Sapir, 2009, Beyond the WTO? An anatomy of EU and US preferential trade agreements, "The World Economy" 33(11).

Meryem Demirel p. Stadt Schwäbisch Gmünd, (12/86), 1987, ECR I-3719.

Słok-Wódkowska M., K. Śledziewska, 2015, Anatomy of the EU Regional Trade Agreements – What really influences economic integration?, http://www.delab.uw.edu.pl/wpcontent/uploads/2015/12/trade_working_paper_Delab.pdf

Słok-Wódkowska M., K. Śledziewska, 2014, European Bilateral Investment Agreements – Is There a Real Value Added?, http://papers.ssrn.com/sol3/papers.cfm?abstract_id=2546411.

Towards a comprehensive European international investment policy, 2012, COM(2012)343.

World Trade Report 2011, http://www.wto.org/english/res_e/booksp_e/anrep_e/world_trade_report11_e.pdf.

Marcin Menkes (Warsaw, School of Economics)

Chapter 3. Regulatory Cooperation Under the TTIP. If You Can Read This, You're Too Close

1. Introduction

One of the paradoxes of economic globalisation is that ever-closer economic ties mean that any significant global agreement would fundamentally reshape the entire picture, which renders highly desired agreements difficult to reach. This is, for instance, the case of the never-ending WTO Doha negotiation round (Lamy 2013). As a result, regionalisation of trade and investment agreements increases transaction costs for business, and hence, the need for regulatory convergence. The easiest and perhaps most democratic way would be to adopt a *quasi*-universal agreement with which at least all states could voice their concerns. In this case, civil society and the business community would probably try to contribute towards the standards-setting.

Although the easiest route does not appear available anytime soon, it does not mean that we are doomed to regulatory havoc. There are at least two alternatives: a trickle-up or trickle-down process. The first would be through voluntary self-regulation by producers and traders. As particular standards gain popularity and become market benchmarks, the pressure on others to comply with such norms increases. What is probably even more intriguing is the opposite, or the trickle-down scenario. Here, several major rule-setters adopt norms they hope will be imposed on others thanks to their relative weight in international economic relations. This is, for instance, the case of regulatory works by the International Standardisation Organisation, an entirely private body (Prakash, Potoski 2006).

The latter could also be the case for the Transatlantic Trade and Investment Partnership (TTIP), whereby the parties undertake to review and compare relevant domestic regulation and cooperate towards the development of new rules. Since, largely due to GATT/WTO achievements, tariffs constitute a negligible obstacle to international trade, regulatory cooperation means striking down the other villain, that is, non-tariff barriers to trade (NTB[1]). Import tariffs in bilateral

1 In WTO, with respect to goods, these are basically covered under the Agreement on Sanitary and Phytosanitary Measures (SPS), dealing with health concerns, and the

relations are set at ca. 3%, with the exception of processed foods (14.6%) and motor vehicles (10%) (European Parliament 2015). However, NTBs on US business services are estimated to be the equivalent of 14.9% of export value, 15.3% on pharmaceuticals and 34.6% on cosmetics (whereas tariff barriers on chemicals average 2.3%), and in terms of communications services they are equivalent to 11.7% (Bertelsmann 2014). According to some estimations, ambitious, comprehensive trade liberalisation would entail the removal of 25% of NTBS costs and 100% of the tariffs (in a less ambitious scenario, these figures stand at 10% and 98%, respectively) (CEPR 2013). Accordingly, the TTIP is more about NTBs than anything else. Most of all, however, it is about a broader vision of economics and politics.

Some sceptics of the TTIP (as well as of the TPP and TISA) fear that it is an instrument of large pan-Atlantic capital possibly attempting to oust China (as the main challenger to US domination) and Brazil (which questioned a certain cooperation model by rejecting the ISDS). Two fundamental questions arise here: what if these voices are wrong, and what if they are right? As for the former, the alternative to failing to conclude the agreement is to see the Atlantic economic influence in the world wane. The TTIP provides an opportunity to jumpstart the Atlantic economy, even though this may materialise at the cost of intra-EU and intra-NAFTA trade (Hübner 2014). If this view is right, the gradual loss of international status may still occur; the question is, though, how should we manage the process (or, as critics would say, whether we engage in damage control).

By adopting the TTIP chapter on regulatory cooperation, the EU and the US hope to acquire the advantage of market standard-setter, as both negotiating parties undertake to "promote international standards".

At the same time, the EU has declared that regulatory cooperation will not lead to lowering of protection standards relating to human health, consumer well-being and rights, the environment or "other things that benefit society as a whole". The threshold for cooperation is set by the public interest and regulatory independence. At least, that is the TTIP principle. The question is, how will the parties understand their regulatory mandates? On the one hand, should it be market-driven, as in the US, that is, let industry set the rules, or rather should one engage in European-style, active policy of increasing protection standards. On the other hand, which regulatory standards reflect social expectations and which merely result from regulatory inertia. Accordingly, institutional setup is not about

Agreement on Technical Barriers to Trade (TBT), concerning other requirements (such as labelling, terminology, packaging, etc.).

laying down actual rules but rather about creating space for their approximation in the future.

Now, the three major concerns in this respect, as identified by the European Commission during its public consultation, relate to the threat of lowering protection standards, limiting the government's capacity to regulate, and circumventing parliaments (European Commission 2015).

2. Regulatory Cooperation Provisions

The principal point of reference in the public debate on the matter at hand is the textual negotiation proposal tabled by the EU and published in February 2015 (European Commission (II) 2015). Although from the perspective of this paper the documents cover the most important part of cooperation, that is, the EU-Brussels and the US-federal levels, it should be noted that the provisions concerning the EU-national and the US-state level cooperation—which may have a significant impact on the government and parliamentary position—will be published later. To some extent, one may refer, however, to the text of the EU-Canada Comprehensive Economic and Trade Agreement (CETA 2014), as it constitutes a benchmark for the TTIP negotiations.

2.1. At the very beginning, the treaty reiterates regulatory autonomy at the level considered by each Party to be "appropriate" to achieve legitimate public policy objectives (TTIP, article 1[2]). A sample list of such goals includes environmental, consumer protection, working conditions, human, animal and plant life, health and safety, personal data, cybersecurity, cultural diversity, and preserving financial stability.

Procedural obligations are set under Section II and Section III.

Section II duties concern Good Regulatory Practices that apply to supply or the use of services (such as authorization, licensing or qualification) and goods (their characteristics, production methods, presentation or use). These practices cover transparency requirements and constitute a toolbox of Regulatory Policy Instruments.

2.2. Transparency denotes the parties' obligation to publically report at least once per year planned regulatory acts at the central level (TTIP Art. 5). If, however, an impact assessment (IA) is planned for such a regulation—and we will see below that the TTIP sends a strong impulse to undertake such an exercise for

2 Since the TTIP proposal's chapters have not been numbered, I am using numeration of these particular documents. Accordingly, by TTIP Art. 1, I refer to the first article of the investment chapter and not of the partnership agreement as a whole.

all regulations important to international business—the information should be made public as early as possible. The parties already undertake to report plans to regulate a relevant aspect and the possible timing. Depending on what the parties understand by a planned action, this could mean a duty of transparency comparable to public scrutiny of an ongoing regulatory process or a general obligation already at the level of strategic analysis. In this respect, it is necessary to reiterate that in accordance with the *general notes,* preceding Article 1, the chapter on regulatory cooperation "may not lend [itself] to the application of dispute settlement rules" (point 5). Accordingly, it is of fundamental importance whether this provision shields parties from liability for breach of cooperation duties. I believe yes, although neither the place of the provision nor its formulation appears to exclude any doubt in this respect.

Above this general right to information, the parties are obliged to undertake open and non-discriminatory public consultation with respect to regulation undergoing IA. Although the parties are obliged to examine the contents of the concerns thus voiced, they are not bound by such demands (TITP Art. 6(1)). Similar to public access to information, public consultation is increasingly considered a standard in a democratic state of law. The problem is, whether such a form of transparency actually leads to a better legislative process and, most of all, increased legitimacy of law-making at an aggregate level in Brussels and Washington D.C. Take, for instance, the experience with TTIP public consultations. Thousands of copy-paste accusations against the partnership were submitted, which makes it difficult both to ignore and to include such a contribution. Hence, one has to ask what public information will look like for it to remain meaningful and to lend itself to abuse by the private or public sectors.

2.3. The second leg of the transparency duty—alongside transparency and public consultation—consists of Regulatory Policy Instruments as an analytical tool. This part starts with both parties affirming their intention to carry out impact assessments for planned regulatory acts at the central level (TTIP Article 7(1)). Given the title, that is, policy instruments, which should denote legally non-binding instruments, and interpreted in good faith, the declaration should not raise concerns. It seems fair, however, to make two observations in this respect. First, as mentioned above, an act undergoing an IA is subject to more stringent obligations in terms of public access to information. Thus, indirectly, this part broadens the application of the "earliest possible" right of access to virtually all regulations at the central level. This, in turn, leads to a second observation in terms of the cost-benefit analysis of undertaking IA with respect to any central regulation. It entails considerable institutional costs for the lawmakers, limiting their capacity to focus on other matters and fragmenting the attention of the analytical branch to a multitude of minor tasks. This situation is to be contrasted with a private perspective in which individual companies, NGOs or think-tanks specialise in one particular matter and, if worried about the normative prospects, can dedicate relatively large resources to raise public attention. It is not to say that CBAs/IAs are not to be made, but it should be taken into account that, both domestically and in the international context, a lawmaker's message is dispersed across many problems and audiences, whereas the other party will streamline its communications efforts by targeting particular recipients.

What is interesting, however, is the declaration of both parties that an IA should take into account relevant international instruments and the regulatory perspective of the counterpart, and that it should consider the impact on international trade and investments (TTIP Art. 7(2)). Although taking into account the regulatory standards of the other side does not have an explanation attached to it similar to the one for taking into account public consultation, another interpretation would give extraterritorial scope to domestic legislation, which would not be legal[3]. This aside, it is an interesting provision that will prod lawmakers to look at law-making from a broader perspective and to routinely take into account the relation between EU/US standards and global regulatory practices. Accordingly, if an IA is desirable at all, this prospect will have an ever greater significance in a globalising economy.

2.4. The core of the chapter is set in Section III on Regulatory Cooperation. These obligations apply to centrally adopted rules on the trade in goods and services mentioned above, which, additionally, have or are likely to have a significant impact on trade or investment between the parties. Here, cooperation covers several elements.

First, by establishing domestic Focal Points, for the purposes of exchanging information concerning envisaged and existing regulation, both parties will thus together create a bilateral cooperation mechanism (TTIP Art. 8). Through this channel, the parties shall seek opportunities for the purposes of increased compatibility and identify cooperation priorities.

Second, with respect to the above need to make public certain regulatory actions, the parties will indicate to each other through the Focal Points which of the acts are likely to have a significant impact on international trade and investments. This obligation is not limited to bilateral economic relations. Should the other

3 The disclaimer concerning the meaning of taking certain circumstances into account appears again with respect to the duty of regulatory and information exchange.

party be interested in acquiring further information about a regulation, including norms adopted by government branches other than the executive, it may request an exchange of information. Although there are additional obligations in terms of timing, such exchanges cannot constitute an obstacle to timely law-making, especially with respect to urgent matters (TTIP Art. 9(3)).

In accordance with the public policy goals (as mentioned with respect to TTIP Art. 1), each party may suggest in the course of the information exchange to adopt measures for the promotion of regulatory compatibility. In such case, the parties may decide to jointly examine ways of increasing normative convergence (TTIP Art. 11(2)):

- Full or partial mutual recognition of equivalence of regulation, if upon analysis both sets of norms allow achievement of equivalent results.
- Harmonisation of regulatory acts, or essential parts thereof, by approximation of domestic rules or, again to reiterate, the referral to or development of international standards. The latter approach is strengthened under TTIP Art. 13, which also calls for international cooperation with third-parties.
- Simplification of a regulation in line with common legal or administrative principles and guidelines.

All of the above works are to be coordinated by the Regulatory Cooperation Body (RCB). The body shall have both prospective (planning) and retrospective (monitoring) powers. The result of the monitoring reviews will be reported to the Joint Ministerial Body (TTIP Art. 14(2b)). The body shall also ensure transparency in regulatory cooperation, which could suggest certain powers with respect to obligations stemming from Section II. The RCB would consist of representatives of both parties.

What may, however, be worrying is the possible effect of opening the RCB annual meetings to Civil Society Contact Groups (if any such are created), which would encompass equal representation of business, consumers, trade unions, environmental groups and other relevant public interest associations, regardless whether the items on the agenda affect their interests or not. Assuming that the number of such seats will be limited, one can hardly imagine a group that would be representative of a spectrum of views within each of these general categories (perhaps the least problematic is the environment). Direct participation cannot be equated with the right of stakeholders to submit their observations to the parties.

3. What is New, Then?

On the positive side, while one should be aware of the possible challenges posed both by the confidentiality and ill-managed transparency in the proposal, it must be first observed that the considerable amount of concern about regulatory cooperation stems from a lack of understanding of the contemporary international regulatory process. I would argue that for a researcher on international economic governance, the most striking feature of the chapter is that the general concept is hardly new at all. Looking even at the relatively late EU-US level (many European states had started bilateral cooperation earlier), regulatory cooperation dates back at least to the 1998 Mutual Recognition Agreement on conformity. The latter lesson is interesting given the current fears, as opposed to the high hopes in the late '90s. However, the effectiveness of that solution proved limited, covering only three out of six areas of cooperation, that is, only one-fifth of the envisaged bilateral trade, even in highly competitive sectors (de Brito, Pelkmans 2015). Later, the two scholars compiled a list of over four pages of regulatory initiatives undertaken jointly by the EU and the US (Chase, Pelkmans 2015), some of them numbering thousands of both formal and informal communications and exchanges annually. Cooperation covered fields such as drugs, aviation safety, toy safety and marine equipment.

Hence, the concept as such is not new. What could constitute the added-value is an awareness of the external aspect of regulatory cooperation. If the EU and the US manage to agree to harmonise certain standards, it would send a strong signal to Canada as well while CETA goes into force. The Canadians may take into account EU/US regulatory convergence, which in turn would constitute a powerful signal for any truly global business.

Having said that, the chapter highlighted several areas—mostly in terms of transparency and prospective actions—where the scope of obligation is as yet unclear and a broader interpretation could prove detrimental. For instance, what does early notice about regulatory initiatives mean (not to mention also the idea to cover law-making under the same provision)? How early would such acts have to be signalled? Does it necessarily mean that the original version would ever see the light of day? Can the entire decision-making process and brainstorming continue smoothly with stakeholder oversight and, possibly, their own contributions to the topic?

Also, the crucial factor of what is important to international trade and investments, that is, the basis for a greater cooperation obligation, is a category broad enough to possibly cover almost any area of regulation.

But arguably, the largest unknown of the chapter are the blank spaces left out for the EU national and US state regulatory and legislative process. On the one hand, the administrative burden of transatlantic regulatory cooperation would constitute a considerable cost for the local communities, on the other hand, it is hard to imagine how such interests could be represented at an aggregate level. This impression, even if strengthened by the fact that protection of public interest at the central level—Brussels and Washington D.C.—is not as clear below.

Although the US negotiating position has not been published, there were some signals that the entire initiative tabled by the EU met with reluctance from the American side. Where Brussels understands regulatory cooperation in a more centralised and institutionalised form, for the US it is something closer to regulatory convergence/coherence, achieved through notices and comments. Allegedly, the scope of local regulatory autonomy constitutes one of the thorny issues (Treat 2015).

Conclusions

Given that the US position has not been released to the public, it is difficult to ascertain which negotiation stage we have actually reached or what the chance is that the final provisions of the TTIP will reflect the provisions discussed above. Not only is it impossible to assess the convergence of views with respect to this chapter but also the problems raised here lead to other concerns and point our attention to other sectors. For instance, while the EU states opened their public procurements sector to entrepreneurs enjoying the freedom of establishment, thus indirectly also to US businesses, the American "local counterparts", i.e., states, appear very concerned about the possible duty of restraining the "buy local" attitude. The Europeans are, in turn, worried about the regulation of GMOs, hormones and beef, cloning of animals, chemical regulation and public health (The Greens EFA 2015).

While we cannot treat these concerns lightly, the point of this chapter is not to lose sight of the big picture of global economic regulation.

References

Bertelsmann Foundation, 2014, TTIP Sectoral Study, http://bit.ly/1gfqbeW (accessed 30.11.2015).

Chase P., J. Pelkmans, 2015, This time it's different: Turbo-charging regulatory cooperation in TTIP, CEPS Special Report No. 110 / June 2015.

CEPR, 2013, Reducing transatlantic barriers to trade and investment, Centre for Economic Policy Research, http://bit.ly/1PqsMWv (accessed 1.12.2015).

CETA, 2014, Consolidated CETA Text, http://bit.ly/1uMnTss (accessed 27.11.2015). European Commission 2015, Factsheet on Regulatory cooperation in TTIP, http://bit.ly/1ScJHYT (accessed 27.11.2015).

de Brito A., J. Pelkmans, 2015, Transatlantic MRAs: Lessons for TTIP?, CEPS Special Report No. 101 / March 2015.

European Commission (II), 2015, TTIP – Initial Provisions for Chapter [on] Regulatory Cooperation, (accessed 27.11.2015).

European Parliament, 2015, TTIP Impacts on European Energy Markets and Manufacturing Industries. Study, IP/A/ITRE/2014-02.

Greens EFA, 2015, Impact of TTIP regulatory cooperation proposals on food policies, http://bit.ly/1ToNK6z (accessed 30.11.2015).

Hübner K., 2014, TTIP and CETA. Remaking of the Atlantic Economy?" [in:] J. Roy, R. Domínguez (eds.), The Transatlantic Trade and Investment Partnership between the European Union and the United State, Miami, pp. 35–50.

Lamy P., 2013, The Geneva Consensus. Making Trade Work for All, Cambridge University Press, Cambridge.

Potoski M., A. Prakash, 2006, Racing to the Bottom? Trade, Environmental Governance, and ISO 14001, American Journal of Political Science vol. 50, iss. 2, pp. 350–364.

Treat S., 2015, Regulatory Cooperation_update_Treat 619Treat TTIP, speaking at Maine's Citizen Trade Policy Commission, http://bit.ly/1NEgfOV (accessed 30.11.2015).

Dominika Bochańczyk-Kupka
(University of Economics in Katowice)

Chapter 4. Geographical Indications in the US-EU TTIP negotiations

Strong intellectual property protection is an essential part of free trade agreements (FTAs). In the current negotiations for the Transatlantic Trade and Investment Partnership (TTIP), one area of intellectual property rights that is certain to create disagreement between the EU and the US is that of geographical indications (GIs). The protection of geographical indications is perceived to be one of the most contentious parts of the TTIP negotiations.

Modern globalised economy seems to reduce the importance of the location or origin of goods. Nevertheless, it plays a crucial role in the ongoing debate around geographical indications in the TTIP, where the EU and the US policy approaches diverge markedly. Additionally the policy makers and scholars worldwide are currently deeply divided over the proper meaning and appropriate level of protection of geographical indications. There are several reasons influencing different approaches to GIs protection in the US and the EU: existing national legal systems, economic interests, historical background, etc. Simply put, the difference in the two approaches is that the European Union prefers *sui generis* protection for GIs, while the US approach is founded on traditional notions of trademark law. These significant differences have caused commentators to speculate over whether the two systems are nowadays at all compatible, as it is hard to see a deep TTIP compromise on geographical indications.

This chapter gives an overview of the European and American systems for protecting GIs. It describes differences in the historical background, explains differences between public and private approaches towards GIs protection and shows the negotiation positions of the USA and the EU in the TTIP.

1. Geographical Indications as part of the system of intellectual property rights

Policy makers and scholars worldwide are currently divided over the proper meaning and appropriate level of geographical indications protection. Central to the GIs concept is the idea that particular regions or localities bestow unique qualities on products. There is a common agreement that a product's quality, reputation or other characteristics can be determined by where it comes from. This origin creates special and unique features and characteristics of the products. Therefore this "origin" should be protected – this is indisputable. The battle arises around the precise meaning of GIs and the right model of protection.

The definition of GIs is provided by the World Trade Organization's Trade Related Intellectual Property Rights (TRIPS) Agreement, adopted in 1994, which recognizes GIs as a private industrial property right[1]. Geographical indications are defined, for the purposes of this Agreement, in Article 22 as indications which identify a good as originating from a particular place (in the territory of the WTO Members), or a region or locality in that territory, where a given quality, reputation or other characteristic of the good is essentially attributable to its geographical origin (Agreement on Trade-Related Aspects of Intellectual Property Rights 1994). In other words, geographical indications can be understood as a source identifier and a protection of the integrity, specialty, and commercial value of products whose uniqueness and singularity are identified by their geographic origin and special process of manufacture. Thus GI acts as a special device that helps the manufacturers to differentiate their products from competing products on the market and enable them to build a reputation and goodwill around them, and often fetch a premium price. GIs are very frequently premium quality products, often expensive to manufacture, produced by small and medium firms locally, and therefore especially exposed to misuse and counterfeiting. It is worth noting that GIs are economically and culturally significant for many countries but not all goods of the same type are equivalent in terms of quality.

Nowadays geographical indications are seen as an important aspect of intellectual property rights. The TRIPS Agreement does not address such issues explicitly, but it is generally recognized that GIs do not share exactly the same meaning of property as classical intellectual properties. This is due to the fact that GIs generally have no single legal owner who would have the same rights as to a trademark or patent. On the one hand, most of GIs are geographical names, and these are usually considered to be administered by the states. On the other hand, the group of legitimate users of GIs should generally be limited according to the GI product's quality, and thus would include anyone able to achieve this quality in the relevant geographical area (Belletti, Marescott 2011).

---

1 The TRIPS Agreement was negotiated during the 1986–94 Uruguay Round of trade negotiations. That Agreement was the first to introduce extensive intellectual property rules into the multilateral trade law system.

2. Models of GIs protection

There is a long history of GIs protection in countries as well as at the international level through international treaties dating back to the end of the 19th century[2]. The following international agreements contain elements of protection for GIs:

- the Paris Convention for the Protection of Industrial Property (1883) (GIs protections under a different label – 'false indications'),
- the Madrid Agreement for the Repression of False or Deceptive Indications of Source on Goods (1891),
- the Lisbon Agreement for the Protection of Appellations of Origin and their International Registration (1958),
- the Agreement on Trade-Related Aspects of Intellectual Property Rights (the TRIPS Agreement) (1994).

Nowadays protection of GIs is guaranteed under the TRIPs Agreement. According to Article 22 members of the WTO shall provide the legal means to prevent the use of any means in the designation or presentation of a good that indicates or suggests that the good originates in a geographical area other than the true place of origin in a manner which misleads the public as to the geographical origin of the good and any use which constitutes an act of unfair competition within the meaning of Article 10*bis* of the Paris Convention (1967). Higher level of protection for wines and spirits is provided by Article 23.

Geographical indications protection is a matter of having exclusive rights to the use of a name. Under the TRIPS, the WTO members have a mandatory responsibility to recognize and protect GIs as intellectual property rights, but there is no universal method of protecting them, nor is there a common international commercial law. Therefore granting of legal protection for GIs lies within the jurisdiction of separate domestic laws and regulations of individual countries. It is thus useful to understand the different options that exist for protecting producers' exclusive right to use a geographical name in trading. Domestic mechanisms vary considerably, therefore different marks, appellations, or designations need to be registered in all relevant countries in order to protect the GIs they represent. GIs can be protected in several different ways. These include certification marks, denominations of origin, collective membership marks, trademarks and formal *sui generis* systems, as well as administrative rulings, registers, or even, under laws on unfair competition, truth in labelling, or consumer protection. Different

2 For a comprehensive survey of the history of GIs in Europe and USA see: Melkonian 2005, Farley 2014, and Monten 2005.

types of protection are used in different countries and may even apply differently to certain products such as wine and spirits as opposed to foods or handicrafts. Multiple forms of protection may also apply in the same country, such as trademarks as well as a *sui generis* system, thereby presenting plenty of opportunities for confusion or conflict (Thévenod-Mottet 2006).

There are 110 countries, including the Member States of the European Union, with specific GI laws in place. Outside the EU, only 22 of the remaining countries have established registers and officially listed geographical indications. There are 56 countries without specific GI protection laws, but which protect GIs through certification marks, collective marks or trademarks[3]. In fact, many countries with *sui generis* systems also have the option of limited or extended protection by means of their trademark systems (*Guide to Geographical Indications Linking Products and Their Origins* 2009, p. 40).

In modern literature there are several approaches to classifying systems which are used to protect GIs. The most general division classifies all legal systems according to the private or public approach (Legal Protection of Geographical Indications 2013). The public law approach appears when public authorities enact legislation dedicated specifically to protection of GIs (a *sui generis* system)[4]. This approach generally consists of an official recognition of GIs by granting them the status of a public seal of quality, often through a common official logo, where governments can protect the use of the GIs *ex officio*. Registration is often free from administrative charge and there is no need to renew it. This protection is created in order to protect authentic product designation. The private law approach entails the use of laws against unfair competition. It is connected with trademark laws, where the protection is primarily based on private actions. Registration is the most common legal tool to define the circle of legitimate users and ensure protection. This is anticipated both in specific GI legislation (the *sui generis* systems) and in

3 These include the Australia, Canada, Japan, United States, parts of Africa and a number of Arab countries.

4 *Sui generis*, from the Latin meaning "of its own kind", is a term used to identify a legal classification that exists independently of other categorizations because of its uniqueness or as a result of the specific creation of an entitlement or obligation. *Sui generis* methods of intellectual property protection may provide legal protection for signs and characteristics associated with a product, such as a logo or a specific shape, by including them in the related product specifications (Legal Protection of Geographical Indications http://www.fao.org/fileadmin/user_upload/foodquality/fichefiles/en/c6.1.pdf).

trademark law. Geographical signs have acquired a "secondary meaning" and certification marks or collective marks are used[5]. Registration must be renewed after a certain period. This protection is created to certify the quality of the particular product. The public approach is generally accepted in the European Union member countries, and the private approach in the USA. Key distinctions between trademarks and GIs are presented in table 1.

Table 1. Key distinctions between trademarks and geographical indications

Feature	Trademarks (private approach)	Geographical Indications (public approach)
Ownership	Anyone. Typically individual entity or corporation, sometimes collective or government.	Producers or government.
Transferability	To anyone, anywhere.	Linked to origin. Cannot be de-localized.
Rights to origin name	First in time – first in rights principle	Distinguishes legitimate rights to origin, not first to apply for name. Registration confers rights to all legitimate producers.
Protection	Private. Burden entirely on owner.	Public. Government responsible but some private burden to identify infringement.

5 GIs may be protected through a registration under trademark law, in the form of a trademark, a certification mark or a collective mark, depending on the categories existing in the country. A trademark is a distinctive sign used by a company to identify itself and its products or services to consumers. It is a type of intellectual property involving a name, word, phrase, logo, symbol, design or image, or a combination of these elements. Trademarks do not refer to generic terms, nor do they refer exclusively to geographical terms. A certification mark is a specific type of trademark. It certifies that the goods or services bearing the mark meet a certain defined standard or possess a particular characteristic. Such marks are usually registered in the name of trade associations, government departments, technical institutes or similar bodies. A collective mark is a specific type of trademark which indicates that the goods or services bearing the mark originate from members of a trade association, rather than just one trader.

Feature	Trademarks (private approach)	Geographical Indications (public approach)
Use	Trademark: typically private, can license. Collective mark: closed group. Certification mark: open according to set rules.	Collective, open to all producers that comply with rules.
Quality	Private. Usually not specified except sometimes for certification marks.	Disclosed in standards or specifications and obligatorily linked to origin.
Name or sign	May be created. May or may not have geographic linkage.	Must exist already and must link to *terroir*.

Source: adapted from: Guide to Geographical Indications Linking Products and Their Origins (2009), International Trade Centre, Geneva, p. 55.

Another classification of means of GI protection is created by the WTO Secretariat. It classifies all diverse means of protection into three broad categories (Das 2007):

- laws focusing on business practices;
- trademark laws;
- *sui generis* protection.

Laws focusing on business practices form a category of GI protection which deals with laws prohibiting business practices involving the misuse of GIs. This category covers a wide range of laws, such as common laws (particularly in relation to passing-off; laws relating to the repression of unfair competition) or laws meant for consumer protection, either in general terms or more specifically with regard to such matters as product-labelling, health protection, and food safety.

Trademark laws are found to provide two types of protection for geographical indications: protection against the registration and use of GIs as trademarks and protection as marks indicating collectivity, certification, or a guarantee against unauthorized use by third parties.

The forms afforded by *sui generis* protection include the laws specifically dedicated to the protection of GIs, i.e. provisions providing special protection to GIs contained in other laws, for example, on trademarks, marketing, labelling, or taxation. Some of these means provide *sui generis* protection for geographical indications that relate to products with specifically defined characteristics or methods of production, while other means apply without such specific definitions.

The protection provided under a *sui generis* system is stronger than that available under the above two categories of modes of protection. Generally, these different categories of protection can coexist in a single country. For instance, the legal forms of protection for GIs available in the US include provisions of laws focusing on business practices and trademark law. In other countries (e.g. in European) there are also *sui generis* regulations , especially regarding foodstuffs, wines and spirits.

These differentiations in the approved methods of GI protection cause problems in international relations, because GIs are variously understood and protected in different legal systems. It is clear that in the TTIP negotiations just only European and American claims are negotiated but the EU and the United States systems together are fairly representative of the diversity of approaches utilized by most countries active in this field today. They can serve as useful examples or models because the US and the EU represent fundamentally different approaches to GI protection. Over the years both the European Union and USA have been trying to promote different GI standards worldwide to provide sufficient protection to their locally produced products. These different approaches have already provoked many disputes, especially in the context of international agreements such as free trade agreements.

Whether one or the other system provides a better protection for GIs is still debatable and it is absolutely impossible to find out which system is better. Arguments are raised in both directions and there seems to be no worldwide consensus on this issue. From the point of view of the level of GI protection, the protection level reached in a *sui generis* system is higher. According to some scholars, previously registered trademarks containing a protected GI can, under some circumstances, be invalidated – using a trademark to mislead the public about the origin of the good carrying it (Flodgren 2009). Additionally the use of a trademark regime to protect a GI name does not provide as comprehensive protection as that offered by a *sui generis* GIs system (Cáceres 2007). The use of a trademark system has proved to be very complicated, costly and not always effective. The *sui generis* approach, as used in the EU countries, treats GIs as belonging to a group in the region (often administered by a government or association), and as a public asset that cannot be bought, sold, transferred or controlled by an individual or corporation. GIs cannot be decoupled from their origin. In this case, the public authorities are likely to be involved in the protection process.

On the other hand, systems oriented toward private means of protection such as the trademark regime may also have some advantages. One occurs when the size and bureaucratic nature of governments could make them slow to respond in correcting a misrepresentative or fraudulent use of a GI (Giovannucci 2009). In contrast, the owners of a mark can take immediate legal action, provided they have the capacity to do so. Also, in absence of a real democratic process, a government may not be fairly responsive to the protection needs of GIs. Private systems put the burden of cost directly on the owner of the mark. This can reduce public costs unless, as often happens, the government owns the mark. Furthermore, the government cannot be expected to efficiently take on many roles that are best handled in the private sector or within a collective organization.

To sum up, it is clear that the systems described above are extremely different. Therefore the EU and the United States have divergent interests in their treatment of GIs. The EU is attempting to consolidate the international reputation of GIs and their increased public protection. The United States has been focusing on increasing open markets and has viewed the EU's GIs efforts as somewhat protectionist.

3. Geographical Indications in the TTIP

Protection of Geographical Indications is one of the most disputed parts of the TTIP talks. The negotiation position of the European Union Council states that the future Agreement shall aim to provide enhanced protection and recognition of EU GIs with the aim of solving existing conflicts in a satisfactory manner. The United States Trade Representative (USTR) in 2014 claimed that they would seek new opportunities to advance and defend the interest of US farmers and producers, with respect to strong protection and effective enforcement of intellectual property rights, including their ability to compete in foreign markets (Office of United States Representatives 2014). The Report of the Eleventh Round of Negotiations for the Transatlantic Trade and Investment Partnership which took place in Miami, indicated many unsolved issues in the negotiations (European Commission 2015). For instance, the EU side recalled that the protection of GIs constitutes a key EU priority in TTIP. The EU also wanted the US to improve its system in several ways, notably by protecting an agreed list of EU GIs. The EU renewed its call to the US to move to negotiating mode on this topic, so as to bring it in line with progress made in other areas of negotiations, in particular on tariffs. The EU explained again the shortcomings of the US trademark system. The US negotiation position remained unchanged. The US commentators and scholars constantly claimed that trade agreements were supposed to tear down barriers to trade and commerce – not erect new ones. For instance Shawna Morris, Senior Director of the International Consortium for Common Food Names (CCFN) claimed that main goal of negotiation should be to promote approaches that protect both legitimate GIs and generic food names and accused the EU of attempts to monopolize common names (Common Food Names 2015).

A major objective for the TTIP is the elimination of regulatory differences that make cross-border trade more difficult. This task may be relatively easy in cases where regulations impose different requirements in pursuit of the same goal. But in situations where the US and the EU have very different goals, achieving regulatory reform through trade negotiations may prove to be impossible. Especially when taking into account that both parties are major producers of GIs nowadays, so that issue has enormous commercial significance for both sides. But it also touches on cultural and ideological differences. Europe's GI protection scheme is part of a much larger policy that seeks to preserve traditional production methods and ways of life in the face of globalization (Watson 2015). The European model of GI protection is very strict and it is justified in theory by a strong belief that the link between place and quality is an objective creation of traditional culture and practices. When others use geographic names in a generic way, they are unfairly using the value created in that name by generations of local manufacturers. Supporters of this point of view claim that strong GI protection is needed to prevent fraud, ensure fairness, and promote economic development. It is easy to under stand why passions are aroused if the EU producers feel that the value inherent in GIs is appropriated by competitors making use of the same designation. However, most of the EU's GIs are unknown outside their region of origin.

The United States takes a very different approach. With some exceptions for wine and spirits, the US protects GIs through trademark law. The main policy goal is to prevent consumer confusion, so unlike the European model, the United States does not protect marks that are generic terms for the product. As a result, many European GIs receive no protection in the United States. That also partly explains the US reluctance to extend GIs protection. Some scholars even claim that idea of protection of GIs is alien to American law and American culture (Chen 1996). That is because American intellectual property law is built on the foundation of disseminating knowledge as widely as possible, in order to spur innovation and favour new entrants to the market. The European system of geographical indications dampens innovation in favour of traditional production.

The issue of GI protection causes strong feelings and uncompromising rhetoric on both sides of the Atlantic. Commentators in America condemn European GIs as trade barriers. The US agricultural industrial lobbies are heavily set against GIs. At the same time, the EU commentators talk about inferior imitations of European GIs in the United States and vows to solve the problem through the TTIP. It is worth remembering that the United States is not demanding that the European Union allow the sale of American products as geographical indications.

It is unlikely that TTIP negotiations over GI protection will result in an outcome that both sides find satisfactory. And it is still unclear how the issue of GIs will be resolved in the TTIP talks or even whether it can be resolved. There is a pressure on the US negotiators to reject completely any EU calls for GIs in the TTIP.

Conclusions

Geographical indications are becoming increasingly recognized, and they play an important role in the world economy nowadays. The progressive globalization of the world economy has dramatically altered agricultural politics and policy. It has also raised hard questions about the place of tradition and locality in a world that seems to be ever-more homogeneous and borderless. GIs, as intellectual property rights, aim to protect both farmers and heritage and have never been more economically and politically important or controversial than they are today.

The present paper explained different approaches to GI protection in the EU and the US systems. GIs and trademarks are different IPRs, and therefore cause both synergies and conflicts in international trade. The recent history of debate between the United States and Europe on the matter of Geographical Indications can lead the commentators to assume that the divide separating the two great trading blocs is unbridgeable. Both sides represent different attitudes to this issue and their aims and interests are extremely opposite. Therefore it seems that a bilaterally satisfactory agreement is impossible to achieve.

References

Agreement on Trade-Related Aspects of Intellectual Property Rights, 1994, <https://www.wto.org/english/docs_e/legal_e/27-trips_04b_e.htm>

Belletti G., A. Marescott, 2011, *The Effects of Protecting Geographical Indications Ways and Means of their Evaluation, Swiss Federal Institute of Intellectual Property* <https://www.ige.ch/fileadmin/user_upload/Juristische_Infos/e/publication_no_7_2nd_ed_Effects-of-Protecting-Geographical-Indications.pdf>

Benka, S., 2015, *Protection of Geographical Indications: How Extensive Should They Be?*, America's Trade Policy website, <http://americastradepolicy.com/protection-of-geographical-indications-how-extensive-should-they-be/#.VHTrgNJ0y71>

Cáceres E. O., 2007, *Perspectives for Geographical Indications*, WIPO GEO/BEI/07/13

Common Food Names, 2015, *Threats to Common Food Names More Widespread in EU Trade Deals and other Geographical Indications Policies*, <http://www.commonfoodnames.com>

Chen J., 1996, *A Sober Second Look at Appellations of Origin: How the United States will Crash France's Wine and Cheese Party*, Journal of Global Trade 29, 58

Das K., 2007, *Protection of Geographical Indications. An Overview of Select Issues with Particular Reference to India*, Centad.

European Commission, 2015, *Report of the Eleventh Round of Negotiations for the Transatlantic Trade and Investment Partnership (Miami, 19–23 October 2015)* < http://trade.ec.europa.eu/doclib/docs/2015/november/tradoc_153935.pdf>

FAO, 2013, *Legal Protection of Geographical Indications*, <http://www.fao.org/fileadmin/ user_upload/foodquality/fichefiles/en/c6.1.pdf>

Farley Ch. H., 2014, *The Protection of Geographical Indications in the Inter-American Convention?*, WIPO Journal 68

Flodgren J., 2009, *Geographical Indications in the 21st century – what, when and how? A Critical Review of the Legal Framework for GI Protection and GI-Related Trade in the International Community*, University of Lund

Giovannucci D., T. Josling, W. Kerr, B. O'Connor, M.T. Yeun, 2009, *Guide To Geographical Indications Linking Products and Their Origins*, International Trade Centre

International Trade Centre, 2009, *Guide To Geographical Indications Linking Products and Their Origins*, Geneva

Melkonian R., 2005, *The History and Future of Geographical Indications in Europe and the United States*. Harvard Law School, Harvard, Students Papers <https://dash.harvard.edu/handle/1/8852204>

Monten L., 2005, *Geographical Indications of Origin: Should They be protected and why? Analysis of the Issue from the US and EU Perspectives*, Santa Clara High Tech.L.J.315, 315.

Office of United States Representatives, 2014, *US Objectives, US Benefits in the Transatlantic Trade and Investment Partnership* <https://ustr.gov/about-us/policy-offices/press-office/press-releases/2014/March/US-Objectives-US-Benefits-In-the-TTIP-a-Detailed-View>

Thévenod-Mottet E., 2006, *WP1 Report. Legal and Institutional issues related to GIs. SINERGI EU Funded Project, final report.*

Watson W., 2015, *Geographical Indications in TTIP: An Impossible Task*, http://www.cato.org/publications/cato-online-forum/geographical-indications-ttip-impossible-task

Jerzy Menkes, Magdalena Słok-Wódkowska
(Warsaw School of Economics, University of Warsaw)

Chapter 5. ISDS and the TTIP—A Polish Perspective

The mechanism of investor-state dispute settlement (ISDS) lately has become one of the most controversial elements of trade and investment agreements. The negotiations of the Transatlantic Trade and Investment Partnership (TTIP) as well as the Transpacific Partnership (TPP)—two of the most important regional trade agreements (RTA) in recent years—have made the discussion even more heated. Many doubts have been raised, mainly in civil society in developed states, which mostly underline that there is no need for additional protection for foreign investors in states with established standards of democracy and rule of law.

This chapter's aim is to present the Polish point of view and that of other Eastern and Central European states' on the issue[1]. To be able to fully describe the differences in perspective, we need to describe the problem. Therefore, we start by presenting problems that seem to be caused by ISDS and then we describe the new EU perspective and ways of solving these problems. The last part concerns the Polish perspective on the issue of ISDS, especially in the TTIP.

1. Critics of ISDS

Bilateral Investment Agreements (BITs) have been signed by various states since 1959. They are perceived as the best way to guarantee a sufficient level of protection for foreign investors. The main goal of a BIT is to prevent host states from discrimination, denial of justice or any other form of unfair treatment.

The concerns indicated by investors are real, despite the fact that legal standards of risk protection constitute the hard core of International Human Rights as well as public international law (Mann 1957 and *Arbitration between Libya and Taxaco Overseas Petroleum Company*). The concerns are also common among those whose "host state" is located in the trans-Atlantic legal area. Foreign investors (from the "home state") fear discriminatory treatment in the host state (Yannaca-Small 2006). Those concerns have not been met by the practice of diplomatic

1 The project is funded by the National Science Centre of Poland based on decision No. DEC-2013/09/B/HS4/01488.

protection (used in Mavrommatis Palestine Concessions (Jurisdiction) and Draft Articles on Diplomatic Protection 2006) — protecting the rights of investors in the legal regime of "State-State Dispute Settlement" (SSDS)[2].

Although in practice there have been abuses of the right of diplomatic protection of citizens abroad, in Latin America and elsewhere, the victims of abuse are not alien but from the host state. In response to specific cases, the "Calvo doctrine" formulated the standard of equal treatment to protect nationals of the host country against *de facto* discrimination (Calvo 1896, p. 231) and it soon became standard with the Treaty of Commerce and Navigation, concluded by Latin American States at the Lima Congress II and supported at numerous inter-American conferences. Yet, similar to the lack of acceptance for abuse of the law and discrimination against citizens of the host country which resulted in the Calvo doctrine, also unacceptable is the abuse, or deprivation of investors' right to diplomatic protection of the host country by their own country (Calvo clause).

On the contrary, investors' expectations from the law evolved towards investor protection within the legal framework of BITs[3] that, predominantly, allow for settlement of investor vs. state disputes before an arbitral tribunal. This process was initiated in 1987 when a Hong Kong investor used a UK BIT against the government of Sri Lanka (Singh, Sharma 2013). Such a regime of dispute settlement is provided both by the new generation BITs (Lowenfeld 2008, pp. 570–2) and by international trade treaties (e.g., NAFTA) as well as international investment agreements (e.g., the Energy Charter Treaty). Most BITs guarantee investors "fair and equitable treatment", "full protection and security" and "free transfer of means" as well as access to ISDS in disputes against the "host state". Most disputes are settled under the International Convention for the Settlement of Investment Disputes and Chapter 11 of NAFTA. Foreign investors do not need to make use of diplomatic protection of the home state, as they are able to protect their rights within the regime of the investor-state dispute settlement mechanism (Tietje, Siporski 2012, p. 237), and they make use of it. However, in recent years the investor-state disputes have substantially changed. On the one hand investors from developing countries started to seek protection for their investments, hence a growing number of cases in which the suing party comes from Turkey or Jordan. On the other hand, there is a growing number of cases against developed states

2 Executed in the regime of Treaties of Friendship, Commerce and Navigation (FCN), The first FCN was concluded with France in 1778 and lasted until the end of the 1960s. Cases of investor-state disputes adjustable earlier as part of FCNs are currently regulated under BITs.

3 Initiated by the 1958 BIT between Germany and Pakistan.

such as EU member states, among which significantly increased the number of cases against i.e., Czechia, Spain, Hungary and Slovakia (UNCTAD 2014).

The new regulations, however, are being criticized. ISDS is often considered unilaterally favourable to foreign investors. It is also considered less favourable for the host state, for example, it is seen as restricting the state's capacity to protect public health, its natural environment and human rights. Recognizing that, for ISDS as a model solution to survive (as indicated by both bilateral and multilateral treaty practice) by balancing the legitimate interests of the parties, i.e., foreign investors and the host state, poses a challenge. The pendulum must be balanced, the dispute settlement regime must likewise protect the interests of the society and its institutions. Otherwise, we get Venezuela's 2012 termination of the agreement of the International Centre for Settlement of Investment Disputes of the World Bank, which is not a single phenomenon and its assessment cannot be limited to considering it the manifestation of a regime[4] that represents a political aberration but one that may testify to a steady divergence from ISDS (Conversation 2013). The regime imposed in the Convention on the Settlement of Investment Disputes between States and Nationals of Other States (ICSID) faces many challenges. One of them is related to its subjective status; on the one hand, the number of parties to the Convention, despite the given notices, are (still) 158 countries. On the other hand, however, the EU is not party to ICSID and that may result in the regime's atrophy.

Investor vs. state dispute settlements must be fair. To that end, transparency of the proceedings, among other solutions, is applied (see Article 29 of US model-BIT 2012), i.e., rejecting confidential in-camera proceedings and instituting the possibility to appeal the decision (Gantz 2005). Those demands mean departing from traditional commercial arbitration rules. Meeting them means the law is evolving, proving the ability to react to challenges.

Another unappreciated and widespread problem in the ISDS regime is discrimination of a national investor relative to a foreign one. The national investor does not have access to ISDS, thus one of the effects may be exodus of investors abroad.

2. Investment dispute settlement in the TTIP

The TTIP is supposed to be one of the most ambitious agreements ever. It is meant to cover not only trade liberalisation but also investment and protection

4 It should be noted that states felt threatened, also in the diplomatic protection regime, as evidenced by the Calvo doctrine. Art. 27 of the Mexican constitution demonstrated that.

of it. A potential ISDS chapter was not excluded, but the EU conditioned it on the results of the negotiations. Already in the negotiations mandate adopted by the EU Council in June 2013, conditions were set that needed to be met by a future ISDS mechanism in order to be agreed by the EU. It was also made clear that ISDS would be applicable only to an investment protection chapter, excluding chapters related to *inter alia* market access.

Although the main challenges of the EU-US ISDS were known by the time the negotiations started (Fact Sheet: Investment Protection and Investor-to-State Dispute Settlement in EU agreements, November 2013), under broad public pressure, negotiations within this field were suspended by the EU in January 2013. The European Commission announced its intention to hold public consultations on the issue. Public online consultations began in March and became an opportunity for the Commission to address the aims and boundaries of ISDS. Results of the consultation were published in January 2015, with rather critical responses. Main problems that were named: protection of the right to regulate, the establishment and functioning of arbitral tribunals, the review of ISDS decisions through an appellate mechanism. These problems were already known before.

Most of the EU objectives to be pushed ahead during the negotiations were already mentioned in a Communication from 2010. First of all, the Commission intends to limit the scope and omit nebulous wording from clauses related to the right to regulate, indirect expropriation, as well as fair and equitable treatment (FET). According to the Commission, these provisions are often misinterpreted or even abused by investors, and their claims might possibly be supported by arbitrators. This thesis seems to be an answer to fears present amongst the European public. It was envisaged, for example, in an analysis prepared for the European Parliament[5], that in such cases the infamous *Metalclad* decision would be invoked. Also, the *Vattenfall v. Germany*[6] case, which has not been finished yet, was mentioned. The problem with these provisions relates to the fact that their

---

5 Legal Implications of TTIP for the Acquis Communautaire in ENVI Relevant Sectors, Policy Department A: Economic and Scientific Policy of the European Parliament, http://www.europarl.europa.eu/RegData/etudes/etudes/join/2013/507492/IPOL-ENVI_ET(2013)507492_EN.pdf

6 The *Vattenfall II* case, in which Germany was sued for phasing out nuclear plants in 2011. Documents from the proceedings are not publicly accessible. For an overview of the case, see: N. Bernasconi-Osterwalder, R. Hoffmann, "The German Nuclear Phase-Out Put to the Test in International Investment Arbitration? Background to the new dispute, Vattenfall v. Germany (II)", http://www.iisd.org/pdf/2012/german_nuclear_phase_out.pdf.

vagueness is essential for their effectiveness. The aim of these provisions, especially the FET standard, is to cover situations that cannot be predicted at the time of the conclusion of the treaty. What can be done (and what the Commission claims to do) is narrowing of the scope of application of these clauses. It is also possible to exclude from investment protection system situations in which a disadvantageous decision will be made by a state in the normal exercise of their regulatory powers and adopted in a non-discriminatory manner, for a general purpose. These criteria were mentioned, for example, in the *Saluka* case.

One achievement that has been mostly endorsed by the Commission itself is more precise wording of a FET clause in all newly negotiated agreements. Canada, Singapore and Vietnam already agreed to the reformed, more detailed wording. It is also present in the EU proposal made to the US.

Their wording is very similar and is combined with the full protection and security standard (which is quite common in other BITs as well). The most important part, though, is a definition of the FET standard as behaviour related to (a) denial of justice in criminal, civil or administrative proceedings; (b) a fundamental breach of due process, (c) manifest arbitrariness[7]; (d) harassment, coercion, abuse of power or similar bad faith conduct[8], (e) targeted discrimination on manifestly wrongful grounds, such as gender, race or religious belief. Hence, this catalogue (as well as in other EU recent agreements) is partly open, as they can be supplemented by mutually agreed situations and premises.

The aim of the clarifications of FET is to diminish the risk of being challenged in investor-state arbitration. The very same objective was an incentive to add clarification to the developed states' second most-criticized element of the investment agreements—the too-broad understanding of the notion of indirect expropriation. As in other agreements, an annexe was added in which the EU proposes to state *expresis verbis* that measures "designed and applied to protect legitimate public policy objectives such as public health, safety and the environment, do not constitute indirect expropriation" unless they appear to be manifestly excessive or discriminatory. In both cases (FET and indirect expropriation), the solution seems to be reasonable as long as it is not misread by the arbitrators (judges).

7 In the EU-Singapore Free Trade Agreement, it is "[m]anifestly arbitrary conduct", which seems to be a little bit narrower, http://trade.ec.europa.eu/doclib/docs/2014/october/tradoc_152844.pdf.

8 Comprehensive Economic and Trade Agreement (CETA) refers here to "abusive treatment of investors, such as coercion, duress and harassment", final text accecible at: http://ec.europa.eu/trade/policy/in-focus/ceta/.

Other problems refer mainly to procedural aspects of the ISDS. Therefore, the Commission issued a breakthrough proposal in October 2015, with an Investment Court System (ICS) draft proposal. Even though it has not been accepted by the US yet, a similar system has been agreed to be introduced under CETA and EU-Vietnam Free Trade Agreement.

ICS was drafted as a new international tribunal, established in order to deal with claims related to investors and investments protection and their rights conferred under the TTIP. It is supposed to consist of two instances – a first-instance tribunal and an appeal tribunal, with permanent judges appointed by both the US and the EU, and not by companies involved in disputes. It should serve two purposes. On the one hand, the existence of second instance should prevent arbitrary and unpredictable decisions, as there would be a chance for revision. On the other hand, it should waive concerns on partiality of arbitrators, which were so far hired to only one case and were able to serve in others as advocates for a party. Though, a caseload for such a court – established for only one agreement – can be scarce, which prompts a question about costs of functioning of such a tribunal. To prevent that, in the proposal there is a provision requiring parties to look for opportunities for establishment of a multilateral investment tribunal, which would serve for various agreements. Taking into account that a similar solution was lately agreed in CETA, that seems possible.

The ICS also addresses problems with transparency of proceedings and public participation. Lately, there is a visible emphasis on transparency of proceedings in all newly concluded BITs. With the exception of confidential or protected information, all documents should be made available to the public. Hearings should also be open to the public. "UNCITRAL Transparency Rules", which came into effect in 2014 will be fully applicable also to the ICS. Also *amicus curiae* briefs should be accepted.

A very important part of the enhanced procedure under ICS is that it addresses also a rarely mentioned problem of very long periods after which arbitrators issue their awards in a standard ISDS. In the ICS procedure, there was a determined timeframe for every step of a dispute, which should enable issuing the awards much faster.

The proposed ICS system addressed the majority of usually raised issues. It also meets criteria for an ISDS in TTIP set out in the Resolution of the European Parliament, which called for a new system "where potential cases are treated in a transparent manner by publicly appointed, independent professional judges in public hearings and which includes an appellate mechanism, where consistency of judicial decisions is ensured, the jurisdiction of courts of the EU and of the Member States is respected, and where private interests cannot undermine public policy objectives".

3. Investment dispute settlement from the Polish perspective

Poland makes a specific case in its relations with the US. Although numerous observations and conclusions regarding ISDS in both universal and inter-regional relations (the EU and a third party) apply to Poland, the comprehensive Polish position regarding dispute settlement (regulated by the Polish-American bilateral agreement – *The Treaty between the United States of America and the Republic of Poland concerning business and economic relations signed 21 March 1990 in Washington*), the regime (an American investor-Poland) or this regime's alteration by a TTIP-created regime, seems specific. Even though there is agreement, the criticism of an ISDS mechanism within the TTIP, and more broadly against the TTIP, and indeed, against tightening cooperation with the US, is joined by Polish critics.

The public opposition to the TTIP in Poland does not follow the standard split into an anti-market and anti-American left and pro-market and pro-American right. This social movement intersects another political and social division in Poland in terms of anti-Americanism because the common denominator of Polish political parties (mainstream) is that they are pro-American and focused on enhancement of the transatlantic link (what differentiates parties on the right from the rest is their attitude towards the EU). However, the significant specific characteristic of the criticism in Poland is a disregard for reality. In case of the non-conclusion of the TTIP covering an investor-state dispute settlement mechanism, the situation of Poland will not change, i.e., Poland, like Canada, Germany and other states, already has an investment arbitration mechanism with the US. Thus, American investors will still be able to continue to implement ISDS in disputes against Poland. For Poland to change the situation, however, would require it to withdraw from the treaty on trade and economic relations. Even then, ISDS will be in force for 10 years (Article XIV). Thus, if TTIP becomes binding it would not worsen Poland's situation as regards the ISDS regime. Adversely, the current trend in the TTIP to settle investor-state disputes through international arbitration, clearly points to a future EU-US agreement changing the present Polish-American mechanism to provide for the shortcomings of ISDS legal solutions.

Poland concluded BITs covering ISDS because in 1990 it was bankrupt in both the international and domestic dimensions (i.e., as regards both foreign and local creditors) and lacked neither the capital nor state institutions to cope with it. The Polish economy needed capital and knowledge and was willing to attract foreign investors, stable ones in particular, and thus it had to provide them not only with potential economic benefits (obviously higher than in highly developed investments exporting states) but also had to ensure those investments had legal and political security, comparable to that in the countries of origin. That is why Poland was bound by a BIT concluded with 61 states, and then foreign capital arrived.

Also significant is the Polish-American context of the ISDS mechanism. In 1990, Poland entered into an agreement with the US within the broadly conceived social and economic transformation and reorientation of Polish politics. Poland wanted to turn to the western hemisphere and expected not only US economic aid but also security, that is, to be covered by the American defence umbrella. The US was perceived as a promoter of EU and NATO accession. The US met those expectations. Currently, Poland expects bigger US involvement in its security and actual equality between the old and new NATO members. It is hard to understand the rationale of the opponents of the TTIP, and specifically those against the ISDS mechanism, in terms of the Polish-American relationship, as they assume that politics and defence are economically independent and that the US will be more committed to providing Poland with security in response to unfriendly business activities.

Poland is relatively rarely sued through international arbitration. For example, in 2014 Poland was party to three arbitration proceedings and was not (in principle) a losing party[9]. Although not much comes from summarising the arbitration awards, it should be noted that Poland has won two cases vitally important for the state. One was *Schooner Capital v. Poland* (November 2015) and an earlier case, *Minolta and Lewis v. Poland* (May 2014). The effect of the proceedings proved Poland was a state with the rule of law. None of the adjudications in Polish courts were outwardly equally convincing.

Therefore, one may claim that ISDS upholds the rule of law. In this context, we recall the case of *Saar Papier Vertriebs Gmbh v. Poland.* Less relevant are the substantive issues of the dispute or the award (Poland was obliged to pay compensation for the indirect expropriation). What was interesting in this case took place in the course of the arbitration proceedings and after its completion. Poland

9 In March 2014, ICSID has handled 463 disputes with 55 cases involving EU members and 39 internal cases. The leading losing side and most sued are Czech Republic, Spain, Slovakia and Hungary, See: *Recent Developments in Investor-State Dispute Settlement (ISDS).* UNCTAD No. 1 April 2014. http://unctad.org/en/PublicationsLibrary/webdiaepcb2014d3_en.pdf as well as *The ICSID Caseload – Statistics (Special Focus – European Union),* https://icsid.worldbank.org/apps/ICSIDWEB/resources/Documents/Stats%20EU%20Special%20Issue%20-%20Eng.pdf .

refused to respect the award and its enforcement. Poland paralysed the proceedings, first by not appointing an arbitrator and then not meeting its obligation to pay. Although obliged in 1995 to pay damages of DEM 2.3 million and lawsuit costs (DEM 4 million), Poland paid only in 2001. There were blockages of accounts, a political dispute and German government intervention.

Poland, both the state and its institutions, behaved like a crook, evading the obligation to execute the award's enforcement. The state's authorities and their representatives' conduct have never been investigated in a competent (domestic) criminal proceeding. Likewise, despite some differences, the case of *Eureko B.V. v. Poland*, where there was no doubt as to Poland's failure to meet its obligations of the agreement, an evaluation of the behaviour of the Polish side is, in my opinion, quite obvious. Moreover, this is not only the Polish experience. Cases such as *TV Nova, Hermitage Capital Management*, or *Jukos* prove the need to not only protect property but also the security of the proprietor (the death of Sergey Magnitsky and the imprisonment of Mikhail Khodorkovsky confirm the need for an international legal enforcement regime). Also, Poland, in a proportional manner, has encountered similar events, although none as dramatic, such as the case of L. Jeziorny and P. Rey (W. Czuchnowski, J. Sidorowicz 2010). Perhaps the ISDS mechanism has the value of a preventive instrument protecting not only property but also the lives and freedoms of proprietors. Perhaps host-state authorities will be less eager to attack property and proprietors if they expect court control (through international arbitration) of such acts. Perhaps public officers will be less likely to benefit from illegal activities because they fear the *Magnitsky Act* and will not be able to benefit from the fruits of crime.

Conclusions

There is no doubt that investor-state dispute settlement and the creation of an appropriate mechanism comprise one of the most burning issues of the TTIP. Therefore, the ISDS mechanism as we know it has to change, and the TTIP—an agreement negotiated by the two leading forces in international relations—may set a standard for reformed mechanisms. As it is still unclear whether United States is going to agree on establishment of the ICS, creation of such a body in the TTIP would be a breakthrough in international investment law. It is also obvious that a new mechanism will have to include not only better, more precise rules of procedure but less nebulous standards of treatment as well. The EU seems to be able to afford to create these new standards designed to save the future of BITs and ISDS. Both CETA and the EU-Singapore and EU-Vietnam agreements already address some of the biggest challenges related to ISDS.

In case of ISDS in the TTIP, a bigger problem is posed by differences in the status of ISDS in various states. There are also different facts: ongoing disputes with investors. In spite of these facts, there is never one universal outcome – there are not always losers and always winners (this is not a zero-sum game). This is also true for Poland, whose best interest is to sign an agreement together with other EU member states.

References

Arbitration between Libya and Taxaco Overseas Petroleum Company and al. (TOP-CO), Award of January 19, 1977, International Legal Materials 1978, No. 17, paragraphs 46–51.

Calvo C., 1896, Le droit international théorique et pratique: précédé d'un exposé historique des progrès de la science du droit des gens, vol. 3, vol. 6, Paris

Central European Media (CME) v. the Czech Republic http://www.italaw.com/documents/CME-2003-Final_001.pdf

Commission draft text TTIP – investment, internal EC document, http://trade.ec.europa.eu/doclib/docs/2015/september/tradoc_153807.pdf

Czuchnowski W., J. Sidorowicz, Bananowa republika w Krakowie czyli sprawa Jeziornego i Reya, Gazeta Wyborcza, 13.02.2010.

Draft Articles on Diplomatic Protection 2006. Yearbook of the International Law Commission, 2006, vol. II, Part Two.

Fact Sheet: Investment Protection and Investor-to-State Dispute Settlement in EU agreements, November 2013, http://trade.ec.europa.eu/doclib/docs/2013/november/tradoc_151916.pdf.

Gantz D. A., 2005, An Appellate Mechanism for Review of Arbitral Decisions in Investor – State Disputes: Prospects and Challenges, bepress Legal Series, Working Paper 703, September 8, http://law.bepress.com/expresso/eps/703

Legal Implications of TTIP for the Acquis Communautaire in ENVI Relevant Sectors, Policy Department A: Economic and Scientific Policy of the European Parliament, http://www.europarl.europa.eu/RegData/etudes/etudes/join/2013/507492/IPOL-ENVI_ET(2013)507492_EN.pdf

Lowenfeld A. F., 2008, International Economic Law, Oxford University Press 2nd ed.

Mann F. A., 1957, Reflection on a commercial law of nations, Brit. Y. B. Int'l L., Vol. 33, No 20, pp. 34–39.

Mavromaatis Palestine Concessions (Jurisdiction), P.C.I.J. Series A, No. 2

Metalclad Corporation v. The United Mexican States, ICSID case No. ARB(AF)/97/1, Award from 30.08.2000

Recent Developments in Investor-State Dispute Settlement (ISDS), 2014, UNCTAD No. 1, April, http://unctad.org/en/PublicationsLibrary/webdiaepcb2014d3_en.pdf.

Report – Online public consultation on investment protection and investor-to-state dispute settlement (ISDS) in the Transatlantic Trade and Investment Partnership Agreement (TTIP), 2015, Commission Working Staff, SWD(2015)3, Brussels, January 13, http://trade.ec.europa.eu/doclib/docs/2015/january/tradoc_153044.pdf.

Resolution of 8 July 2015 containing the European Parliament's recommendations to the European Commission on the negotiations for the Transatlantic Trade and Investment Partnership (TTIP) (2014/2228(INI)), http://www.europarl.europa.eu/sides/getDoc.do?pubRef=-//EP//NONSGML+TA+P8-TA-2015–0252+0+DOC+PDF+V0//EN

Saluka Investments B.V. vs. The Czech Republic, UNICITRAL PCA case, Partial award from 17.03.2006, http://www.pca-cpa.org/showpage.asp?pag_id=1149,

Singh S., S. Sharma, 2013, Investor-State Dispute Settlement Mechanism: The Quest for a Workable Roadmap, Utrecht Journal of International and European Law, Vol. 29, Issue 76.

Tietje Ch., E. Siporski, 2012, The evolution of investment protection based on public international law treaties: lesson to be learned. (in:) A. K. Bjorklund, A. Reinisch (eds.), International Investment Law and Soft Law, Edward Elgar PL.

Transparency and Third Party Participation in Investor-State Dispute Settlement Procedures, OECD Working Papers on International Investment, 2005/01, OECD Publishing, http://dx.doi.org/10.1787/524613550768

Treaty between the United States of America and the Republic of Poland concerning business and economic relations signed 21 March 1990 in Washington, text accessible at: http://www.state.gov/documents/organization/210528.pdf.

UNCITRAL Rules on Transparency in Treaty-based Investor-State Arbitration, http://www.uncitral.org/pdf/english/texts/arbitration/rules-on-transparency/Rules-on-Transparency-E.pdf.

When trade agreements threaten sovereignty: Australia beware, The Conversation 14 November 2013, Australian government position from 2011, http://theconversation.com/when-trade-agreements-threaten-sovereignty-australia-beware-18419.

Yannaca-Small K., 2006, Improving the System of Investor-State Dispute Settlement, OECD Working Papers on International Investment 2006/01, http://dx.doi.org/10.1787/631230863687.

Elżbieta Czarny, Paweł Folfas, Katarzyna Śledziewska
(Warsaw School of Economics, Warsaw School of Economics,
University of Warsaw)

Chapter 6. Will Polish Exports Be Affected by Trade Diversion Resulting from the Transatlantic Trade and Investment Partnership?

In this chapter[1], we analyse the potential substitution of Polish goods exported to the EU with American goods after tariffs are eliminated within the framework of the TTIP (the so-called trade diversion effect). We believe that this effect will be limited only to a small number of commodity groups; nonetheless, it will be present. The main reason for this expectation are the different structures of Polish and American exports to the EU. The survey reviews data from 2014, which is the last year that annual data were available during the research period. Statistics for the HS2 classification come from TRAINS (tariffs) and COMTRADE (exports) databases. The remainder of this chapter contains an analysis of Polish and American exports of the EU's most tariff-protected product groups and EU tariff protection of the top Polish export products, including their positions against US exports.

In the analyses, we assume that the EU that buys Polish goods has 27 Member States (EU-28 minus Poland) and, at the same time, the EU that trades with the US has 28 members (as it is at present).

1. Polish and American exports of the EU's most tariff-protected product groups

In the first part of this chapter, we examine the shares of Polish and American exports to the EU of fifteen of the Union's most tariff-protected HS2 product groups (Table 1). Because the top ten commodity groups consist only of agri-food products, we present a top-fifteen list and include manufactured goods (in this case, textiles). This analysis might show that the TTIP's entry into force will negatively affect the competitive position of Polish products that were previously tariff protected.

1 The project is funded by the National Science Centre of Poland based on decision No. DEC-2013/09/B/HS4/01488.

Table 1. Product groups most tariff-protected on the EU market (average tariff in %) and their share of exports to the EU from Poland and the US in %, in 2014

HS	Product group	Average* tariff** on US products	Polish share of exports to the EU-27***	US share of exports to the EU-28
2	meat and edible meat offal	37.12	2.05	1.29
17	sugars and sugar confectionery	36.88	0.32	0.16
24	tobacco and manufactured tobacco substitutes	36.23	1.20	0.11
4	dairy produce; birds' eggs; natural honey; edible products of animal origin not included elsewhere	35.07	1.29	0.45
11	milling industry products; malt; starches; inulin; wheat gluten	31.17	0.10	0.07
16	preparations of meat, fish or crustaceans, etc.	23.08	0.66	0.17
20	preparations of vegetables, fruit, nuts or other parts of plants	22.77	0.63	0.37
10	Cereals	14.91	0.62	1.67
19	preparations of cereals, flour, starch or milk; pastry products	14.58	0.83	0.31
23	residues and waste from food industries; prepared animal fodder	14.34	0.42	0.88
7	edible vegetables and certain roots and tubers	11.85	0.55	0.27
61	articles of apparel and clothing accessories, knitted or crocheted	11.68	0.85	0.11
62	articles of apparel and clothing accessories, not knitted or crocheted	11.31	1.19	0.11
64	footwear, gaiters and the like; parts of such articles	11.06	0.48	0.06
15	animal or vegetable fats and oils and their cleavage products; prepared edible fats; animal or vegetable waxes	10.91	0.33	0.24

* Simple average (to visualize the role of the highest tariffs in each product group)
** Non-tariff measures are not included
*** EU-28 minus Poland
Source: http://databank.worldbank.org/data/views/variableselection/selectvariables.aspx?source=UNCTAD-~-Trade-Analysis-Information-System-%28TRAINS%29 and http://wits.worldbank.org (both accessed on 19 March 2016).

In the EU in 2014, the highest tariffs were imposed on US agri-food products (meat, sugar, tobacco, dairy products). Of the fifteen product groups, twelve with the highest level of EU tariff protection belong to the agri-food sector, with the majority being processed food products (the three remaining groups are related to the textile industry). This material structure of EU protection is compatible with the Common Agricultural Policy.

The highest tariffs are imposed on meat, which also comprised the biggest share of Polish EU exports in the analysed sample (group 2: 2.05%). Shares exceeding 1% were recorded in groups 4 and 24 (dairy products, tobacco). These three groups are among the EU's most tariff-protected products, each carrying a rate of more than 35%. Also, one product group from the textile industry plays a fairly important role in Polish exports to the EU. It is group 62 (articles of apparel and clothing accessories), amounting to 1.19% of Polish exports to EU-27. However, EU's tariffs are much lower on textile products than on agri-food goods, in this case, not exceeding twelve percent.

The US shares of exports in those four product groups (2, 4, 24 and 62 as well as the majority of the other products listed in Table 1) are considerably lower than the Polish exports (group 2 at 1.29%; 4 at 0.45%; 24 at 0.11%; and 62 at 0.11% respectively)[2]. The exceptions among the top fifteen are groups 10 (cereals) and 23 (residues and waste from the food industries), where the EU tariff exceeds 14% and the American shares of exports to the EU-28 are more than twice that of the Polish share. Although meat is highly protected, it also has a relatively high share of American EU exports. When TTIP is concluded, Poland can expect tougher competition on the EU meat market. This may be expected for cereals as well as in residues and waste from food industries (groups 10 and 23) because of the Americans' better position in EU exports than Poland. However, the possible worsening of Poland's competitive position against the US will not be so painful because these groups are a much smaller part of Polish exports than meat.

Next, we investigate how the EU's most tariff-protected product groups are represented in American exports to non-EU countries. This helps eliminate its relatively weak position in exports elsewhere as a reason for the lack of US success in the EU. If so, fears connected with a possible trade diversion effect would not be justified. A comparison of the respective US shares with Poland's reveals the

2 We are aware of the fact that the comparison of Poland's and the US's shares of exports conceals their absolute values, which differ considerably due to differences in the economic potentials and levels of technological advancement of both countries. We are convinced that a comparison of such different countries in relative and not absolute terms is a better option.

latter's position in the analysed groups for third markets where no preferences are granted, such as the Single European Market (Table 2). If Polish goods are able to compete with American ones on third markets, why should they be crowded out in the EU?

Table 2. Shares of the EU's most tariff-protected product groups in Polish and US exports to non-EU countries, in %, in 2014

HS	Share of Polish exports	Share of US exports
2	1.26	1.53
17	0.41	0.19
24	0.45	0.11
4	1.73	0.54
11	0.11	0.08
16	0.23	0.20
20	0.63	0.40
10	1.08	1.97
19	0.98	0.37
23	0.29	0.97
7	0.63	0.30
61	0.39	0.11
62	0.43	0.11
64	0.65	0.07
15	0.05	0.25

Source: http://wits.worldbank.org (accessed on 19 March 2016).

Shares of Polish exports to non-EU markets in eleven out of fifteen of the EU's most tariff-protected product groups are higher than for the US. The relatively better position of Poland than that of the US in the sectors of tobacco, dairy products, and articles of apparel and clothing accessories (groups 24, 4 and 62) is especially important, as these goods comprise relatively large shares of Polish exports. Moreover, dairy products, which amount to 1.73% of Polish non-EU exports, are the leading group of exports from Poland among the analysed commodities and its share is more than three times that of comparable US exports.

The share of Polish meat exports to non-EU countries is lower than the US's (1.26% compared to 1.53%), but the difference is not very big (just 0.27 percentage points, or p.p.) and Poland's position on this market is relatively good, with the second-highest share among the analysed groups. Nevertheless, this sector should be prepared to face tougher competition after the TTIP is agreed, although it is expected that agri-food products will still be protected to an extent. These data show a possible US challenge to Poland on the EU market for meat under the TTIP.

Table 3. Average tariff rates in the years 2014, 2013 and 2004 (in %) on most EU-tariff-protected product groups on the EU market.

HS	Product groups	Average* tariff** on US products in 2014	Average* tariff** on US products in 2013	Average* tariff** on US products in 2004
2	meat and edible meat offal	37.12	36.79	35.49
17	sugars and sugar confectionery	36.88	42.29	48.47
24	tobacco and manufactured tobacco substitutes	36.23	36.33	32.67
4	dairy produce; birds' eggs; natural honey; edible products of animal origin not included elsewhere	35.07	45.13	60.27

*Simple average (to highlight the role of the highest tariffs in each product group).
** Non-tariff measures are not included.
Source: http://databank.worldbank.org/data/views/variableselection/selectvariables.aspx?source=UNCTAD-~-Trade-Analysis-Information-System-%28TRAINS%29 (accessed on 19 March 2015).

Although it has been announced that agri-food products will enjoy special treatment under the TTIP, meat along with sugars, dairy products and tobacco are crucial commodities within the context of the agreement. The reason is not just an interest in constraining the liberalization of trade in these goods but because there is much controversy between the EU and the US as far as standards and even brand names are concerned[3].

Trade in these products is strongly affected not only by tariffs imposed by the EU but also by US import tariffs. However, tariffs applied by the EU to imported

3 The analysis of the controversy over the standards used by both parties and of brand names goes beyond the scope of this chapter. Some aspects of these issues are examined in Chapter 4 of this book.

agri-food imports from the US are much higher than the respective US tariffs (Beckman et. al 2015, p. 7; Bureau et. al 2014, p. 21). Consequently, the reduction of tariffs under the TTIP seems to be more important for the EU as an exporter (also for Poland) than for the US. Table 3 shows tariffs imposed by the EU on US products in the long run. We analyse how these tariffs changed since the year 2004 (Poland's EU-accession). We also include data from the year 2013, when TTIP negotiations started. The last year of the analysis remains 2014.

The average protection rate applied by the EU to US imports of dairy products fell from 60.27% in 2004 to 45.13% in 2013, and then to 35.07% in 2014. That means that the tariff rates decreased by 25.2 p.p. (almost 42%). Over the same period, EU protection on US imports of sugars declined from 48.47% to 42.29%, and then to 36.88%. Overall, during the years 2004–2014, the tariff rate decline was equal to 11.59 p.p., or about 24%.

In 2004, the average tariff imposed on tobacco was lower than in 2014 (the increase was equal to 3.56 p.p., or almost 11%). However, the highest tariff in the analysed period was actually imposed in just 2013 (0.1 p.p. higher than in 2014). In the case of meat, the average protective rate was the highest in 2014, increasing by 1.63 p.p. (4.6%) since 2004.

Consequently, the current protection of the EU meat market appears to be the strongest across all products and it is possible that it will remain at a non-zero level even under the TTIP, which could be crucial to Poland in keeping its competitive position on the EU-market.

2. Tariff protection of the top Polish export products and their position vs. US exports

The second part of the study refers to the 15 product groups with the highest shares of Polish exports to the EU in 2014. We analyse EU tariff protection of these products and their shares of Polish exports (Table 4), and then compare them with the respective shares of US exports. This analysis allows us to evaluate the competitive position of the most important product groups in Polish exports compared with the American ones.

*Table 4. Product groups with the highest shares of Polish expor ts to the EU, Polish shares of exports of these products to EU and non-EU countries, and shares of these goods in US exports to EU and to non-EU countries, in %, in 2014**

HS	Product group	Average** tariff*** imposed on US products	Share of Polish exports to the EU-27 in 2014	Share of Polish exports to non-EU countries in 2014	Share of US exports to the EU-28 in 2014	Share of US exports to non-EU countries in 2014
84	nuclear reactors, boilers, machinery and mechanical appliances; parts	1.71	12.96	16.10	12.88	13.13
85	electrical machinery and equipment; sound recorders and reproducers, television image and sound recorders and reproducers; parts and accessories	2.57	11.77	10.40	8.01	8.42
87	vehicles other than railway or tramway rolling stock; parts and accessories	5.86	10.52	6.59	9.25	9.97
94	furniture; bedding, mattresses, etc.	2.10	5.57	3.81	0.71	0.79
39	plastics and articles thereof	6.20	4.48	3.68	4.43	4.65
27	mineral fuels and oils and distilled products, etc.	0.61	4.15	3.47	11.35	11.66
73	articles of iron or steel	1.67	3.30	3.07	1.49	1.64
89	ships, boats and floating structures	1.12	2.63	8.71	0.23	0.24
40	rubber and articles thereof	2.44	2.44	1.92	0.99	1.03
72	iron and steel	0.26	2.14	1.07	1.32	1.50
2	meat and edible meat offal	37.12	2.05	1.26	1.29	1.53
48	paper and paperboard; articles of paper pulp, of paper or of paperboard	0.00	2.02	1.80	1.17	1.27
44	wood and articles of wood; wood charcoal	2.41	1.96	1.11	0.70	0.73

HS	Product group	Average** tariff*** imposed on US products	Share of Polish exports to the EU-27 in 2014	Share of Polish exports to non-EU countries in 2014	Share of US exports to the EU-28 in 2014	Share of US exports to non-EU countries in 2014
74	articles of iron or steel	1.67	1.93	2.18	0.60	0.65
30	pharmaceutical products	0.00	1.68	2.05	3.08	1.76

*Product groups' order: shares of Polish exports to the EU-27 in 2014.
**Simple average (to highlight the role of the highest tariffs in each product group).
*** Non-tariff measures are not included.
Source:http://databank.worldbank.org/data/views/variableselection/selectvariables.aspx?source=UNCTAD-~-Trade-Analysis-Information-System-%28TRAINS%29 and http://wits.worldbank.org (both accessed on 19 March 2016).

The most important groups in Polish exports to the EU are processed goods (groups 84, 85, 87, 94 and 39, i.e., nuclear reactors, electrical machinery, vehicles, furniture and plastics). In fact, on this level of aggregation (HS2) we cannot see exactly the items exported. They can be processed finished goods as well as parts and accessories. Delving deeper into less aggregated data might change the researchers' point of view and possibly their evaluation as well[4]. These leading groups are followed by less-processed commodities (e.g., mineral fuels and oils, iron, steel, and rubber as well as articles thereof). Among the top fifteen product groups in the Polish exports to EU-27 there is just one group from the sample with the highest EU tariffs in trade with the US (group 2: meat, ranking 11th).

EU tariffs imposed on the majority of the top fifteen product groups in Polish exports to the EU market are low. As mentioned before, the highest tariffs are on meat (37.12%), which is the only agri-food product group in the top fifteen (meat appears again as an area of special concern). In the case of non-agri-food goods, the highest tariffs are imposed on plastics (6.2%) and vehicles (5.86). As the share of US exports to the EU of plastics is only slightly lower than the respective share of Polish exports (0.05 p.p.) and the US has a higher share than Poland in

4 Microeconomic (disaggregated to HS6) analysis of Polish exports of goods from product group 84 reveals that the most important items in Polish exports to the US are not nuclear reactors, machines or even engines but parts of engines and turbines. The majority is produced by affiliates of American enterprises located in Poland because of, i.a., tax relief enjoyed by companies in so-called "special economic zones" (specjalne strefy ekonomiczne, SSE); for more, see: Czarny, Śledziewska (2016).

exports to non-EU markets (by 0.97 p.p.), this American product can be treated as a potential rival to Polish goods on the EU market. The situation is not much different for vehicles. Although that group's share in US exports to the EU is considerably lower than the respective share of Polish vehicles (by 1.27 p.p.), in exports to non-EU countries the American share is much larger than the Polish one (by 3.38 p.p.). It may make American vehicles an effective competitor to Polish vehicles on the EU-market under the TTIP. This confrontation will not deprive Poland of opportunities, though, as these product groups comprise a relatively large portion of Polish exports to third countries as well (6.59%).

Table 5. Product groups with the highest shares of Polish exports to the EU and Polish imports from the EU in 2014

HS	Product group	Share of Polish exports to the EU-27 in 2014 (%)	Share of Polish imports from the EU-27 in 2014 (%)
84	nuclear reactors, boilers, machinery and mechanical appliances; parts	12.96	13.24
85	electrical machinery and equipment; sound recorders and reproducers, television image and sound recorders and reproducers; parts and accessories	11.77	8.58
87	vehicles other than railway or tramway rolling stock; parts and accessories	10.52	11.70

Source: http://wits.worldbank.org (accessed on 19 March 2016).

It is worth noting that three product groups with the highest shares of Polish exports to the EU (84, 85 and 87) are also the groups with the highest shares of Polish imports from the EU (Table 5). Probably, in the case of these groups Poland actively participates in EU production networks and the majority of its exports and imports of these products are accounted for by foreign affiliates of transnational corporations (TNC) located in Poland (and also by Polish companies cooperating with these affiliates). Thus, a lion's share of Polish trade in products from groups 84, 85 and 87 might be intra-firm trade. For example, assembly firms in Poland import intermediaries from foreign factories and export final products (the assembly firm and factory belong to the same TNC). Consequently, the future performance of Polish exports and imports depends on how TTIP will affect international production networks and Poland's position in them. At the same time, these three product groups, which have similar shares in Polish exports and imports, can have relatively high intra-industry trade (IIT) with EU countries. Depending on the concrete streams of IIT, the position of Poland in this trade can be weaker or stronger (for more, see Czarny, Śledziewska 2016).

Conclusions

To sum up, we may say that the most protected goods on the EU market are agri-food products. This is compatible with Common Agricultural Policy. However, the reasons for the smaller shares of the fifteen most highly EU tariff-protected product groups in US exports to the EU can be as more than the Union efficiently protecting its products. The long distances between trading partners prevents the transport of (often) perishable food products and the weak position of some groups in overall US exports plays an important role, too. Nevertheless, it should be remembered that agri-food products will retain some protection even after the TTIP is implemented. Because many of these products are perishable or have relatively low value per weight unit (especially unprocessed ones), they are impossible or too expensive to transport, thus giving Polish products a long-lasting advantage on the EU market over comparable American goods.

The analysis shows that strong EU tariff protection is evident for the agri-food and textile sectors. The highest tariffs (over 37%) are levied on agri-food products such as meat, dairy products and tobacco. Among the 10 most tariff-protected products, the largest share in Polish exports to the EU is meat (group 2: over 2% in 2014). Tobacco and dairy products account for, respectively, 1.2% and 1.29%. The US shares of those products in its exports to the EU do not exceed 1.3%.

Also relatively highly protected in the EU are textiles, which are exported by Poland as well (of the country's exports to the EU, groups 61, 62 and 64 comprised 2.85%, and of its exports to the rest of the world, it was 1.47%). However, the three groups of textiles mentioned play only a marginal role in overall US exports (in 2014, the combined share of these three in US exports to the EU was 0.28%, and to third countries it was 0.29%). This comparison of the Polish and American positions in the export of textiles gives reason for optimism as far as the Polish position in this sector in the EU is concerned.

Plastics and vehicles are among the goods with the highest shares of Polish exports (in 2014, the combined share of these products in exports to the EU was 15%, and in exports to third countries it was 10.27%), and thus they are most at risk under the TTIP. They enjoy a relatively high level of EU protection (with tariff rates, respectively, of 6.2% and 5.86%). The share of these groups in US exports to the EU is already not very different than for Poland (13.68%), and to the rest of the world it is even higher, at 14.62%.

In the other most important groups of Poland's exports, the tariffs are relatively low (not higher than 2.57%) and its exports to non-EU countries perform as well as or better than the US's (except for mineral fuels and oil, but these are not good candidates for Polish exports because of the dependence on foreign—mainly Russian—raw materials and the instability of world prices for them).

Our analysis supports the initial hypothesis. Since Polish and US exports to the EU and to non-EU countries differ, the diversion effect is expected to be limited for the product groups important in their respective exports.

References

Beckman J., S. Arita, L. Mitchell, M. Burfisher, 2015, Agriculture in the Transatlantic Trade and Investment Partnership: Tariffs, Tariff-Rate Quotas, and Non-Tariff Measures, United States Department of Agriculture, Washington

Bureau J-Ch., A-C. Disdier, Ch. Emlinger, J. Foure, G. Felbermayr, L. Fontagne, S. Jean, 2014, Risk and opportunities for the EU Agri-food Sector in a Possible EU-US Trade Agreement, European Parliament, Strasburg and Brussels.

Czarny E., K. Śledziewska, 2016, Reaktory jądrowe, kotły, maszyny, urządzenia mechaniczne, czy ich części – na jakim produkcie opiera się polski eksport do USA?, mimeo

COMTRADE <http://wits.worldbank.org> accessed 19 March 2016.

TRAINS <http://databank.worldbank.org/data/views/variableselection/selectvariables.aspx?source=UNCTAD-~-Trade-Analysis-Information-System-%28TRAINS%29> accessed 19 March 2016.

Jan Hagemejer, Katarzyna Śledziewska[1] (University of Warsaw and the National Bank of Poland[2], University of Warsaw)

Chapter 7. Trade Barriers in Services and Merchandise Trade in the Context of the TTIP: Poland, the EU and the United States

After remarkable reductions in tariffs resulting from the General Agreement on Tariffs and Trade (GATT) and World Trade Organization (WTO) negotiating rounds, technical barriers to trade (TBTs) represent factors that hamper trade relations. Recent studies identify non-tariff measures (NTMs) or, alternatively, non-tariff barriers to trade (NTBs) as the major sources of import protection and, therefore, considerable distortions of trade. This issue is especially significant for the two main economic powers in the world, the EU and the US, since the proposal of the Transatlantic Trade and Investment Partnership, a free trade agreement between them. The Partnership implies alignment of NTMs and regulatory divergences by cutting non-tariff costs imposed by bureaucracy as well as from liberalising the trade in services and public procurement.

Already in 2003 Bradford estimated that US NTMs added twelve percent to the cost of trade with the United States, while European NTMs add between 48 and 55 percent to the cost of traded consumer goods. In the context of the European Single Market, a study by Copenhagen Economics (2005) underlines that removal of NTMs for the EU services directive might yield remarkably positive economic impacts. Likewise, according to the studies conducted by ECORYS (2009) and Francois, Manchin, Norberg, Pindyuk and Tomberger (2013) the removal of non-tariff barriers through the Transatlantic Partnership might bring remarkable trade expansion and considerable welfare gains.

Based on the theoretical framework of the gravity model, we extend the analyses of the topic from the Polish perspective. We analyse the sectoral trade flows between the EU and the US by employing the Global Trade Analysis Project

---

1 Corresponding author: k.sledziewska@uw.edu.pl.

2 The views presented here are those of the authors and not necessarily of the National Bank of Poland. The project is funded by the National Science Centre of Poland based on decision No. DEC-2013/09/B/HS4/01488.

(GTAP) dataset covering the period 1999–2013. Based on the estimation results, we compute the non-tariff measures. This chapter is organised in the following way: section 1 provides a literature review and a theoretical framework of the analyses. In section 2, we discuss the EU and US tariff profiles. Section 3 contains a data description and section 4 has estimation results. Section 5 summarizes the findings of the chapter.

1. Review of methods

The most popular framework for empirical analyses of trade remains the gravity model, introduced by the crucial work of Jan Tinbergen (1962). Reflecting the relationship between the size of economies, their distance and the value of their trade, the gravity equation can be expressed in the following form:

$$X_{ij=} GS_j M_j \emptyset_{ij}$$

where X_{ij} is the monetary value of exports from *i* to *j*, M_j controls for all importer-specific factors that make up the total importer's demand (for example, the importing country's GDP) and S_j comprises exporter-specific factors (for example, the exporting country's GDP) that represent the total amount exporters are willing to supply. G is a variable independent from *i* and *j*, such as the level of world trade liberalisation. Finally, ϕ_{ij} represents the ease of exporter *i* to access of market *j* (trade costs).

Typically, trade costs are measured by the bilateral distance, suggesting that transport costs increase with the distance between countries. In addition, empirical studies reveal the existence of information costs. For example, firms are more likely to search for new markets in countries with a familiar business environment. In other words, similar business practices, common cultural features or a common language decreases the information costs of trade. Finally, a very important role is played by tariff rates. However, after the repeated reductions of tariffs due to the WTO negotiations, analyses of NTMs is of special importance.

According to the definition provided by the WTO, technical barriers to trade are "regulations, standards, testing and certification procedures, which could obstruct trade". They consist of NTBs such as quotas, import-licensing systems, sanitary regulations, prohibitions, etc. Computations of tariff equivalents reveal the existing protection that distorts the trade flows. However, because NTMs are not directly computable, a measurement of their impact is not easy.

The recent literature reveals two possible computation procedures. First, as suggested by Park (2002), the distribution of the residuals of an estimated gravity equation can be used for the computation of the equation of tariff equivalents.

Alternatively, we can compute the average protection applied by each importer, from the importer fixed effects coefficients (Fontagne, Guillin and Mitaritonna 2011).

In the first case, following Anderson (2001) and Park (2002), some constraints have to be imposed on the sum of the residuals for a given importing country in a given year, namely it should be equal to zero and the sum of all residuals for a given year must also be equal to zero:

$$\sum_i \varepsilon_{ij} = 0$$

$$\sum_i \sum_j \varepsilon_{ij} = 0$$

According to Anderson and Wincoop (2003), as well as Park (2002), we may define the residual as the difference in log values of actual and predicted import values from country i to country j. Then the difference between the total actual and predicted value of country imports may indicate the level of distortion to trade caused by the existence of trade barriers. However, the absolute differences should be normalized relative to a benchmark free-trade country case. Finally, the relative trade barrier (t_j) of country j can be measured by the following equation (Park 2002):

$$-\sigma ln t_j = ln\frac{X_j^a}{X_j^p} - ln\frac{X_b^a}{X_b^p},$$

where the sub-indexes a, p and b represent actual, predicted and benchmarks, respectively, X_j is country j's simple average imports and σ stands for the constant elasticity of substitution. Following the assumption made by Park (2002), we take the value of σ equal to 5.6. The countries with the greatest positive differences between actual and predicted imports are considered to be the free trade "benchmark" countries in the regression.

In the second, fixed effect, methodology, (Fontagne, Guillin and Mitaritonna 2011) we can obtain tariff equivalents by the difference between the fixed effects of the country j and the benchmark country. Specifically,

$$-\sigma ln t_j = Fe\gamma_j - Fe\gamma_{benchmark}.$$

As in the first approach, σ stands for the constant elasticity of substitution, assumed to be equal to 5.6. However, in this methodology the benchmark country is the one that yields the highest importer fixed-effect coefficient.

The above theoretical approaches provide the main framework for the recent empirical analyses of impacts of non-tariff barriers between the EU and the US. According to a study conducted by ECORYS (2009), in case of the alignment of

50% of the NTMs and regulatory divergences, US exports are expected to go up by 6.1% and EU exports by 2.1%, yielding a trade balance improvement for both. As a result of extended bilateral trade flows, EU GDP could increase by 0.7% and US GDP by 0.3% per year, bringing an additional 122 billion EUR to the EU and 41 billion EUR to the US as an annual gain. The study also reports the effects on sectoral levels. For the EU, trade flows in motor vehicles, chemicals, cosmetics and pharmaceuticals, food and beverages as well as electrical machinery are found to be mostly constrained by the NTMs. For the US case, the report outlines that trade in goods and in services is also hampered by non-tariff barriers. Namely, together with electrical machinery, chemicals, cosmetics and pharmaceuticals, insurance and financial services are mainly constrained by NTMs.

More recently, Francois, Manchin, Norberg, Pindyuk and Tomberger (2013) analysed the role of NTBs in EU-US bilateral trade. As the study shows, 80% of the total potential gains are expected to come from removal of trade costs imposed by bureaucracy and regulations. Estimations of the expected increases in trade flows as a result of the removal of NTMs are close to those provided by ECORYS (2009). The study estimates that removal of NTBs could bring 119 billion EUR for the EU and 95 billion EUR for the US per year. Additionally, the predictions are extended by outlining that the benefits for the EU and the US would not be at the expense of the rest of the world. On the contrary, according to the study, liberalizing trade between the EU and the US would increase GDP in the rest of the world by almost 100 billion EUR. The sectoral analyses on the GTAP level also reveal that the motor vehicles sector is characterized by an initial combination of high tariffs and high non-tariff barriers, mainly such as different safety standards. In this sector, EU exports to the US are expected to increase by 149%. As the authors explain, this partly reflects the importance of two-way trade in parts and components and the further integration of the two industries across the Atlantic.

Putting the emphasis on trade in services, Ghodsi, Hagemejer and Kwiecinska (2015) assessed the degree of trade liberalization and its impact on bilateral trade of rail transportation services during the period 2002–2010 for 27 European countries. Together with the standard gravity variables to explain the bilateral trade, the authors used four indices measuring the market liberalization in rail transport services as elaborated by IBM Consulting Services. Estimation results of Fixed and Random effects reveal that among all the measures, only the liberalization of the legal framework has a significant impact on the volume of imports. Additionally, estimations of tariff equivalents did not reveal a clear downward trend in the levels of non-tariff barriers between EU countries and OECD countries over the analysed period.

As the literature highlights, the cost of NTMs in the trade relations between the EU and the US is considerable. Based on the actuality and importance of the issue at hand, we extend the analyses of the topic from the Polish perspective. We employ the GTAP dataset to provide calculations of tariff equivalents on the sectoral level for the period 2005–2013.

2. Tariff Profiles: the EU and the US

We can analyse trade costs between the EU and the US by considering the tariffs applied on the import of goods in the different sectors based on the GTAP classification. Table 1 shows the tariff rates applied on the imports from the EU in the US and to all other trade partners in 1999 and in 2013. The tariff rates represent the effectively applied simple average tariffs, averaged over all the partners. First of all, we may observe, that the tariff rates applied by the US are remarkably lower than those applied by the other trade partners in 1999 as well as in 2013. Second, the table shows that compared to 1999, in 2013 tariff rates are reduced by all trade partners of the EU. However, the tariffs applied by countries other than the US still remain at a much higher level than tariffs applied by the US. The reduction in tariff rates is also observed in the case of the US, however with few exceptions. Namely, compared to 1999, in 2013 tariff rates applied by the US slightly increase for fuels, nonferrous metals, transport equipment n.e.c. and manufacturing n.e.c.

Table 1. Tariffs applied to imports from the EU in 1999 and 2013

	1999		2013	
GTAP sectors	**US**	**Other Trade Partners**	**US**	**Other Trade Partners**
Agriculture	0.7	8.2	0.5	6.2
Mining	8.6	26.4	5.5	25.0
Food	8.5	15.8	7.5	13.5
Textiles	11.2	19.1	10.7	17.6
Wearing apparel	8.6	16.5	8.9	15.3
Leather	1.3	15.0	1.2	11.5
Wood	1.1	12.5	0.0	9.4

	1999		2013	
GTAP sectors	**US**	**Other Trade Partners**	**US**	**Other Trade Partners**
Paper, publishing	3.0	7.8	3.5	6.1
Fuels	2.8	12.3	2.6	9.7
Chemicals	4.1	13.7	4.1	11.4
Minerals n.e.c.	1.5	10.4	0.9	8.1
Steel	2.3	9.4	2.6	7.7
Nonferrous metals	2.4	13.7	2.2	11.4
Metal products	2.3	14.0	1.3	11.5
Motor vehicles	1.0	9.5	1.3	8.5
Transport equipment n.e.c.	0.9	8.0	0.6	6.0
Electrical appliances	1.4	9.9	1.3	8.1
Machinery and equipment	0.7	8.2	0.5	6.2
Manufacturing n.e.c.	2.2	14.5	2.3	12.6

Source: World Integrated Trade Solution (WITS), own calculations.

Table 2 shows the tariff rates applied by the EU and by the all other trade partners to imports from the US in 1999 and in 2013. As in the previous case, the tariff rates represent the effectively applied simple average tariffs, averaged over all the trade partners. Again, we may observe, that the tariff rates applied by the EU are remarkably lower than those applied by the other trade partners in both years 1999 and 2013. Second, the table shows that compared to 1999, in 2013 tariff rates were reduced by all trade partners of the US, however the tariffs applied by countries outside the EU still remain at a much higher level compared to the bloc's tariffs. The reduction in tariff rates is also observed in the case of the EU, however, again, there are a few exceptions. Specifically, compared to 1999, in 2013 tariff rates applied by the EU slightly increased on agricultural products, mining, fuels, metal products, and motor vehicles. The increase in tariffs on leather as well as paper and publishing is negligible (0.03 for the former and 0.04 for the latter), so we can consider them unaffected.

Table 2. Tariffs applied to imports from the US in 1999 and 2013

	1999		2013	
GTAP sectors	**EU**	**Other Trade Partners**	**EU**	**Other Trade Partners**
Agriculture	0.0	7.5	0.1	6.7
Mining	10.9	27.4	10.0	21.0
Food	8.0	18.0	6.9	15.2
Textiles	11.3	21.8	10.9	17.5
Wearing apparel	6.7	17.0	6.7	15.5
Leather	2.8	16.2	2.7	13.3
Wood	0.1	14.4	0.1	8.9
Paper, publishing	0.5	8.9	1.5	5.2
Fuels	4.4	12.7	4.5	8.6
Chemicals	3.5	13.8	3.6	11.9
Minerals n.e.c.	0.4	11.6	0.4	9.2
Steel	2.9	9.1	2.8	9.8
Nonferrous metals	2.8	14.3	2.9	12.8
Metal products	6.4	17.2	6.4	13.5
Motor vehicles	2.4	10.2	2.4	8.7
Transport equipment n.e.c.	2.7	9.6	2.3	5.9
Electrical appliances	2.1	10.1	2.1	8.1
Machinery and equipment	3.0	14.6	2.9	13.2
Manufacturing n.e.c.	0.0	7.5	0.1	6.7

Source: World Integrated Trade Solution (WITS), own calculations.

To conclude, the tariff data on the sectoral level demonstrate that the tariffs applied by the EU to imports from the US as well as tariffs applied by the US to imports from the EU are considerably lower than those applied by the other trade partners. Even though the dynamics from 1999 till 2013 show an apparent overall decrease in tariff rates, in the case of the EU and the US, the reduction is not remarkable since initially the rates were already low. This trend suggests that tariffs do not represent the main trade barriers between the EU and the US and, therefore, they cannot be considered a main tool for further trade liberalisation between these two partners.

3. Estimation method and data

We follow the Park methodology using importer fixed effects in order to obtain the average trade levels for the countries under investigation as well as for the reference country. In our estimation equations for both merchandise trade and services, we use standard gravity variables, such as (logs of) reporter and partner GDP, population, distances between group of countries, contiguity, common language and colonial ties. Besides reporter fixed effects, we also include partner dummies as well as year dummies to capture variation in trade over time. In the merchandise trade equation, we also include the bilateral level of effectively applied tariffs.

The merchandise trade data comes from Comtrade through the WITS database. The tariff levels come from WITS. Services data are taken from Francois and Pindyuk (2013). We match the trade data with the macroeconomic characteristics of partners and reporters that are taken from World Development Indicators Database. The geopolitical gravity variables are provided by CEPII in their Mayer and Zignago (2011) paper.

We limit the year time span of the database to start from 2005. We do this in order to provide fairly recent estimates of trade barriers (including the effects of EU enlargement) while at the same time to maximize the number of observations. The resulting merchandise trade database is much larger than the one for services: it includes over 350 thousand observations as opposed to only 78 thousand observations for services. We initially planned to focus on extra-EU trade data, but this was possible only in the case of merchandise trade as in the case of trade in services the number of observations dropped sharply. Therefore, the services data estimations include both intra- and extra-EU trade, but we add an additional dummy variable corresponding to both importer and partner having membership of the EU, in order not to inflate the importer fixed effect in the case of EU members. The merchandise trade database covers the period 2005–2013 and the services trade data is from 2005–2010. All estimations are performed in GTAP sectors to facilitate the use of the obtained tariff equivalents in trade policy simulations. While the WITS database offers GTAP aggregation as one of the standard choices, the Francois and Pindyuk services dataset is also aggregated into that classification.

The obtained importer fixed effects are then sorted for each sector to identify the reference (most liberal country). The tariff equivalent is computed as the difference of the country's fixed effect and the reference country's fixed effect multiplied by the elasticity of substitution. While the estimation equation enables us to identify the elasticity of substitution from the tariff coefficient, it does not prove to be very reliable. Instead, we use GTAP sectoral elasticity of substitution in order to increase the compatibility with CGE simulations.

Table 3. Gravity estimations for merchandise trade, part 1

VARIABLES	Total	Agricul-ture	Mining	Food	Textiles	Apparel	Leather	Wood	Paper	Coal Petrol
log(GDP Reporter)	1.066***	0.886***	0.508***	0.474***	1.098***	1.910***	1.303***	1.145***	0.999***	0.599***
	(0.0220)	(0.0615)	(0.110)	(0.0578)	(0.0617)	(0.0647)	(0.0732)	(0.0600)	(0.0632)	(0.128)
log(GDP Partner)	0.0529	-0.0106	0.000107	-0.0870	-0.0362	0.455***	-0.222*	-0.492***	0.250**	-0.608***
	(0.0370)	(0.108)	(0.187)	(0.102)	(0.0982)	(0.0976)	(0.119)	(0.102)	(0.104)	(0.192)
log(Population Rep.)	0.161***	0.272***	1.235***	0.563***	0.178***	-0.705***	0.0507	-0.0564	0.256***	0.571***
	(0.0200)	(0.0585)	(0.107)	(0.0567)	(0.0571)	(0.0605)	(0.0672)	(0.0567)	(0.0587)	(0.125)
log(Population Part.)	-0.509***	-0.620	-1.770**	-1.277***	-0.463	-0.882***	-0.735**	-0.743**	-1.382***	0.656
	(0.110)	(0.418)	(0.853)	(0.391)	(0.287)	(0.310)	(0.373)	(0.341)	(0.322)	(0.763)
log(distance)	-1.540***	-1.570***	-2.278***	-1.468***	-1.485***	-1.176***	-1.250***	-1.673***	-1.933***	-2.941***
	(0.00834)	(0.0263)	(0.0399)	(0.0234)	(0.0239)	(0.0253)	(0.0281)	(0.0264)	(0.0277)	(0.0483)
Contiguity	0.663***	0.662***	0.621***	0.423***	0.703***	0.668***	1.066***	0.614***	0.651***	0.691***
	(0.0256)	(0.0870)	(0.125)	(0.0760)	(0.0755)	(0.0864)	(0.0958)	(0.0817)	(0.0963)	(0.117)
common language	0.546***	0.434***	0.568***	0.761***	0.478***	0.702***	0.351***	0.461***	0.960***	0.0937
	(0.0193)	(0.0567)	(0.0947)	(0.0523)	(0.0528)	(0.0579)	(0.0592)	(0.0573)	(0.0617)	(0.109)
colony(1945)	0.878***	1.346***	0.331**	1.098***	1.072***	1.147***	1.141***	0.892***	0.966***	0.0336
	(0.0370)	(0.107)	(0.141)	(0.121)	(0.129)	(0.129)	(0.124)	(0.124)	(0.126)	(0.206)
log(Tariff_Weighted)	-1.900***	0.0946	-2.753***	-0.843***	-1.745***	-0.344	-3.023***	-2.526***	-1.746***	-1.249***
	(0.0698)	(0.161)	(0.420)	(0.124)	(0.220)	(0.227)	(0.292)	(0.242)	(0.293)	(0.449)
Constant	-4.581**	-1.284	18.57	17.49***	-3.655	-21.57***	-4.363	13.95**	6.716	14.06
	(1.853)	(6.632)	(13.24)	(6.262)	(4.921)	(5.152)	(6.303)	(5.627)	(5.299)	(12.23)
Observations	357,139	19,186	16,654	19,821	19,695	19,035	18,345	19,025	19,738	14,044
R-squared	0.463	0.688	0.573	0.725	0.767	0.782	0.723	0.735	0.746	0.534

Standard errors in parentheses
***** p<0.01, ** p<0.05, * p<0.1**

4. Estimation results

Our gravity estimations focus on the flows of imports. In the merchandise trade estimation, the results seem to be fairly plausible. The standard gravity variables have, in general, the expected signs. The GDP of the reporter is positively related to its imports. The overall elasticity across all sectors is close to 1, however there are visible differences, e.g. in agriculture, food, petrol, and mining, as well as chemicals have coefficients that are significantly smaller than 1, in line with the idea of the non-homothetic demand for basic goods and, at the same time, the fuel intensity of GDP decreasing with income. Partner size is not as important in explaining trade flows, and the signs vary across sectors. However, we have to keep in mind that due to the inclusion of reporter and partner fixed effects, the cross-country size variation is already embedded in those effects and, therefore, the macro-coefficients are related to within-pair changes. Therefore, as there is a one-to-one reporter size-imports relationship, we do not find anything like that for the exporter-size link. Distance elasticity is negative across the estimations and, in most cases, it is much larger than the one indicating that trade dies out fairly quickly with increasing distance. Contiguity, common language and the colonial aspect are positive, significant and rather large in most estimations.

The calculated tariff equivalents of the trade barriers are presented in table 5. Column 2 of that table gives the reference country (the country with the highest importer fixed effects). In most cases, the reference countries are South-East Asian states such as Malaysia, Vietnam and Thailand but also Australia and Chile. We base our calculation on GTAP Armington elasticities, as we believe that the estimated elasticities of substitution as identified by the coefficient on the tariff yield values that are too low as judged by common sense.

Table 4. Gravity estimations for merchandise trade, part 2

VARIABLES	Chemicals	Minerals	Steel	Metals	Met. Prod.	Motor Veh.	Tr. Eq. Nec	Electric	Machinery	Mnfcs Nec
log(GDP Reporter)	0.789***	1.141***	0.761***	1.399***	1.322***	1.276***	1.293***	1.861***	1.461***	1.477***
	(0.0513)	(0.0594)	(0.0805)	(0.0884)	(0.0568)	(0.0675)	(0.0862)	(0.0600)	(0.0492)	(0.0540)
log(GDP Partner)	0.235**	-0.0800	0.0388	0.398***	0.285***	-0.163	0.274**	0.825***	0.133	0.174*
	(0.101)	(0.0936)	(0.129)	(0.136)	(0.0973)	(0.111)	(0.136)	(0.0988)	(0.0891)	(0.0973)
log(Population Rep.)	0.468***	0.0263	0.511***	0.157*	0.0501	0.0683	-0.0233	-0.463***	-0.158***	-0.278***
	(0.0489)	(0.0557)	(0.0757)	(0.0842)	(0.0520)	(0.0644)	(0.0819)	(0.0556)	(0.0453)	(0.0518)
log(Population Part.)	-0.0815	0.342	0.796*	0.149	-0.603**	-0.375	-0.417	-2.499***	-0.373	-0.872**

VARIABLES	Chemicals	Minerals	Steel	Metals	Met. Prod.	Motor Veh.	Tr. Eq. Nec	Electric	Machinery	Mnfcs Nec
	(0.255)	(0.277)	(0.459)	(0.470)	(0.296)	(0.352)	(0.478)	(0.384)	(0.261)	(0.409)
log(distance)	-1.406***	-1.597***	-2.023***	-2.072***	-1.608***	-1.872***	-1.390***	-1.075***	-1.248***	-1.202***
	(0.0196)	(0.0235)	(0.0288)	(0.0324)	(0.0234)	(0.0290)	(0.0325)	(0.0243)	(0.0199)	(0.0234)
contiguity	0.585***	1.188***	0.378***	0.396***	0.529***	0.383***	0.710***	0.500***	0.495***	0.617***
	(0.0693)	(0.0859)	(0.0859)	(0.0922)	(0.0749)	(0.0887)	(0.0954)	(0.0924)	(0.0674)	(0.0741)
common language	0.698***	0.530***	0.502***	0.755***	0.692***	0.458***	0.651***	0.544***	0.540***	0.905***
	(0.0496)	(0.0560)	(0.0669)	(0.0748)	(0.0548)	(0.0643)	(0.0713)	(0.0558)	(0.0463)	(0.0535)
colony(1945)	0.596***	1.177***	0.641***	0.426***	1.136***	1.151***	1.559***	0.901***	0.989***	1.141***
	(0.106)	(0.134)	(0.119)	(0.142)	(0.126)	(0.158)	(0.139)	(0.138)	(0.135)	(0.122)
log(Tariff_Weighted)	-1.218***	-1.162***	-2.023***	-2.705***	-1.518***	1.213***	-3.242***	-0.0404	-0.827***	-1.610***
	(0.190)	(0.226)	(0.311)	(0.335)	(0.262)	(0.251)	(0.327)	(0.306)	(0.213)	(0.240)
Constant	-12.09***	-12.71***	-18.84**	-26.27***	-12.68**	-2.492	-17.01**	-7.499	-14.23***	-8.808
	(4.534)	(4.695)	(7.528)	(7.636)	(4.979)	(5.828)	(7.717)	(6.110)	(4.390)	(6.352)
Observations	20,881	19,122	17,764	17,241	19,944	18,958	17,142	20,132	20,981	19,431
R-squared	0.762	0.767	0.653	0.619	0.783	0.771	0.624	0.803	0.834	0.794

Standard errors in parentheses
***** p<0.01, ** p<0.05, * p<0.1**

The estimated tariff equivalents are, in general, higher than the corresponding tariffs. The overall tariff equivalent of NTBs for the EU-15 is 21 percent, compared to 23 percent in the US. This overall tariff equivalent is visibly higher in Poland (at 26 percent) and lower for the New Member States (NMS, eighteen percent). However, the differences across countries and regions are, in general, not systematic, i.e., one cannot clearly observe the same ordering of tariff equivalents across sectors. We also believe that there are at least two sectors that deserve additional comments.

Table 5. Calculation of tariff equivalents in merchandise trade

Sector	Reference country	Importer Effects (log)						Tariff Equivalent			
		Ref.	EU-15	NMS	Poland	USA	Elasticity	EU-15	NMS	Poland	USA
Total	MYS	1.3	-0.2	0.1	-0.5	-0.3	7.1	21%	18%	26%	23%
Agriculture	VNM	3.1	1.6	1.4	0.1	1.0	4.8	31%	36%	33%	44%
Mining	AUS	2.7	0.7	0.0	-0.9	-0.2	11.9	17%	22%	30%	24%
Food	AUS	3.6	1.8	1.3	0.0	2.3	5.0	36%	46%	46%	25%
Textiles	CHL	1.7	-0.3	0.1	0.1	-0.6	7.5	27%	22%	21%	32%
Apparel	VNM	3.2	0.8	1.2	0.1	0.1	7.4	33%	27%	26%	42%

Sector	Reference country	Importer Effects (log)						Tariff Equivalent			
		Ref.	EU-15	NMS	Poland	USA	Elasticity	EU-15	NMS	Poland	USA
Leather	VNM	3.5	1.1	1.7	-0.4	0.1	8.1	30%	23%	28%	43%
Wood	AUS	2.0	0.3	0.2	-0.4	0.6	6.8	25%	27%	33%	21%
Paper	MYS	1.8	-0.4	-0.1	-0.9	-0.9	5.9	37%	32%	47%	46%
Coal Petrol	USA	1.5	-1.6	-2.3	-1.8	1.5	4.2	73%	91%	133%	0%
Chemicals	CHL	0.5	-0.8	-0.6	-0.2	-1.0	6.6	19%	17%	19%	23%
Minerals	ZAF	1.2	-0.8	-0.3	-0.3	-0.4	5.8	35%	26%	32%	28%
Steel	MYS	1.9	-0.5	-0.8	-0.5	-0.3	5.9	40%	45%	54%	37%
Metals	THA	2.7	-0.6	-0.2	-0.8	-1.1	8.4	40%	35%	44%	46%
Met. Prod.	CHL	1.3	-0.8	0.1	-0.8	-1.6	7.5	29%	16%	27%	39%
Motor Veh.	VNM	1.2	-1.0	-0.3	-0.5	-1.3	5.6	38%	26%	35%	44%
Tr. Eq. n.e.c.	MYS	2.1	0.3	0.1	0.0	-0.4	8.6	21%	23%	23%	29%
Electric	MYS	2.7	-0.4	1.1	-1.0	-1.8	8.8	35%	18%	29%	51%
Machinery	VNM	1.3	-1.0	0.0	-0.8	-1.8	8.1	27%	15%	25%	38%
Mnfcsn.e.c.	THA	1.9	0.0	0.6	-0.7	0.7	7.5	26%	17%	26%	15%

GTAP elasticities. Poland's fixed effect is the difference between NMS and Poland fixed effects
Source: own calculations using Comtrade data.

First of all, we believe that the tariff equivalents for agricultural goods may be underestimated, i.e., trade in agricultural products is, overall, low across the world and it may be the case that even the reference country is trading relatively little. We also observe that in the estimated regression for that sector, the coefficient on tariff is not significantly different from zero. While the overall weighted tariff level in agriculture does not reflect the possibility of tariff peaks and therefore underestimates the effective tariffs, the same sort of argument can be made on the estimates of NTB tariff equivalents. We also believe that flows in processed fuels (CoalPetrol) are largely driven by the allocation of natural resources and that the ability of the gravity model in explaining these trade flows is limited. In that sector, the US is the reference country but imports of processed fuels in the European countries are *ceteris paribus* low, leading to somewhat large tariff equivalents.

Turning to trade in services, the coefficients on standard gravity variables are also in line with the intuition. It is quite surprising, though, that the coefficient on reporter GDP in the aggregate flow of services trade significantly exceeds one, while in sectoral regressions it is only in the business services where that happens. One has to note, however, that unlike the merchandise trade regressions, the overall regression is done on aggregate trade and not on the pooled sample across sectors and, therefore, it also includes trade in services that is not necessarily included in the sectoral estimations. Moreover, services trade estimations are performed on intra- and extra-EU countries. It is also interesting that in trade in services, distance has a visibly lower elasticity that in merchandise trade and the size of the contiguity and language coefficients is also visibly lower. The EU dummy variable is significant only in some cases and shows that EU membership increases bilateral services trade between partners by roughly 10% overall. However, in sectoral trade, this coefficient is not always positive and significant. This is so in the case of trade (82 percent higher imports), transport (over 30 percent), financial services and non-market services. It is rather surprising to find a negative and significant EU dummy variable in the case of construction.

Table 6. Gravity estimations for services trade

VARIABLES	Overall	Const-ruction	Trade	Trans-port	FinServ	Insuran-ce	BusNec	RecOth	NmktSvc
log_GDP_REP	1.303***	0.540***	0.485***	0.619***	0.732***	0.450***	1.341***	0.542***	0.497***
	(0.0422)	(0.0900)	(0.0776)	(0.0505)	(0.0847)	(0.0772)	(0.0597)	(0.0737)	(0.0632)
log_GDP_PAR	-0.509**	1.720***	0.452	0.108	-0.365	1.293***	0.679*	1.221***	-0.0820
	(0.215)	(0.459)	(0.426)	(0.306)	(0.525)	(0.468)	(0.350)	(0.396)	(0.360)
log_population_REP	-0.527***	0.297***	0.213***	0.172***	-0.0777	0.160**	-0.591***	0.264***	0.313***
	(0.0414)	(0.0887)	(0.0763)	(0.0494)	(0.0825)	(0.0745)	(0.0585)	(0.0726)	(0.0623)
log_population_PAR	-0.119	-3.607***	-0.499	-0.385	3.714***	-0.879	-1.783*	-1.611	-0.888
	(0.539)	(1.331)	(1.228)	(0.850)	(1.347)	(1.270)	(0.944)	(1.172)	(1.019)
log_dist	-0.886***	-0.881***	-0.679***	-1.013***	-0.951***	-0.827***	-1.027***	-0.710***	-0.734***
	(0.0196)	(0.0374)	(0.0353)	(0.0276)	(0.0384)	(0.0357)	(0.0294)	(0.0304)	(0.0297)
contig	0.550***	0.750***	0.217**	0.0715	0.103	0.292***	0.0845	0.373***	0.535***
	(0.0556)	(0.0878)	(0.0919)	(0.0579)	(0.0837)	(0.0776)	(0.0708)	(0.0783)	(0.0663)
comlang_off	0.515***	-0.0985	0.650***	0.210***	0.696***	0.877***	0.170***	0.602***	0.305***
	(0.0401)	(0.0923)	(0.0807)	(0.0670)	(0.0815)	(0.0794)	(0.0646)	(0.0698)	(0.0673)
col45	1.014***	0.00210	-0.0339	0.763***	0.712***	0.466***	0.822***	0.775***	0.890***
	(0.0652)	(0.166)	(0.179)	(0.0993)	(0.172)	(0.162)	(0.137)	(0.144)	(0.104)
eupair	0.0968**	-0.263***	0.821***	0.345***	0.251**	0.104	0.0311	0.104	0.174**
	(0.0476)	(0.0947)	(0.0865)	(0.0808)	(0.102)	(0.0931)	(0.0713)	(0.0758)	(0.0757)
Constant	-5.101	5.031	-15.38	-6.426	-57.55***	-25.06	-0.391	-17.91	0.768
	(6.612)	(19.88)	(17.55)	(11.87)	(20.29)	(19.72)	(15.33)	(17.48)	(14.33)

VARIABLES	Overall	Construction	Trade	Transport	FinServ	Insurance	BusNec	RecOth	NmktSvc
Observations	18,337	7,253	9,811	21,649	6,657	6,652	10,082	8,668	8,011
R-squared	0.799	0.536	0.579	0.570	0.664	0.654	0.774	0.586	0.663

Standard errors in parentheses
*** $p<0.01$, ** $p<0.05$, * $p<0.1$

The estimated tariff equivalents are calculated with respect to the reference country. This time, the reference countries are Thailand and Singapore, which is in line with previous estimates of trade barriers. The overall level of trade barriers in services is roughly twice as high as in the case of merchandise trade. Moreover, we also observe that in most cases, imports of services are the most liberalised in the US (except construction) and the trade barriers are usually lower in the EU-15 than in the NMS and Poland.

Table 7. Calculation of tariff equivalents in services trade

Sector	Reference country	Importer Effects (log)						Tariff Equivalent			
		Ref.	EU-15	NMS	Poland	USA	Elasticity	EU-15	NMS	Poland	USA
Total	THA	1.4	-0.1	-0.3	-0.1	0.1	3.8	38%	43%	46%	33%
Construction	SGP	-1.2	-2.8	-3.2	0.0	-3.5	3.8	41%	53%	53%	62%
Trade	THA	2.4	0.5	-0.6	-0.5	1.1	3.8	48%	78%	91%	33%
Transport	SGP	0.3	-1.6	-2.6	-0.1	-1.0	3.8	50%	77%	80%	35%
Financial Svcs	SGP	1.9	-0.2	-0.7	-0.1	1.5	3.8	55%	67%	69%	9%
Insurance	SGP	0.3	-1.2	-2.0	-0.2	-0.9	3.8	40%	58%	63%	30%
Business Svcs n.e.c.	SGP	1.3	0.1	-0.2	0.2	0.3	3.8	32%	39%	34%	26%
Recreation & Other	SGP	0.8	-0.5	-0.7	-0.6	0.0	3.8	33%	39%	54%	21%

GTAP elasticities. Poland's fixed effect is the difference between NMS and Poland fixed effects
Source: own calculations using Francois & Pindyuk data.

Conclusions

The Transatlantic Trade and Investment Partnership is aimed *inter alia* at facilitating trade between the signing parties. However, due to overall significant progress in liberalising trade in many manufacturing industries within the framework of GATT and WTO, especially in advanced economies, further tariff liberalisation is not expected to bring sizeable gains. Indeed we show that in most sectors, overall tariff levels are below 10%. At the same time, there is some anecdotal and empirical evidence that non-tariff barriers still matter a lot in international trade between advanced economies and are even more important in the services trade, where no tariffs *per se* exist.

In order to assess the possible gains from trade liberalisation through the TTIP, we evaluate both tariff and non-tariff barriers in the bilateral trade of the EU members and the United States. We differentiate between the EU-15, the New Member States and Poland to account for their structural differences and different trading patterns. We use a standard gravity framework and attribute the differences in importer fixed effects to non-tariff barriers.

We find that the level of non-tariff barriers in general trumps that of tariffs across different sectors and among the analysed groups of countries. The overall tariff equivalent in merchandise trade is around twenty percent or at least twice the level of tariffs. However, there are sectoral differences and in many cases the NTBs exceed 40 percent. We also find that non-tariff barriers in services trade are overall higher than those in merchandise trade. At the same time, Poland and the remaining NMS exhibit higher barriers to trade in services than the EU-15 and the US.

One has to keep in mind that these estimates are based on actual trade flows. Therefore, a country that imports less, all else being equal, is going to have a higher estimated NTB tariff equivalent. However, when one thinks of the effects of NTB removal, countries with overall high NTBs have more potential for trade liberalisation within the TTIP. Keeping everything else equal, reaching the same target level of NTBs will give a higher trade boost in an initially more restrictive importer country. However, this is only true in percentage terms—when one analyses the volume of trade, the initially restrictive countries traded less initially and, therefore, from an aggregate point of view, the size of the response cannot be easily evaluated. This has to be taken into consideration when employing trade-based tariff equivalents in trade liberalisation simulations—non-linearities in the response may matter (e.g., in switching from prohibitive to non-prohibitive NTBs) and they are difficult to be implemented in simulation frameworks.

References

Anderson J., E. van Wincoop, 2003, Gravity with Gravitas: A Solution to the Border Puzzle, American Economic Review, 93, issue 1, pp. 170–192.

Copenhagen Economics, 2009, Assessment of barriers to trade and investment between the EU and Japan report prepared for the European Commission, DG Trade.

Francois J., O. Pindyuk, 2013, Consolidated Data on International Trade in Services, IIDE Discussion Papers 20130101, Institute for International and Development Economics.

Francois J., M. Manchin, H. Norberg, O. Pindyuk, P. Tomberger, 2013, Reducing Transatlantic Barriers to Trade and Investment: An Economic Assessment, No 20130401, IIDE Discussion Papers, Institute for International and Development Economics.

Ghodsi M., J. Hagemejer, A. Mach-Kwiecińska, 2015, The Implications of the Liberalization of Rail Services in Europe, in: A. Cieślik, J. J. Michałek (eds.), Liberalization of Transportation Services in the EU: The Polish Perspective, Polish Studies in Economics, Volume 6, Peter Lang, Frankfurt.

Fontagné L., A. Guillin, C. Mitaritonna, 2011, Estimations of Tariff Equivalents for the Services Sectors, Working Papers 2011-24, CEPII research center.

Mayer T., S. Zignago, 2011, Notes on CEPII's distances measures: the GeoDist Database, CEPII Working Paper 2011-25.

Park S.-C., 2002, Measuring Tariff Equivalents in Cross-Border Trade in Services, Trade Working Papers 353, East Asian Bureau of Economic Research.

Jan Hagemejer
(University of Warsaw and National Bank of Poland[1])

Chapter 8. Liberalization of trade flows under the TTIP from a small country perspective. The case of Poland

The Transatlantic Trade and Investment Partnership is a free trade agreement between the European Union and the United States. The initiative of the TTIP seems to be one of the proliferating trade agreements that the EU has been negotiating in the recent years with other developed (e.g. Canada, Japan and Singapore) and developing countries (ACP, MENA and the CEEC) as a result of the stall in the multilateral negotiations of the Doha round of the WTO.

The TTIP is a broad economic agreement. It covers trade, investment and government procurement facilitation. As far as international trade is concerned, apart from elimination of most of the overall low bilateral tariffs (except some tariff peaks in the agricultural trade), the focus of the agreement is on reduction in the non-tariff barriers both in merchandise trade and in services. This includes regulatory cooperation, in the form of review of existing rules and increased mutual regulation and standards recognitions, while cooperating on joint elaboration of newly introduced technical and safety regulations. Separate chapters of the negotiated agreements will be devoted to technical barriers to trade (TBT) and sanitary and phytosanitary measures (SPS). Some sectors require sector-specific chapters and these include inter alia chemicals, pharmaceuticals and motor vehicles where the national regulations are usually the most frequent. The agricultural sector is believed to be one of the most difficult chapters due to protectionist SPS measures.

The public debate in Poland and other European countries has been dominated by the somewhat political discussion fostered by several non-governmental organizations mostly on issues related to protection of investments and harmonization of regulations, but most of all, the lack of transparency of the negotiations

---

1 The views presented here are those of the author and should not be associated with the views of the National Bank of Poland, j.hagemejer[at]uw.edu.pl. The project is funded by the National Science Centre of Poland based on decision No. DEC-2013/09/B/HS4/01488.

(despite the fact that TTIP negotiations are much more transparent that most of the previous trade negotiations). The negotiation chapters were made public in 2015 by the European Commission.

As far as international trade is concerned, there have been numerous attempts to evaluate the possible effects of the TTIP. CEPR (2013b) provides an EU-commissioned impact assessment, mainly focused on trade and investment for the aggregate economy of the EU and the US. The results of elimination of tariffs and a partial elimination of non-tariff barriers (NTBs) show that under the most ambitious scenario, the TTIP may lead to changes in the GDP of roughly 0.4 to 0.5 percent of the GDP of the US and EU respectively, most of which is attributed to the reduction of non-tariff barriers.[2]

The methodology of both the EU-wide and country-specific evaluations found in the literature is to some extent standard: most of them use global computable general equilibrium models. The impact scenarios involve tariff liberalization and partial removal of NTBs (that are either estimated or based on external sources). While the overall effects of the EU vary to some extent but are close to the ones provided by CEPR (2013b), the distribution of gains from the TTIP across the EU members seems to be uneven. Fontagné et al. (2013) estimate the trade impact of roughly 50 percent in the EU-US trade and the overall level of GDP gains at 0.3 percent of the GDP, with Germany gaining the most (0.4 percent of the GDP) and the NMS in the ballpark of 0.2 percent of the GDP. Kinnman and Hagberg (2012) provide detailed estimates for Sweden using a GTAP model and show that due trade liberalization extra GDP gain are at the level of 0.2 percent, close to the EU-26 average in this study. CEPR (2013a) shows a percentage gain in GDP for the United Kingdom of roughly half the gain for the aggregate of remaining EU-26 countries.

In this study, we aim to provide a comprehensive evaluation of the possible TTIP effects for the economy of Poland. We use the GTAP computable general equilibrium model, a widely used CGE modelling framework. In order to capture the country specificity, in our simulation scenarios we use the estimates of NTBs (estimations are described in an auxiliary paper) that allow us to differentiate the impact of NTBs on trade of Poland, the remaining NMS aggregate, Germany, the largest trading partner of Poland and the rest of EU-15. This way we can

2 While these estimates are not available at disaggregated country level, CEPR provided some selected results for Poland's Ministry of Economy that evaluate the TTIP impact at 0.2 percent of the GDP.

extensively analyze not only the bilateral impact of the TTIP on Poland and the US but also on the bulk of bilateral trade relations of Poland.

We show that from a point of view of a small country, where most of international trade is concentrated on exchange with one or several neighbouring partners, such as Poland, simultaneous trade liberalization with a third partner will not bring sizeable gains to its economy. We observe US-EU-15 trade expansion to be crowding out some of the trade in the most important Polish trading sectors, such as chemicals and motor vehicles. The unfavourable change in the terms of trade makes the gains from trade small, while some sectors reduce output by a considerable amount.

This chapter is organized as follows. In the first section we provide a Poland-EU-USA trade profile, where we analyze bilateral trade relations to identify the reciprocal importance of each of the analyzed trading partners with the US and vice versa, provide sectoral analysis of relative trade balances and comparative advantages. We proceed with a brief discussion the model and simulation scenarios. In the subsequent section we provide detailed results. We conclude with a brief discussion of the main features of the simulations.

1. Poland-EU-USA trade profile

The potential of the benefits from the TTIP to a large extent depends on the intensity of existing trade relations. Table 1 shows the shares of total US trade with the particular EU members and shares of EU members trade with the US in their total trade. These shares are very diversified both in merchandise trade and services. First of all, EU as a whole is an important trade partner for the US, responsible for roughly 20% of US services trade and 14% of US merchandise trade. Most of it is, however, due to trade with Germany and the rest of the EU-15, while Poland and the remaining NMS contribute very little. Trade with Germany is relatively more intensive in merchandise trade than in services, compared to the remaining EU-15 aggregate.

EU as a whole is more important to the US than the US to the EU in terms of bilateral trade relations. The overall share of the EU-28 exports to the EU both in services and in merchandise trade stands at 5–6%. However, US share of Poland and the NMS is considerably lower than in the EU-15. From the point of view of relative importance, German involvement in trade of the US is significant, especially on the export side of merchandise trade but also in services.

Table 1. Importance of Bilateral Trade Relations, 2011 (Services), 2013 (Merchandise Trade)

	USA trade		EU countries trade	
Country	**Share of imports**	**Share of exports**	**Share of imports**	**Share of exports**
Merchandise trade				
Poland	0.2	0.2	2.7	2.4
Germany	4.3	2.5	5.7	8.3
rEU-15	9.2	10.9	5.6	6.7
rNMS	0.5	0.4	1.7	2.2
Overall	14.3	13.9	5.1	6.5
Services				
Poland	0.3	0.3	3.9	2.8
Germany	5.4	4.5	7.0	6.8
rEU-15	14.9	14.3	5.5	4.2
rNMS	0.6	0.6	3.3	2.5
Overall	21.2	19.7	5.6	4.5

USA trade: country/region share in total US trade, EU trade: US share in total trade
Source: Comtrade, Francois' services data

We analyze the sectoral split of bilateral trade from two angles. First, we compute the revealed comparative advantage indices and second, we analyze the balance of trade in each sector as a percentage of total bilateral trade. The first column of Table 2 shows the relative RCA's of the EU countries in their exports to the US (relative competitiveness of analyzed regions in their trade to US). The pattern of trade is fairly clear. EU-15 countries have slight comparative advantages in most manufacturing sectors. That excludes Germany, where RCA's are concentrated within the automobile industry, machinery and metal industry. On the other hand, Poland reveals a comparative advantage in agriculture, light manufacturing including food, textiles, wood but also in the some heavy industries such as minerals, metals, metal products, and in the production of remaining transport equipment and electrical equipment. Similar patterns emerge for the remaining NMS. While there seems to exist a certain degree of specialization among the NMS and the EU-15, one has to bear in mind that NMS trade with the US is somewhat negligible compared to the EU-15. As far as services are concerned, business services reveal a comparative advantage in Poland and Germany as well as recreation. Construction seems to be an important export service sector in Germany and so does communication, to a smaller extent.

Table 2. Revealed Comparative Advantage Indices

	RCAs of EU countries in trade to US				RCAs of US in trade to EU			
sector	**Germany**	**Poland**	**rEU-15**	**rNMS**	**Germany**	**Poland**	**rEU-15**	**rNMS**
Agriculture	0.6	1.8	1.1	1.9	0.9	0.7	0.8	1.0
Mining	0.0	0.2	1.5	0.2	0.2	0.2	0.2	0.3
Food	0.3	1.5	1.4	0.4	0.4	1.1	0.3	0.5
Textiles	0.7	1.1	1.1	1.4	0.3	0.4	0.3	0.4
Apparel	0.0	0.9	1.3	3.4	0.1	0.0	0.1	0.1
Leather	0.1	0.2	1.4	1.1	0.1	0.1	0.1	0.1
Wood	0.5	6.7	1.0	2.4	0.2	0.2	0.4	0.3
Paper	0.9	0.7	1.1	0.3	0.6	1.0	0.9	0.9
Coal Petrol	0.1	0.9	1.4	1.6	0.6	0.1	1.3	1.7
Chemicals	0.8	0.3	1.1	0.5	1.5	1.0	1.6	1.0
Minerals	0.7	1.7	1.1	1.4	1.6	0.9	0.7	1.4
Steel	0.8	0.3	1.1	1.8	0.2	0.1	0.2	0.1
Metals	1.3	1.2	0.9	0.5	0.5	0.5	0.9	0.4
Metal Products	1.3	1.6	0.9	1.0	0.9	1.0	0.8	0.7
Motor Vehicles	2.2	0.5	0.4	1.0	1.0	0.4	0.2	0.6
Transport Eq. Nec	0.7	2.6	1.2	0.3	2.9	6.4	5.5	5.5
Electrical Eq.	0.8	4.1	0.8	4.5	0.9	0.6	0.7	1.3
Machinery	1.2	1.0	0.9	1.3	1.6	1.6	1.7	1.8
MnfcsNec	0.3	0.4	1.4	0.4	1.0	0.5	1.5	1.0
Construction	2.2	0.3	0.6	0.7	0.3	0.1	0.2	0.0
Trade	1.2	0.1	0.9	2.8	0.3	0.1	0.1	0.2
Transport	0.6	0.9	1.1	0.6	0.7	0.9	0.6	0.4
Communication	1.1	0.9	0.9	1.2	1.6	0.6	0.5	2.0
Fin. Svcs	0.6	0.7	1.2	1.2	0.4	2.6	0.8	0.7
Insurance	0.8	0.2	1.1	0.2	0.3	1.6	0.2	0.5
Business Svcs	1.2	1.3	0.9	1.1	1.4	1.2	1.5	1.2
Recreation, Nec	1.4	1.7	0.7	4.2	2.2	1.7	0.9	5.8

EU RCA's are relative to total EU-27 exports to US.US RCA's are relative to total countries imports

Source: own calculation using Comtrade trade database and Francois services data.

There are only several sectors where the US has a notable comparative advantage in exports to the EU compared to other EU trade partners including the EU itself. These are most notably, transport equipment n.e.c. (RCA across all analyzed EU countries/regions, due mostly to trade in aircraft) but also machinery and equipment. For the EU-15 including Germany, an important sector in imports from the US is the chemical industry. As far as services are concerned, business services imports from the US are relatively large across all analyzed country groupings. US exports also reveal a comparative advantage in communication (NMS including Poland), financial services and insurance (Germany) and recreation.

The sectoral trade balance shows a competitive position in the bilateral exchange of EU members and the United States. Table shows that the important exporting sectors for Germany and the EU where there is a trade surplus are mostly motor vehicles, machinery and products of the metal industry but also apparel, textiles, leather and wood. Trade deficits are mostly in agriculture, mining and electrical and transport equipment n.e.c. In Poland, trade deficits span across a larger number of sectors and include also motor vehicles, food, textiles and steel. On the other hand one can observe a significant trade surplus in the remaining NMS aggregate.

Table 3. Sectoral Trade Balances

	Germany	**Poland**	**Rest of EU-15**	**Rest of NMS**
Agriculture	-75.1	-58.0	-63.2	-32.7
Mining	-97.4	-97.0	-33.3	-92.7
Food	13.9	-11.4	51.5	-21.1
Textiles	20.4	-10.9	32.4	17.1
Apparel	31.0	68.1	71.4	80.4
Leather	58.9	-9.5	76.2	77.8
Wood	46.9	90.7	31.1	78.5
Paper	10.2	-64.7	-19.0	-52.0
Coal Petrol	-82.0	97.9	6.7	23.8
Chemicals	14.8	-51.7	3.4	4.0
Minerals	-4.8	23.8	38.8	21.6
Steel	63.9	-20.2	59.1	84.9
Metals	29.1	11.2	-26.1	14.7
Metal Products	29.3	-13.7	16.0	6.8

	Germany	Poland	Rest of EU-15	Rest of NMS
Motor Vehicles	70.7	-23.2	65.2	58.4
Transport Eq. Nec	-20.0	5.9	-18.4	5.7
Electrical Eq.	-20.1	-47.9	-18.9	3.9
Machinery	35.4	-14.1	7.1	5.0
Manufacturing nec	5.9	35.8	17.5	36.3
Construction	9.1	-38.0	4.8	68.5
Trade	43.2	-43.0	59.3	67.8
Transport	-1.5	1.4	35.7	9.4
Communication	-24.2	22.4	22.4	-45.1
Fin. Svcs	15.2	-49.2	-8.4	40.5
Insurance	57.9	-70.7	52.3	-40.0
Business Svcs	-5.3	-6.7	-32.9	-10.3
Recreation, Nec	-32.3	-59.5	-35.4	-63.2

Share in percent of total sectoral trade = 100* (X–M)/(X+M)
Source: Trade – Comtrade, Services Francois' data

The analysis presented in this section shows that Poland has a relatively more imbalanced trade towards the US; it reveals few comparative advantages and trades less than the other EU countries under consideration, despite its size. This simple analysis shows that the benefits from direct trade liberalization with the US may be small with the benefits expected for other EU countries. Moreover, intensification of trade between other EU members and the US may lead to a decrease in Poland's intra-EU trade relations due to the initial asymmetry.

2. The model and data

To evaluate the effects of trade liberalization, we employ the GTAP computable general equilibrium model and database developed by the Global Trade Analysis Project at Purdue University. The GTAP is a commonly used framework for trade policy analysis. The structure of the model is relatively simple while allowing for a large range of simulations[3]. The basic economic agent in the model is the so-called regional household that maximizes the regional utility subject to income

3 For a complete description of the model, consult Hertel, Tsigas (1997).

constraints. This regional household takes all the expenditure decisions within the region's economy, by choosing the levels of private consumption, government expenditures and savings.

The regional household preferences are multiply nested. In the top nest the private consumption, public consumption and overall regional savings are aggregated using a Cobb-Douglas function (this assumption ensures that within each region the respective consumption and saving shares are constant). While within the government consumption, the sectoral structure is preserved by a lower level Cobb-Douglas composite, private consumption demand is governed by a Constant Difference of Elasticity preferences to account for the non-homothetic nature of consumption demand. Each of the goods and services consumed is in fact a constant-elasticity of substitution aggregate of domestic and foreign goods and services according to the Armington setting.

Firms produce using intermediate goods and primary factors purchased from the regional household. The sources of primary factors are purely domestic – it is assumed that the factors are strictly immobile internationally and mobile within a region (with the exception of land and natural resources). The intermediate goods can either be domestically produced or imported.

The GTAP database has information on 57 sectors in 129 regions. The data include information on the production volume, sales both domestic and international, intermediate use and primary factor use. It also contains information about bilateral trade between countries in both goods and services. Version 8 of the database uses the year 2007 as a reference year[4]. For the purpose of this chapter, we have created an aggregated database (regional and sectoral aggregation, mainly in the agriculture and food sectors).

All the descriptive statistics presented in the previous sectors are produced on the basis of the Comtrade statistics taken from the WITS database. Services trade data come from Francois, Pindyuk (2013).

3. Simulation scenarios

Tariffs are low overall. Table 4 shows bilateral effectively applied tariffs in each of the analyzed sectors weighted by the respective trade flows (at HS6 digit level). Overall, the tariffs applied by the EU towards the US are higher than those applied on US imports from the EU. There are some product categories, where overall tariffs are higher and they include the processed food sector, the automotive sector

4 Database details can be found here: https://www.gtap.agecon.purdue.edu/databases/v8/

in the EU and textiles and apparel in both US and the EU. We update the tariff rates in the GTAP database to reflect the 2011 rates (however, the baseline 2007 tariff levels in the original data did not differ to a large extent). All our simulation scenarios feature a complete tariff removal. However, given the low level of pre-liberalization tariffs and the moderate level of trade between US and the EU, the sole removal of tariffs brings virtually zero macroeconomic effects.

What matters are the non-tariff barriers. In order to assure consistency with the database used in the simulations, we apply a common methodology to estimate NTBs both for merchandise trade and services trade within the GTAP sectors. We follow (Park 2002) and (Fontagné, Guillin and Mitaritonna 2011) by calculating the tariff equivalents based on the importer fixed effects in the gravity equation. We base the estimations for the merchandise trade data on Comtrade bilateral trade statistics aggregated to GTAP sectors. The gravity control variables come from the World Development Indicators database and the CEPII dataset. The details of the estimations are provided in Hagemejer and Śledziewska (Chapter 7).

Our estimates allow us to differentiate between the NTB estimates for the EU-15, NMS and Poland. Since gravity estimations are based on the residuals of regression equation, countries with less than average trade (controlling for gravity factors) will exhibit larger tariff equivalents. This is the case for the NMS and Poland, where the estimated NTBs are in many cases higher than those of the EU-15.

Ecorys (2009) presents a study on non-tariff barriers in the EU-US trade. While their EU aggregate estimates of NTB's also come from a version of the gravity model, they also perform a thorough analysis of NTBs actionability. This actionability is estimated at roughly 50% of the initial level of NTBs. We treat the 50% actionability as the baseline scenario in our simulation. We consider three scenarios: Partial, Actionable and Complete. They correspond to a removal of respectively 25, 50 and 100 percent of non tariff barriers on top of the complete removal of tariffs. We treat the complete removal of NTBs as an upper bound for long-run possible effects of the TTIP. However, we do not impose any shocks on the Coal-Petrol sector of the manufacturing industry as we believe that the analysis within this sector goes beyond the scope of our modelling. Moreover, in our scenarios we include the agriculture and food sectors. However, the estimated tariff equivalents in this sector seem low contrary to the anecdotal evidence. This may stem from the fact that international trade in agricultural goods is highly protected around the world, and therefore the gravity model underestimates the tariff equivalents. In such a case, the effects of trade liberalization for those sectors may be underestimated.

Table 4. Bilateral tariffs, 2011

	US vs EU				EU vs US			
Sector	**Poland**	**NMS**	**Germany**	**EU-15**	**Poland**	**NMS**	**Germany**	**EU-15**
Agriculture	2.1	19.1	1.9	2.9	5.2	5.6	3.4	3.5
Mining	0.3	0.1	0.5	0.0	0.0	0.0	0.0	0.0
Food	4.3	6.4	3.7	3.0	11.8	24.7	10.2	13.7
Textiles	5.2	6.0	5.5	7.2	6.1	6.6	7.1	6.8
Apparel	11.8	11.6	9.0	9.5	10.7	10.3	10.0	10.0
Leather	6.2	5.8	8.1	7.4	5.6	6.2	4.4	3.8
Wood	0.3	0.3	0.4	0.5	3.1	1.6	2.7	1.5
Paper	0.0	0.0	0.0	0.0	0.0	0.0	0.0	0.0
Coal Petrol	0.7	1.3	1.3	1.3	0.9	2.1	2.1	1.9
Chemicals	1.6	1.4	1.3	1.1	2.7	2.9	2.0	2.1
Minerals	9.8	4.7	2.9	5.0	2.3	3.5	3.2	3.0
Steel	0.2	0.5	0.2	0.1	0.5	0.6	0.6	0.4
Metals	1.7	3.6	2.4	1.4	4.1	3.5	2.5	1.4
Metal Products	1.1	2.2	2.0	1.9	2.4	3.1	1.4	2.4
Motor Vehicles	0.8	1.2	1.2	1.2	8.8	9.0	9.4	6.5
Transport Eq. Nec	0.1	0.4	0.2	0.1	1.4	1.4	1.3	1.3
Electrical Eq.	0.9	0.1	0.3	0.3	0.5	0.5	0.4	0.6
Machinery	1.2	1.2	0.9	0.8	1.2	1.4	1.3	1.2
Manufacturing nec	1.5	1.1	0.9	0.7	2.7	1.9	1.4	1.0

Source: TRAINS

In addition to the three short run scenarios, we also provide a long-run scenario where we allow for investment-triggered capital accumulation as described by Baldwin (1992) and applied by Francois and McDonald (1996), where capital stock increases at the rate that is equal to investment, mimicking the steady-state in a dynamic growth model.

The simulation scenarios assume that iceberg transport costs go down as a result of the removal of trade barriers. This translates directly to a drop in import prices. For example, if the initial tariff equivalent was ten percent and we assume complete liberalization, then the prices have to decrease accordingly. If the gross import price before liberalization was $P_0=1.1$, then the price after liberalization will be equal to $P_1=1$. So the price has to go down by $0.1/1.1 \approx 0.09$, i.e. nine percent.

Table 5. Estimated tariff equivalents of NTBs

Sector	Tariff Equivalent			
	EU-15	NMS	Poland	USA
Total	21%	18%	26%	23%
Agriculture	31%	36%	33%	44%
Mining	17%	22%	30%	24%
Food	36%	46%	46%	25%
Textiles	27%	22%	21%	32%
Apparel	33%	27%	26%	42%
Leather	30%	23%	28%	43%
Wood	25%	27%	33%	21%
Paper	37%	32%	47%	46%
Coal Petrol	73%	91%	133%	0%
Chemicals	19%	17%	19%	23%
Minerals	35%	26%	32%	28%
Steel	40%	45%	54%	37%
Metals	40%	35%	44%	46%
Met. Prod.	29%	16%	27%	39%
Motor Veh.	38%	26%	35%	44%
Tr. Eq. Nec	21%	23%	23%	29%
Electric	35%	18%	29%	51%
Machinery	27%	15%	25%	38%
MnfcsNec	26%	17%	26%	15%
Construction	43%	52%	52%	58%
Trade	32%	51%	60%	22%
Transport	28%	43%	45%	20%
Communication	16%	27%	26%	3%
Fin. Svcs	24%	29%	30%	4%
Insurance	15%	23%	24%	11%
Business Svcs	11%	14%	12%	9%
Rec. Svcs	10%	13%	18%	7%

Source: Hagemejer, Śledziewska (Chapter 7)

Therefore, the shock to the import price will be equal to $AT/(1+T)$, A – the is the depth of liberalization (100%, 50%, 25%) and T – initial level of tariff equivalent. The shocks in the GTAP model are imposed on the *ams* parameter. "Shocks to ams(i,r,s) represent the negative of the rate of decay on imports of commodity or service *i* from region *r* imported by region *s*. When ams(i,r,s) is shocked by 20%, then 20% more of the product becomes available to domestic consumers – given the same level of exports from the source country. In order to ensure that producers still receive the same revenue on their sales, effective import prices (pms) fall by 20%".[5]

4. Simulation results

The overall impact on the macroeconomic aggregates is moderate but it varies slightly across the analyzed economies. In the actionable scenario, the gains range from 0.2% of an increase in GDP of Poland and the NMS, through 0.4 and 0.3 for Germany and the rest of EU-15 respectively to 0.5 in the US. The policy shock has a minor effect on the third countries. In the partial liberalization scenario, the gains amount to roughly half of the scale of the actionable scenario, whereas in the complete scenario they reach 1.1 percent of the GDP in the case of the US and considerably less in the other countries and regions involved. The distribution of the gains is somewhat in line with the overall involvement in the bilateral trade. US gains slightly more than the EU-15, while the NMS and Poland gain the least. The extra capital accumulation in the long run scenario brings additional welfare gains to all economies involved and they amount to roughly 0.1% of extra GDP for Poland and the NMS and proportionately more for Germany, EU-15 and the US.

Table 6. Changes (%) in GDP

scenario	Poland	NMS	Germany	EU-15	US	rEurope	Turkey	rAmerica	Asia	RoW
Partial	0.1	0.1	0.2	0.2	0.2	0.0	0.0	0.0	0.0	0.0
Actionable	0.2	0.2	0.4	0.3	0.5	0.0	0.0	-0.1	0.0	0.0
Complete	0.4	0.4	0.8	0.7	1.1	-0.1	0.0	-0.1	-0.1	-0.1
Actionable – LR	0.3	0.3	0.9	0.7	0.9	-0.1	-0.3	-0.4	-0.3	-7.8

LR – long run
Source: own simulation.

5 Hertel T. R., McDougall R. and Itakura K., GTAP Model Version 6.0 https://www.gtap.agecon.purdue.edu/resources/res_display.asp?RecordID=576

There is a large discrepancy in the size of the shock to the total international trade of the involved partners and it is easily explained by the initial trade shares. The large output effects in the US are largely due to a rather significant increase in the overall exports of 8.1% in the actionable trade liberalization scenario. In the EU-15 economies including Germany, the increase in trade is much more moderate at the level of close to 1%, while for Poland and the NMS the mild increase in exports is below 0.5 percent. It is, however, worth noting that due to important trade linkages with Turkey, as a result of the increase in bilateral trade between the EU and the US, exports of Turkey increase by more than those of the NMS in percentage terms. In the remaining country groupings beyond the partners involved in the TTIP, there is a substantial fall in imports.

Table 7. Changes (%) in Overall Exports

scenario	Poland	NMS	Germany	EU-15	US	rEurope	Turkey	rAmerica	Asia	RoW
Partial	0.3	0.2	0.7	0.7	4.3	0.0	0.3	-0.2	0.1	0.1
Actionable	0.4	0.3	1.2	1.3	8.1	0.0	0.6	-0.3	0.1	0.1
Complete	0.9	0.7	2.5	2.8	17.4	0.0	1.3	-0.6	0.3	0.3
Actionable – LR	0.3	0.3	1.9	1.6	10.3	-0.7	-0.6	-1.8	-0.8	-5.2

LR – long run
Source: own simulation.

Table 8. Changes (%) in Overall Imports

scenario	Poland	NMS	Germany	EU-15	US	rEurope	Turkey	rAmerica	Asia	RoW
Partial	-0.1	0.0	1.2	0.8	4.8	-0.6	-0.5	-1.6	-0.5	-0.6
Actionable	-0.2	0.0	2.2	1.5	9.1	-1.1	-0.9	-3.1	-1.1	-1.1
Complete	-0.5	0.1	4.8	3.1	19.9	-2.4	-1.8	-6.7	-2.5	-2.4
Actionable – LR	0.1	0.2	2.4	1.7	8.2	-0.9	-1.1	-2.7	-1.3	-8.0

LR – long run
Source: own simulation.

The nature of the response in overall imports is also interesting. The increase in US imports is roughly in-line with the increase in its exports. However, while the boost in bilateral trade with the US leads to an increase in overall imports in Germany and the EU-15, the Polish overall imports fall while there is virtually no effect on the overall imports of the NMS. There are some trade diversion effects, mainly stemming from the changes in relative prices that lead to such an asymmetric outcome.

If we observe the relative prices, we can see while the scale of the fall of the aggregate import price is roughly the same for all the EU members, the response of the export prices is not (the detailed tables are placed in the appendix). Germany is the only trade partner of the analyzed country groupings, where export prices in fact increase. The fall in export prices in the EU-15 is also much smaller than the one for Poland and the NMS. While the terms of trade of the EU-15 including Germany improves, it significantly deteriorates in Poland and the NMS, which drives the import response.

Table 9. Changes in the Terms of Trade

region	Partial	Actionable	Complete	Action-LR
Poland	-0.1	-0.2	-0.4	-0.2
NMS	0.0	-0.1	-0.1	-0.1
Germany	0.2	0.5	1.0	0.3
EU-15	0.1	0.3	0.6	0.1
USA	1.0	1.9	3.9	1.3
Rest Europe	-0.3	-0.5	-1.2	-0.2
Turkey	-0.2	-0.4	-0.8	-0.5
America	-0.7	-1.3	-2.7	-0.9
Asia	-0.2	-0.4	-0.9	-0.5
RoW	-0.3	-0.5	-1.1	0.6

LR – long run
Source: own simulation.

The limited impact on output exports and imports leads to a moderate effect on welfare as measured by the equivalent variation. The overall gain for Germany and the rest of the EU-15 is in the ballpark of 0.5% of the initial value of GDP which is in line with other studies. However, for the NMS including Poland, the overall welfare effect is close to zero. While there certainly is some exports expansion that is welfare-improving, the deterioration of terms of trade and the resulting fall in overall exports dampens the welfare effect that was expected to be small from the very start, to an even larger extent.

Table 10. Welfare Changes (in % of GDP, equivalent variation)

scenario	Poland	NMS	Germany	EU-15	US	rEurope	Turkey	rAmerica	Asia	RoW
Partial	0.0	0.1	0.2	0.2	0.4	-0.1	-0.1	-0.2	-0.1	-0.1
Actionable	0.1	0.1	0.5	0.4	0.7	-0.3	-0.1	-0.4	-0.2	-0.2
Complete	0.2	0.4	1.2	0.9	1.7	-0.6	-0.2	-0.8	-0.5	-0.5
Actionable – LR	0.1	0.2	0.8	0.6	0.9	-0.2	-0.3	-0.5	-0.4	-6.0

LR – long run
Source: own simulation.

Trade between the US and the EU is focused mainly on manufactured goods. Trade liberalization leads to an overall increase in rents of factors involved in the production of these goods. However, while analyzing the patterns of changes across countries one can see some differences that are mostly due to initial relative factor endowments: Germany and the US experience an increase in the real wages of labour and capital as the trade liberalization allows those regions to exploit their comparative advantages. Aside from a smaller scale of overall change, the NMS experience a larger increase of the price of skilled labour to that of capital and of unskilled labour. In Poland, the land rents increase the most while other factor gain relatively less. This is due to the fact that while the output of agriculture is not changing in Poland due to the TTIP, it falls in the remaining country groupings involved in the TTIP as most trade moves towards the manufacturing industry. The changes in real wages suggest that while in Poland the manufacturing sector expands as well, the structure of comparative advantage is relatively more shifted towards land-based economic activity than in other EU countries.

Table 11. Changes in Real Factor Wages (Actionable Scenario)

factor	Poland	NMS	Germany	EU-15	USA	Rest Europe	Turkey	America	Asia	RoW
Land	0.40	-0.50	-5.30	-3.10	-2.30	0.60	0.60	4.00	0.60	0.40
Unskilled Labour	0.10	0.20	0.70	0.60	0.90	-0.20	-0.20	-0.50	-0.20	-0.20
Skilled Labour	0.10	0.30	0.70	0.60	0.90	-0.20	-0.10	-0.50	-0.20	-0.10
Capital	0.10	0.20	0.50	0.50	0.90	-0.20	-0.10	-0.40	-0.20	-0.20
Natural Resources	-1.90	-3.00	-6.20	-3.00	-6.90	-0.30	-0.10	2.90	0.70	-0.10

Source: own simulation.

We provide a more detailed analysis of the response of the simulated Polish economy to the trade policy shock of the TTIP. Table 12 shows the geographic decomposition of Polish exports and imports in the "Actionable" scenario. One can see that the increase in exports and imports to the US is substantial (respectively by 66.2 and 61.3 percent) and contributes to overall 1.7 p.p. increase to both imports and exports. However, at the same time there is a slight exports diversion towards the US from other trading partners, especially Germany and the EU-15 that overall corresponds to more than one percent of the fall in exports, leading to an overall increase of a mere 0.4 percent.

A similar pattern can be found for Polish imports, where a large boost in imports from the US is dampened by a fall in imports from Polish main trading partners. Here, due to unfavourable developments in terms of trade, the fall in imports from Germany and the EU-15 combined contributes to an over 2 p.p. fall in total exports, which is only partially outweighed by the expansion of transatlantic trade.

Table 12. Overall Import and Export Changes in Poland, Actionable Scenario

Exports	**NMS**	**Germany**	**EU-15**	**USA**	**Rest Europe**	**Turkey**	**America**	**Asia**	**RoW**	**Overall**
% change	-0.1	-2.0	-1.7	66.2	0.0	-0.6	-0.6	-2.1	-0.9	0.4
pp contribution	-0.02	-0.5	-0.6	1.7	0.0	0.0	0.0	-0.1	0.0	0.4
Imports	**NMS**	**Germany**	**EU-15**	**USA**	**Rest Europe**	**Turkey**	**America**	**Asia**	**RoW**	**Overall**
% change	-1.4	-4.4	-3.3	61.3	0.5	2.2	3.1	3.1	0.3	-0.2
pp contribution	-0.1	-1.2	-1.1	1.7	0.0	0.0	0.0	0.4	0.0	-0.2

Source: own simulation.

As far as the sectoral composition of trade is concerned, the overall sectoral changes are small (and patterns similar to Table are found also on sectoral level with Poland-EU-15 trade shrinking and Poland-US trade expanding). Table show the changes in Polish exports and imports including their contribution to overall export change in the actionable scenario. One can observe, that overall export changes are small. There are some exceptions: exports are expected to go up substantially in food, wearing apparel, wood, metal products, transport equipment n.e.c., and machinery sectors. However, only few of these sectors matter for the overall export change. On the other hand, sectors with the largest negative contribution to Polish exports change are metals, motor vehicles and electrical equipment, where the fall in exports may reach up to roughly five percent. A similar analysis of the change in imports reveals that large imports expansion is expected mostly in the transport equipment n.e.c. sector. At the same time, the largest negative contribution to imports is found in motor vehicles, electrical equipment and machinery. In the services sectors, all sectors excluding construction increase exports, while their contribution to overall exports is rather negligible.

The changes in relative prices, exports and imports lead to changes in sectoral output. While these changes are not particularly large, one can observe that the sectors that are expanding include mostly textiles, apparel, wood, metal products and machinery – these are the sectors where import reduction accompanies export expansion. Output falls to the largest extent in the metal industry, motor vehicles, transport equipment n.e.c., and electrical equipment. Tables 18–20 in the appendix show the detailed bilateral exports and imports changes, as well as the changes in bilateral trade balance. One can see that the TTIP scenarios are indeed largely trade-enhancing as far as the bilateral exports and imports with the US are concerned. However, in many production sectors trade expansion between EU-15 including Germany and the US is crowding out Polish exports to the EU-15.

This is especially the case in chemicals, motor vehicles and electrical equipment. Combined with a relatively large expansion in imports from the US, this leads to a deterioration in the bilateral trade balance with the US and an overall drop in output. Motor vehicles and chemicals together contribute to overall over 24 percent of Polish exports according to the GTAP database and therefore the negative contribution to welfare gains is substantial. On the other hand, in another important export sector: machinery and equipment, the overall effect on trade balances is positive across Polish trading partners, which leads to an increase in output.

Table 13. Sectoral Changes in Poland's Overall International Trade

Sector	Partial	Actionable	(contribution)	Complete	Action-LR
Agriculture	-0.5	-1.0	0.0	-2.0	-1.8
Mining	-0.6	-1.4	0.0	-3.4	0.7
Food	0.8	1.5	0.1	3.4	1.2
Textiles	1.6	2.4	0.0	4.6	2.4
Apparel	3.1	4.9	0.1	9.9	4.7
Leather	1.1	1.5	0.0	2.2	1.2
Wood	1.1	2.0	0.1	4.3	1.8
Paper	0.9	1.6	0.0	3.3	1.1

Sector	Partial	Actionable	(contribution)	Complete	Action-LR
Coal Petrol	0.1	0.2	0.0	0.7	0.5
Chemicals	-0.3	-0.4	0.0	-0.5	-0.8
Minerals	1.2	1.8	0.0	3.3	2.1
Steel	0.6	1.0	0.0	1.6	1.6
Metals	-2.1	-4.8	-0.2	-12.5	-2.0
Metal Products	1.1	2.1	0.1	4.4	1.9
Motor Vehicles	-1.2	-1.6	-0.2	-3.0	-1.5
Transport Eq. Nec	0.7	1.6	0.0	4.3	0.5
Electrical Eq.	-1.9	-4.2	-0.2	-9.3	-4.1
Machinery	1.0	1.7	0.2	3.2	1.4
MnfcsNec	1.1	1.5	0.0	2.5	1.6
Utilities, Energy	0.5	0.8	0.0	1.9	1.0
Construction	0.1	-0.1	0.0	-0.3	-1.6
Trade	0.8	1.5	0.0	3.2	1.1
Transport	0.6	1.1	0.0	2.4	0.6
Communication	0.4	0.6	0.0	1.3	0.9
Fin. Svcs	0.1	-0.1	0.0	0.1	-0.6
Insurance	0.6	1.0	0.0	2.1	0.6
Business Svcs	0.9	1.5	0.1	3.2	1.1
Recreation, Nec	0.8	1.4	0.0	2.9	0.7
Non-market Svcs	1.1	1.9	0.0	3.9	1.2

Contribution in percentage points to overall change in exports. LR – long run
Source: own simulation.

Table 14. Output Changes in Poland

Sector	Partial	Action	Complete	Act – LR
Agriculture	0.0	0.0	0.1	-0.1
Mining	-0.1	-0.3	-0.9	0.1
Food	0.1	0.2	0.6	0.2
Textiles	1.1	1.7	3.3	1.7
Apparel	0.9	1.4	2.8	1.4
Leather	0.4	0.5	0.6	0.4
Wood	0.7	1.3	2.9	1.3

Sector	Partial	Action	Complete	Act – LR
Paper	0.3	0.5	0.9	0.4
Coal Petrol	0.1	0.2	0.5	0.2
Chemicals	-0.1	-0.1	0.1	-0.1
Minerals	0.2	0.3	0.5	0.6
Steel	0.3	0.5	0.8	0.9
Metals	-1.3	-2.9	-7.8	-1.2
Metal Products	0.3	0.6	1.3	0.7
Motor Vehicles	-0.9	-1.3	-2.5	-1.2
Transport Eq. Nec	-2.3	-4.2	-7.8	-4.5
Electrical Eq.	-1.3	-3.0	-6.8	-2.8
Machinery	0.3	0.4	0.6	0.5
MnfcsNec	0.2	0.2	0.3	0.4
Utilities, Energy	0.0	0.1	0.2	0.2
Construction	-0.2	-0.4	-0.8	0.2
Trade	0.0	0.1	0.3	0.2
Transport	0.1	0.2	0.5	0.1
Communication	0.0	0.0	0.1	0.2
Fin. Svcs	0.0	0.0	0.0	0.1
Insurance	0.0	0.0	0.1	0.2
Business Svcs	0.0	0.1	0.2	0.2
Recreation, Nec	0.0	0.1	0.2	0.2
Non-market Svcs	0.0	0.0	0.1	0.1

LR – long run
Source: own simulation.

Conclusions

In this chapter we have used a computable general equilibrium model to assess the possible effects of the international trade part of the TTIP on the economy of Poland. We have used the country-specific estimates of the tariff equivalents of non-tariff barriers both in services and merchandise trade, which have proved to exhibit some important differences in selected sectors. Our simulation scenarios assume complete tariff liberalization plus a partial liberalization of NTBs.

Our results show that the overall effects of the TTIP for the EU as a whole will be similar to those found in other empirical studies using a similar methodology.

However, we show that there is a clear asymmetry of results, as far as individual countries are concerned. First, the gain in Poland and the New Member States is considerably smaller than that in the western part of the EU. Second, the German gains from the TTIP stand out from all analyzed regions. The TTIP is in fact an across-the-board trade liberalization, in spite of some sectoral differences. In such cases, the existing pattern of comparative advantage is amplified by CGE models. Therefore large US trading partners (such as Germany) will naturally gain more than small ones (such as Poland and other NMS).

However, we also see some other changes in the pattern of trade. First of all, we observe some trade diversion: while trade between Poland and the US goes up substantially, what is disturbing is the reduction of trade with the EU. The main cause of is the unfavourable change in terms of trade: it deteriorates in Poland, mainly through a relative increase in the imports prices. This is mainly caused by a shift of resources in Germany and the EU-15 towards the production of US-destinated goods and an increase in the cost of Polish imports from those partners. While a decrease in terms of trade has a direct negative welfare effect, one has to keep in mind that production in Poland is import-intensive and this unfavourable change in the terms of trade indirectly affects the competitiveness of Polish exports. Together with the negative initial trade balance with the US in many sectors, some important export-oriented sectors reduce exports and subsequently output. With moderate direct gain of 0.2 percent in output in the central simulation scenario, the terms-of-trade effect brings down the overall gain in welfare in that scenario to just 0.1 percent of the GDP.

While the overall effects are small for Poland to the extent of being almost negligible, one has to keep in mind that some sectoral reallocations are likely to occur across sectors and this may have non-zero effects, depending on wage rigidity and labour market flexibility. Moreover, such simulations as the one presented in this paper are subject to certain risks both on the part of modelling and simulation scenarios. One that comes to one's mind is the level of initial NTBs and the scope of their liberalization: however, as those barriers include all the possible determinants of bilateral trade that are not captured by gravity variables, these might be overestimated – therefore reducing the overall impact. This is probably not the case for agriculture, where trade is generally protected in many countries and the underlying econometric model may not be able to assess the benchmark "free trade" levels. A deeper liberalization in agriculture may lead, however, to an amplification of the differences between Poland and other economies, due to the relative structure of Polish factor endowment. Another source of uncertainty is the treatment of the intermediate goods in the GTAP model: the GTAP database does not structurally distinguish trade in intermediates with the trade in final goods. Therefore the effects of the EU-15 trade expansion on the output of Poland's production of intermediate goods may be underestimated. This is a promising avenue for further research.

References

Baldwin R. E., 1992, Measurable Dynamic Gains from Trade, Journal of Political Economy 100, no. 1, February, pp. 162–74.

CEPR, 2013a, Estimating the Economic Impact on the UK of a Transatlantic Trade and Investment Partnership (TTIP) Agreement between the European Union and the United States, Centre of Economic Policy Research, London.

CEPR, 2013b, Reducing Transatlantic Barriers to Trade and Investment. An Economic Assessment, Centre of Economic Policy Research, London.

ECORYS, 2009, Non-Tariff Measures in EU-US Trade and Investment – An Economic Analysis, OJ 2007/S 180–219493, http://trade.ec.europa.eu/doclib/docs/2009/december/tradoc_145613.pdf

Fontagné L., A. Guillin, C. Mitaritonna, 2011, Estimations of Tariff Equivalents for the Services Sectors, Working Papers, CEPI, Paris.

Fontagné L., J. Gourdon, J. Sebastien, 2013, Transatlantic Trade: Whither Partnership, Which Economic Consequences, CEPII Policy Brief No 1, CEPII, Paris.

Francois J., B. McDonald, 1996, Liberalization and Capital Accumulation in the GTAP Model, GTAP Technical Papers, Center for Global Trade Analysis, Department of Agricultural Economics, Purdue University.

Francois J., O. Pindyuk, 2013, Consolidated Data on International Trade in Services, IIDE Discussion Papers, Institue for International and Development Economics.

Hagemejer J., K. Śledziewska, 2015, Trade barriers in services and merchandise trade in the context of TTIP: Poland, EU and the United States, mimeo, University of Warsaw.

Kinnman S., T. Hagberg, 2012, Potential Effects from an EU–US Free Trade Agreement –Sweden in Focus, Kommerskollegium National Board of Trade Stockholm.

Park S.-C., 2002, Measuring Tariff Equivalents in Cross-Border Trade in Services Trade, Tech. rep., East Asian Bureau of Economic Research.

Appendix: additional tables

Table 15. Changes in Import Prices

scenario	Poland	NMS	Germany	EU-15	US	rEurope	Turkey	rAmerica	Asia	RoW
Partial	0.1	0.1	0.2	0.2	0.2	0.0	0.0	0.0	0.0	0.0
Actionable	-0.3	-0.4	-0.4	-0.3	-0.9	-0.4	-0.6	-0.3	-0.8	-0.6
Complete	-0.7	-0.8	-0.8	-0.7	-1.9	-1.0	-1.3	-0.7	-1.7	-1.3
Actionable – LR	-0.2	-0.3	-0.3	-0.2	-0.6	-0.3	-0.3	-0.2	-0.4	-0.3

LR – long run
Source: own simulation.

Table 16. Changes in Export Prices

scenario	Poland	NMS	Germany	EU-15	US	rEurope	Turkey	rAmerica	Asia	RoW
Partial	-0.3	-0.3	0.0	-0.1	0.5	-0.5	-0.5	-0.8	-0.6	-0.5
Actionable	-0.6	-0.5	0.1	-0.1	0.9	-1.0	-1.0	-1.5	-1.2	-1.1
Complete	-1.2	-0.9	0.2	-0.1	1.9	-2.1	-2.1	-3.3	-2.6	-2.4
Actionable – LR	-0.5	-0.4	0.0	-0.1	0.6	-0.5	-0.8	-1.0	-0.9	0.3

LR – long run
Source: own simulation.

Table 17. Output Changes, Actionable Scenario

Sector	Poland	NMS	Germany	EU-15	US	rEurope	Turkey	rAmerica	Asia	RoW
Agriculture	0.0	-0.1	-1.3	-0.8	-0.6	0.1	0.2	0.8	0.1	0.1
Mining	-0.3	-0.6	-1.0	-0.5	-1.1	0.0	-0.1	0.4	0.1	0.0
Food	0.2	-0.2	-0.5	0.2	-0.1	0.2	0.1	0.5	0.1	0.1
Textiles	1.7	1.9	-0.4	1.5	-4.0	1.0	1.4	1.3	0.5	0.2
Apparel	1.4	2.7	-0.8	3.3	-3.3	0.8	1.4	0.1	0.2	-0.1
Leather	0.5	2.7	1.4	5.5	-8.6	1.5	0.9	0.7	-1.9	0.6
Wood	1.3	0.8	-1.4	-0.5	-0.8	1.0	0.7	3.1	0.8	0.3
Paper	0.5	0.4	-0.6	-0.2	-0.9	1.2	0.6	1.4	0.5	0.5
Coal Petrol	0.2	0.3	0.1	0.6	0.2	0.0	0.1	0.1	0.0	0.0
Chemicals	-0.1	0.2	-1.8	-0.4	-0.9	0.0	0.6	0.8	0.3	0.3
Minerals	0.3	0.2	-0.3	0.3	-1.4	-0.1	-0.7	-1.1	-0.5	-0.4

Sector	Poland	NMS	Germany	EU-15	US	rEurope	Turkey	rAmerica	Asia	RoW
Steel	0.5	0.8	-0.7	-0.4	-4.1	0.6	0.3	-0.2	-0.1	0.1
Metals	-2.9	-3.6	0.7	-1.4	2.7	-3.2	-1.8	-2.3	-0.2	-2.0
Metal Products	0.6	0.4	0.1	0.0	-1.3	1.2	0.5	0.2	-0.1	0.1
Motor Vehicles	-1.3	-0.5	3.1	0.4	-0.2	0.0	0.2	-2.6	-0.7	-0.1
Transport Eq. Nec	-4.2	-6.5	-5.3	-1.3	1.6	-2.3	-4.3	-3.8	-0.6	-1.3
Electrical Eq.	-3.0	0.1	-1.4	-0.4	-0.7	-0.7	-0.8	1.7	-0.3	-0.1
Machinery	0.4	0.1	1.4	0.7	-3.1	0.1	0.7	-2.1	-0.1	0.8
MnfcsNec	0.2	0.5	-1.6	0.5	-0.4	0.5	0.0	0.5	0.3	-0.3
Utilities, Energy	0.1	0.1	-0.5	-0.1	0.0	0.3	0.1	0.2	0.0	0.0
Construction	-0.4	-0.4	0.6	0.1	1.5	-0.8	-1.1	-1.8	-0.9	-1.0
Trade	0.1	0.1	-0.1	0.1	0.3	-0.1	-0.1	-0.2	0.0	-0.1
Transport	0.2	-0.1	-0.5	-0.2	0.0	0.1	-0.1	0.3	0.2	0.0
Communication	0.0	0.0	-0.2	-0.3	0.2	0.2	0.1	0.2	0.2	0.2
Fin. Svcs	0.0	-0.2	-0.5	-0.7	0.3	0.3	0.1	0.3	0.2	0.2
Insurance	0.0	0.0	0.0	0.4	-0.5	0.3	0.6	1.0	0.3	0.3
Business Svcs	0.1	0.1	-0.1	-0.1	-0.3	0.4	0.1	0.4	0.4	0.3
Recreation, Nec	0.1	0.1	0.0	-0.1	0.6	0.2	0.3	0.3	0.1	0.2
Non-market Svcs	0.0	0.1	0.1	0.1	0.2	0.0	0.0	0.0	0.0	0.0

Source: own simulation.

Table 18. Bilateral Export Changes in Poland, Actionable Scenario

sector	NMS	Germany	EU-15	USA	Rest Europe	Turkey	America	Asia	RoW
Agriculture	-0.9	-1.9	-1.8	100.1	-0.8	-0.7	-0.1	-1.2	-1.8
Mining	-2.0	-1.5	-0.9	186.0	-1.6	-1.2	-2.3	-1.8	-1.3
Food	-0.9	0.9	0.6	59.0	-0.8	-0.8	-1.6	-2.1	-1.9
Textiles	1.9	-1.5	0.2	189.5	-1.0	-1.7	-2.3	-3.9	-3.8
Apparel	0.6	-0.7	-0.2	352.4	-1.4	-3.0	-5.6	-4.5	-3.9
Leather	2.0	0.4	0.8	247.6	-1.0	-2.1	-6.2	-4.5	-3.8
Wood	0.9	0.8	0.7	64.5	0.6	-1.3	-1.8	-3.3	-2.8
Paper	1.7	1.4	1.0	88.5	0.9	0.5	-0.3	-1.8	-1.1

sector	NMS	Germany	EU-15	USA	Rest Europe	Turkey	America	Asia	RoW
Coal Petrol	0.0	0.3	0.2	26.0	0.1	-0.1	-0.1	-0.2	-0.2
Chemicals	0.8	-3.1	-2.3	54.0	0.9	0.2	-0.5	-2.1	-1.2
Minerals	0.1	-1.8	0.6	81.1	-0.8	-1.7	-3.2	-3.1	-2.5
Steel	0.4	1.5	0.2	66.5	-1.1	-0.6	-3.1	-3.2	-2.5
Metals	-2.1	-6.2	-11.7	173.8	-3.8	-3.5	-4.7	-4.5	-4.2
Metal Products	1.2	-0.4	-0.4	135.7	0.3	-0.6	-2.5	-3.9	-2.8
Motor Vehicles	-1.4	-5.0	-0.9	79.9	-1.2	-0.5	-2.2	-2.7	-1.9
Transport Eq. Nec	-7.4	-10.7	-12.8	80.5	2.8	4.3	2.8	4.2	3.6
Electrical Eq.	-1.7	-10.7	-6.2	218.9	-0.2	-2 .0	-2.6	-3.4	-1.9
Machinery	0.2	-3.1	-3.8	111.8	0.3	-0.6	0.4	-3	-0.4
MnfcsNec	0.5	-0.1	-3.2	51.6	-0.3	-2.2	-3.4	-3.6	-2.7
Utilities, Energy	0.7	2.3	2.3	3.7	-0.4	-2.4	-3.0	-2.1	-1.9
Construction	-1.1	0.7	-0.5	44.1	-1.8	-2.7	-3.0	-1.9	-1.7
Trade	0.2	1.6	1.1	26.9	-0.7	-0.9	-2.1	-1.8	-0.7
Transport	-1.7	-1.0	-0.9	18.2	-0.2	-0.5	-1.3	-0.6	-0.3
Communication	-0.1	0.6	0.8	6.4	-0.3	-0.7	-1.2	-0.9	-0.5
Fin. Svcs	-0.9	-0.5	-1.7	8.3	0.6	0.3	0.0	0.1	0.4
Insurance	-0.6	1.0	0.7	12.4	-0.1	-0.3	0.2	-0.5	0.1
Business Svcs	0.7	1.8	1.5	12.5	0.4	-1.0	-1.8	-0.7	-0.2
Recreation, Nec	0.3	2.0	1.3	10.1	-0.3	0.1	-0.7	-0.6	0.1
Non-market Svcs	1.2	2.7	3.0	2.2	-0.2	0.4	-0.4	0.1	0.8

LR – long run

Source: own simulation.

Table 19. Bilateral Import Changes in Poland, Actionable Scenario

sector	NMS	Germany	EU-15	USA	Rest Europe	Turkey	America	Asia	RoW
Agriculture	-0.5	-2.6	-2.3	67.9	1.2	1.7	2.9	2.3	2.1
Mining	-1.4	-3.0	-7.5	199.4	-0.3	0.2	-0.5	-0.4	0.0
Food	-1.6	-4.6	-3.7	180.1	0.9	1.3	4.2	2.1	1.7
Textiles	0.0	-3.6	-2.6	146.7	3.4	4.4	9.3	6.0	5.1
Apparel	-1.2	-4.8	-4.1	243.0	2.7	3.4	9.1	5.1	4.3

sector	NMS	Germany	EU-15	USA	Rest Europe	Turkey	America	Asia	RoW
Leather	-1.0	-5	-4.1	164.4	3.2	3.8	10.5	5.6	4.9
Wood	0.7	-3.8	-2.2	90.3	3.6	4.4	9.1	5.8	5.1
Paper	-0.3	-4.5	-3.2	87.7	2.9	3.0	7.7	4.5	3.8
Coal Petrol	0.2	-0.4	-0.4	5.5	0.4	0.5	1.5	0.6	0.5
Chemicals	-0.2	-3.3	-2.3	65.1	2.5	2.6	7.2	4.3	3.6
Minerals	0.1	-3.6	-2.5	87.1	3.0	3.2	7.6	4.2	3.7
Steel	0.3	-2.9	-1.8	111.6	3.1	2.7	7.3	4.4	3.8
Metals	-1.7	-4.3	-1.8	215	1.6	2.0	7.0	3.4	2.8
Metal Products	-0.1	-4.8	-3.0	102.5	3.8	3.9	10.1	5.9	4.9
Motor Vehicles	-1.3	-2.9	-2.7	148.2	0.5	0.9	3.6	2.4	1.3
Transport Eq. Nec	-26.8	-29.4	-28	43.5	-25.6	-25	-21.5	-23.8	-24.8
Electrical Eq.	-3.2	-6.7	-5.7	113.7	-0.1	0.6	6.5	2.1	1.3
Machinery	-2.1	-6.0	-4.7	90.4	1.7	2.0	7.7	4.0	2.8
MnfcsNec	-1.0	-5.9	-3.6	82.8	3.2	3.6	9.5	5.3	4.0
Utilities, Energy	1.0	-3.1	-2.1	-8.4	4.3	4.5	8.9	5.5	4.7
Construction	-0.7	-3.1	-2.7	44.5	1.5	1.8	4.9	2.6	1.9
Trade	-1.1	-4.8	-3.3	47.6	1.2	1.4	4.9	2.3	1.6
Transport	-4.1	-6.1	-5.2	37	-2.6	-2.4	0.3	-1.7	-2.3
Communication	-1.5	-4.4	-3.7	20.3	1.0	1.3	4.7	2.2	1.5
Fin. Svcs	1.6	1.8	3.6	22.6	1.0	1.1	4.9	2.1	1.5
Insurance	-1.4	-4.5	-3.4	18.2	1.3	1.4	4.9	2.3	1.7
Business Svcs	-0.2	-3.4	-2.6	7.1	2.3	2.6	6.4	3.5	2.9
Recreation, Nec	-1.0	-4.2	-3.3	14	1.4	1.6	5.3	2.6	1.8
Non-market Svcs	0.0	-3.2	-2.4	-7.6	2.8	3.0	6.8	4.0	3.2

LR – long run

Source: own simulation.

Table 20. Bilateral Trade Balance Changes in Poland, Actionable Scenario

sector	NMS	Germany	EU-15	USA	Rest Europe	Turkey	America	Asia	RoW
Agriculture	-0.2	0.1	0.8	-39.1	-1.0	-1.7	-2.7	-2.0	-2.1
Mining	-0.8	-1.0	2.9	-193.8	0.3	-0.2	0.4	-0.4	-0.1
Food	-0.3	2.3	1.9	-1.2	-0.8	-0.9	-3.7	-2.1	-1.8
Textiles	1.0	1.8	1.9	40.6	-1.5	-4.3	-5.2	-6.0	-4.8
Apparel	0.8	1.3	1.7	295.0	-1.6	-3.4	-6.8	-5.1	-4.0
Leather	1.5	3.3	3.4	-2.7	-1.5	-3.6	-10.4	-5.6	-4.4
Wood	0.5	1.4	1.0	58.1	-0.1	-2.2	-3.4	-5.2	-3.0
Paper	1.1	3.3	2.5	-56.8	0.4	-0.1	-2.3	-3.5	-1.3
Coal Petrol	-0.1	0.4	0.3	3.7	-0.3	-0.2	-1.3	-0.4	-0.5
Chemicals	0.5	1.5	1.0	-28.9	-0.6	-0.9	-3.1	-3.7	-2.6
Minerals	0.0	1.4	1.5	51.4	-1.1	-2.5	-4.8	-3.9	-2.6
Steel	0.1	2.3	1.3	19.6	-2.5	-1.7	-3.4	-4.2	-2.7
Metals	-0.8	-1.2	-5.1	50.6	-2.2	-2.9	-6.8	-4.3	-2.9
Metal Products	0.8	2.4	1.3	54.8	-0.4	-2.6	-4.8	-5.7	-3.1
Motor Vehicles	-0.3	-0.5	0.6	-77.9	-1.2	-0.7	-3.1	-2.5	-1.8
Transport Eq. Nec	16.4	-2.4	-3.5	-22.9	6.9	4.4	8.1	18.2	12.6
Electrical Eq.	1.8	2.8	-1.6	-45.4	-0.1	-1.6	-5,.1	-2.1	-1.6
Machinery	1.1	2.8	1.2	3.1	-0.3	-1.2	-2.0	-3.9	-1.2
MnfcsNec	0.7	3.3	0.9	21.3	-0.8	-3.4	-5.9	-5.2	-3.0
Utilities, Energy	0.5	3.0	2.2	4.9	-3.5	-4.5	-5.2	-4.1	-2.9
Construction	-0.6	1.5	0.8	32.4	-1.7	-2.2	-3.5	-2.3	-1.7
Trade	0.7	2.7	2.5	-10.1	-1.0	-1.3	-3.8	-2.2	-1.3
Transport	1.1	1.0	2.0	-3.8	1.0	2.0	-0.8	1.0	0.9
Communication	0.9	2.3	2.4	-12.6	-0.7	-1.2	-3.6	-1.7	-1.2
Fin. Svcs	0.3	1.1	2.2	-11.8	-0.5	-1.0	-3.5	-1.5	-0.7
Insurance	0.2	3.1	2.6	-8.8	-0.7	-1.4	-4.2	-1.9	-1.1
Business Svcs	0.5	2.5	2.1	1.1	-0.8	-1.9	-3.9	-1.8	-1.1
Recreation, Nec	0.6	2.5	2.3	-2.6	-0.6	-1.5	-3.1	-1.9	-1.0
Non-market Svcs	0.6	2.9	2.6	6.6	-1.9	-1.3	-5.3	-3.3	-1.9

Trade balance changes expressed as 100*(dX- dM)/(X+M). LR – long run
Source: own simulation.

Michał Przybyliński (University of Lodz)

Chapter 9. How Can the TTIP Affect the Polish Economy. A Study Based on Input-Output Tables

The final shape of the TTIP agreement is not yet established and, what is more, the negotiators are not eager to disclose their positions and details of the ongoing discussion[1]. The results of the previous rounds are published with a substantial delay and thus, studies assessing the effects of the implementation of the TTIP result in a range of projections. The assumptions adopted in the models come from the more or less subjective expectations of the authors as to the results of the negotiations (i.e., Transatlantic… 2013). Under these circumstances, it is quite reasonable to present the results as variants (e.g., Hagemejer 2015), giving a picture of the likely range of the effects of the agreement. Another approach that allows for an estimation of the effects when the changes are not specified in detail is to use analogies to previously concluded agreements (mainly NAFTA) with the assumption that the scope of the negotiated agreement will be similar. This approach has been applied by Felbermayr (2013a and 2013b).

One of the primary objectives of the TTIP is to reduce the cost of trade between the EU and the US. This objective can be achieved by lowering tariffs as well as through a series of regulatory actions that result in the reduction or complete removal of existing non-tariff barriers.

The duty on some products, usually agricultural, may constitute a significant barrier to trade. A list of related product groups was compiled by Czarny and Śledziewska (2015), and in this book see Chapter 6. However, at the macroeconomic level, tariffs have a rather minor influence on trade. The average, effective overhead on US imports was 1.32 percent (in 2014) and 1.38 percent on EU imports (in 2013), while in recent years there has been a downward trend. What really matters are non-tariff barriers (NTBs).

There is a vast variety of NTBs, so it is extremely difficult to determine equivalents among such barriers. There are obviously protectionist tools of government policies, such as import quotas, as well as regulations that do not

1 The project is funded by the National Science Centre of Poland based on decision No. DEC-2013/09/B/HS4/01488.

intentionally protect the domestic market but result in discrimination of foreign companies nonetheless. A foreign producer's adaptation to the administrative requirements of the importer country generates costs. Such regulations cover a variety of aspects of the economy, such as the health and safety of consumers, impact on the environment, standards used in the production process and in transport, rules for handling claims, and others. So, standardizing regulations in areas that apparently have nothing to do with trade can lead to a significant reduction in trading costs. A fairly common and convenient solution to the problem with the calculation of equivalents of non-tariff barriers is the *posteriori* estimation using an econometric model, usually a gravity model (see Hagemejer, Śledziewska 2015).

This study is a continuation of the works published by Hagemejer (2015), who estimated the possible effects of the TTIP for the Polish economy using the Global Trade Analysis Project (GTAP) model, based on the CGE framework. With the help of this model, he performed simulations showing the results of a reduction of non-tariff barriers. Before that, the existing NTB equivalents were estimated by Hagemejer and Śledziewska (2015). Assuming various degrees of reduction of these barriers, Hagemejer estimated the changes in Polish imports, exports, and output for 29 sectors, according to the classifications applied in GTAP, and their macroeconomic sums (including GDP). His simulations were performed under the assumption that there were four scenarios. Three of them followed short-term mechanisms and assumed the partial (25%), actionable (meaning most probable at 50%) and complete (100%) removal of NTBs. The fourth scenario was based on an actionable variant but had a long-term character, allowing for capital accumulation.

Here, the results obtained by Hagemejer (as percentage changes in imports and exports) were transferred to an input-output table for Poland. The table used in this study shows the Polish economy in 2010 (GTAP reference year is 2007), using much more detailed information (77 product groups).

Turnover with the US is a small share of Polish exports and imports[2] and this fact can lead to extreme speculation about future developments. On the one hand, it may seem that the impact of the TTIP will be weak, as the US is not a significant trading partner for Poland, but on the other, the removal of barriers can unleash a huge amount of trade potential[3]. Most likely, a large percentage increase in the

---

2 According to Eurostat data these shares in 2014 were about 1.6% and 2.2% respectively.

3 This is similar to the well-known anecdote about shoe companies, which long time ago sent their sales representatives to Africa in order to explore the possibility of entering that market. All the representatives reported: People here do not wear shoes, no chance

turnover between Poland and the US as a result of the TTIP probably would result in quite modest effects for the Polish economy as a whole.

1. Input-output tables

The popularity and availability of input-output tables has increased year to year. One of the reasons for this is the global process of unification of the methods for collecting and processing statistical data. National statistical offices produce various sets of data, starting from flash estimates, published within several days after the end of a reporting period, and ending with statistical yearbooks and revised National Accounts data. The last and ultimate picture of an economy is provided by a set of input-output tables, created by balancing all the available source materials. This, of course, requires time to compile, which results in long delays in publication, reaching up to four years.

The source of the most detailed and uniform input-output tables is Eurostat. Tables published by Eurostat are the most precise (over 60 sectors) and reliable, as they are prepared by national statistical offices, juxtaposed with primary data (Compilation… 2015). Other sources of data give less detailed aggregation and are prepared based on secondary data, generally taken from Eurostat. One such source is the World Input Output Database (WIOD, see Timmer 2012; Timmer et al. 2015) which provides a time series of tables for the years 1995–2011. They may seem very attractive but were created through simple interpolation procedures (as well as extrapolations). On the other hand, the WIOD balances trade flows on a global scale, which is a great advantage. The same remarks apply to the STAN database, a joint enterprise of the OECD and WTO.

The set of input-output tables used in this study comes from the Polish Statistical Office. It shows the transactions in the economy split into 77 product groups according to the Polish version of the Classification of Products by Activity (CPA)[4]. It consists of an input-output table at basic prices for domestic output and a use table of imported goods and services (Input-output table… 2014). Additionally, for the purpose of recalculating the data on employment, the supply table was applied (Supply and use… 2014).

for selling our products. But one of them drew the opposite conclusion: Everyone walks barefoot, it means lack of competition and huge sales opportunities!

4 It is called the Polish Classification of Goods and Services (Polska Klasyfikacja Wyrobów i Usług, PKWiU)

2. Method and results

The first step was to recalculate the changes in exports and in imports of the 29 product groups simulated by Hagemejer (2015) as 77 product groups. In the Polish I-O table, there was no information to distinguish steel from metal products, which is why the figures for output and number of employees for steel and metal together, were split in two equal parts.

The second step was to calculate the changes in output that balance the changes in imports and exports, assuming that the overall technology of production had not changed. Technology in an input-output model is represented by a set (matrix) of input-output coefficients (for details, see Miller, Blair 2009):

$$a_{ij} = \frac{z_{ij}}{x_j},$$

where z_{ij} is the value of products classified to the *i*th group, used for the production of products classified to the *j*th group (the flow from branch *i* to branch *j*) and x_j is the output of products classified to *j*th group. The columns of matrix **A** show the cost structures of particular branches, except for value added. It is important to distinguish between flows of domestic and imported intermediate products, so the above equation should be rewritten with the superscripts D and M, respectively:

$$a_{ij}^D = \frac{z_{ij}^D}{x_j},\ a_{ij}^M = \frac{z_{ij}^M}{x_j},$$

$$a_{ij} = a_{ij}^D + a_{ij}^M.$$

The second step technically was done by introducing the changes in imports simulated by Hagemejer (2015) to the $\boldsymbol{A}^M$ matrix. All elements in a row were modified according to the same scale. Then, a new $\boldsymbol{A}^D$ matrix was calculated, keeping the **A** matrix constant. Thus, the overall cost structure remained unchanged, allowing for substitution between domestic and imported intermediates. The same procedure was applied to final demand, i.e., domestic final outputs were adjusted to keep the final demand constant, while imports of final products were modified. Then changes in exports were introduced. The new output was the result of applying the modified $\boldsymbol{A}^D$ matrix and modified domestic final output ($\boldsymbol{y}^D$) to the classic Leontief model:

$$\boldsymbol{x} = (\boldsymbol{I} - \boldsymbol{A}^D)^{-1}\boldsymbol{y}^D$$

The model ensures consistency of the results, which means that input-output tables might be recreated with new values and the sums of the rows would remain equal to the sums of the columns. The results are shown in Table 1.

Table 1. Changes in output, balancing Hagemejer's (2015) changes in imports and exports within the framework of the 2010 input-output table for Poland

		Changes in output (%)				Deviations from the results of the GTAP model, in p.p.			
	Sector	**Partial**	**Action**	**Complete**	**LR**	**Partial**	**Action**	**Complete**	**LR**
1	Agriculture	0.0	0.0	0.1	-0.1	0.0	0.0	0.0	0.0
2	Mining	-0.2	-0.6	-1.4	0.0	-0.1	-0.3	-0.5	-0.1
3	Food	0.1	0.3	0.8	0.2	0.0	0.1	0.2	0.0
4	Textiles	1.6	2.4	4.5	2.5	0.5	0.7	1.2	0.8
5	Apparel	2.4	3.7	7.2	3.6	1.5	2.3	4.4	2.2
6	Leather	0.9	1.4	2.0	1.0	0.5	0.9	1.4	0.6
7	Wood	0.6	1.0	2.0	0.9	-0.1	-0.3	-0.9	-0.4
8	Paper	0.5	0.9	1.8	0.6	0.2	0.4	0.9	0.2
9	Coal Petrol	0.1	0.1	0.2	0.1	0.0	-0.1	-0.3	-0.1
10	Chemicals	0.0	0.0	0.3	-0.3	0.1	0.1	0.2	-0.2
11	Minerals	0.3	0.5	1.0	0.5	0.1	0.2	0.5	-0.1
12	Steel	-0.4	-1.0	-3.0	-0.1	-0.7	-1.5	-3.8	-1.0
13	Metals	-0.4	-1.0	-3.0	-0.1	0.9	1.9	4.8	1.1
14	Metal Products	0.5	0.9	1.9	0.7	0.2	0.3	0.6	0.0
15	Motor Vehicles	-0.8	-0.9	-1.7	-1.0	0.1	0.4	0.8	0.2
16	Transport Eq. n.e.c	-4.1	-6.6	-9.8	-4.4	-1.8	-2.4	-2.0	0.1
17	Electrical Eq.	-1.2	-2.7	-6.2	-3.3	0.1	0.3	0.6	-0.5
18	Machinery	1.3	2.1	4.1	1.6	1.0	1.7	3.5	1.1
19	Mnfcs n.e.c.	0.4	0.5	0.8	0.6	0.2	0.3	0.5	0.2
20	Utilities Energy	0.1	0.1	0.3	0.1	0.1	0.0	0.1	-0.1
21	Construction	0.0	0.0	0.1	-0.1	0.2	0.4	0.9	-0.3
22	Trade	0.2	0.4	0.8	0.2	0.2	0.3	0.5	0.0
23	Transport	0.1	0.2	0.4	0.1	0.0	0.0	-0.1	0.0
24	Communications	0.1	0.1	0.3	0.1	0.1	0.1	0.2	-0.1

		Changes in output (%)				Deviations from the results of the GTAP model, in p.p.			
	Sector	Partial	Action	Complete	LR	Partial	Action	Complete	LR
25	Fin. Svcs	0.0	0.0	0.1	0.0	0.0	0.0	0.1	-0.1
26	Insurance	0.0	0.0	0.1	0.0	0.0	0.0	0.0	-0.2
27	Business Svcs	0.2	0.3	0.6	0.2	0.2	0.2	0.4	0.0
28	Recreation n.e.c.	0.0	0.0	0.1	0.0	0.0	-0.1	-0.1	-0.2
29	Non-market Svcs	0.0	0.0	0.0	0.0	0.0	0.0	-0.1	-0.1
	Total	0.1	0.1	0.2	0.0	x	x	x	x
	GDP	0.1	0.1	0.2	0.0	0.0	-0.1	-0.2	-0.3

Source: own calculations based on Hagemejer (2015) and Input-output table…(2014)

The macroeconomic results are slightly positive, but their scale is so small that they should be considered neutral. Changes at the sector level are differentiated. The most obvious winners are producers of apparel, textiles and machinery. On the other side, we can see transport equipment and electrical equipment. This recalculation has magnified the original results but regardless of this, the maximum growth in output slightly exceeds seven percent and the most spectacular decrease does not reach ten percent. For sixteen sectors, or more than half, the impact of the complete removal of NTBs is insignificant (one percent or less).

The third step was to calculate changes in employment under the assumption of constant labour productivity. The data on jobs were taken from Employment… (2011) and recalculated into product classification using a supply table (Supply… 2014). Table 2 shows the results.

Table 2. Changes in employment

	Sector	Partial	Actionable	Complete	Action-LR
1	Agriculture	-277	137	1690	-2022
2	Mining	-250	-559	-1438	-153
3	Food	680	1543	3966	1187
4	Textiles	783	1188	2258	1244
5	Apparel	2399	3790	7317	3636
6	Leather	258	382	566	279
7	Wood	718	1255	2587	1107

	Sector	Partial	Actionable	Complete	Action-LR
8	Paper	526	904	1826	602
9	Coal Petrol	14	14	38	33
10	Chemicals	50	82	685	-1066
11	Minerals	463	716	1364	648
12	Steel	-329	-836	-2560	-64
13	Metals	-329	-836	-2560	-64
14	Metal Products	1379	2575	5353	1976
15	Motor Vehicles	-1577	-1860	-3391	-2066
16	Transport Eq. n.e.c.	-1952	-3132	-4602	-2092
17	Electrical Eq.	-1991	-4643	-10565	-5547
18	Machinery	1346	2273	4389	1684
19	Mnfcs n.e.c.	1570	2012	3132	2192
20	Utilities Energy	275	443	962	367
21	Construction	219	236	469	188
22	Trade	3742	6869	14654	4455
23	Transport	769	1139	2492	710
24	Communications	361	542	1182	543
25	Fin. Svcs	105	127	282	18
26	Insurance	9	11	23	7
27	Business Svcs	3166	5072	10938	3197
28	Recreation n.e.c.	94	144	299	81
29	Non-market Svcs	343	529	1097	322
	Total	12564	20117	42453	10726
	Loss	-6705	-11866	-25116	-13562

Source: own calculations based on Hagemejer (2015), Input-output table…(2014), Employment…(2011) and Supply and use tables… (2014)

Depending on the scale of the reduction of NTBs, the net increase in the number of jobs varies from 12500 up to 42500. Up to 25100 people will have to change their sector of employment.

The results are, of course, in line with Table 1, but in Table 2, the size of the sector matters. Almost 15,000 jobs might be created in the trade sector and over 10,000 in business services. The percentage leader, i.e., apparel sector, can count on up to 7300 new jobs. The electrical equipment sector would suffer the most.

Conclusions

The results were obtained using a simulation procedure that combines calculations based on the huge, international CGE system with simple but more detailed calculations using the national input-output table.

The effects of removing NTBs under the TTIP are hardly noticeable at the macroeconomic level. The increase in output (and assuming a constant in production technology and in GDP) in the most far-reaching variant is 0.2 percent. Also, job growth of 42,000 (in the long-term option, only 10,000), does not seem large (compared to the 14.1 million people working in Poland in 2014). A macroeconomic assessment of the removal of NTBs is, therefore, rather neutral. However, there may be some effects visible at the sector level, which can lead to changes in the structure of production. The strength of these changes will be determined by the results of the negotiations adopted at the level of industries and for particular products. The results presented show changes in 29 branches, so the study shows some more details of the economy than a typical macroeconomic model, but they are, of course, sector averages. Particular firms or sub-sectors might be affected on a much greater scale. For example, according to the results, agriculture as a whole should not be affected by the examined aspect of the TTIP, but it does not mean that major (sometimes even dramatic) changes in the case of particular products are unlikely. The devil (or in another version, God) is in the details.

References

Compilation of national accounts supply, use and input-output tables, 2015, European Commission Eurostat, Unit C.2: National and regional accounts production – Balance of payments. http://ec.europa.eu/eurostat/documents/51957/51999/Summary-questionnaire.pdf.

Czarny E., K. Śledziewska, 2015, Shall Polish export be affected by trade diversion resulting from Transatlantic Trade and Investment Partnership? Paper presented at "The impact of the Transatlantic Trade and Investment Partnership (TTIP) on international cooperation – conclusions for EU members from Central and Eastern Europe". Warsaw, 30 November – 1 December 2015, http://kolegia.sgh.waw.pl/pl/KGS/struktura/IMSG/konferencje/Documents/Czarny%20and%20Sledziewska.pdf.

Employment in national economy in 2010, 2011, Statistical information and elaborations, Central Statistical Office, Warsaw.

Eurostat Manual of Supply, Use and Input-Output Tables, 2008, Eurostat Methodologies and Working papers, http://ec.europa.eu/eurostat/documents/3859598/5902113/KS-RA-07–013-EN.PDF/b0b3d71e-3930–4442-94be-70b36cea-9b39?version=1.0.

Felbermayr G., B. Heid, S. Lehwald, 2013a, Transatlantic Trade and Investment Partnership (TTIP). Who benefits from a free trade deal? Part 1, Bertelsmann Stiftung, Gütersloh.

Felbermayr G., B. Heid, S.Lehwald, 2013b, Transatlantic Trade and Investment Partnership (TTIP). Who benefits from a free trade deal? Part 2, Bertelsmann Stiftung, Gütersloh.

Hagemejer J., 2015, Liberalization of trade flows under TTIP from a small country perspective. The case of Poland, Faculty of Economic Sciences, University of Warsaw, Working Papers 17 (2015)/165.

Hagemejer J., K. Śledziewska, 2015, Trade barriers in services and merchandise trade in the context of TTIP: Poland, EU and the United States, mimeo, University of Warsaw.

Input – output table at basic prices in 2010, 2014, Statistical information and elaborations, Central Statistical Office, Warsaw .

Miller R. E., P. D. Blair, 2009, Input-Output Analysis. Foundations and Extensions, Cambridge University Press.

Supply and use tables in 2010, 2014, Statistical information and elaborations, Central Statistical Office, Warsaw.

Timmer M. P. (ed.), 2012, The World Input-Output Database (WIOD): Contents, Sources and Methods, WIOD Working Paper No. 10, http://www.wiod.org/publications/papers/wiod10.pdf.

Timmer, M. P., E. Dietzenbacher, B. Los, R. Stehrer, G. J. de Vries, 2015, An Illustrated User Guide to the World Input–Output Database: the Case of Global Automotive Production, Review of International Economics, 23: 575–605. doi: 10.1111/roie.12178.

Transatlantic Trade and Investment Partnership. The Economic Analysis Explained, 2013, European Commission, http://trade.ec.europa.eu/doclib/docs/2013/september/tradoc_151787.pdf.

Bożena Pera (Cracow University of Economics)

Chapter 10. The Potential Effects of the TTIP on Polish and other CEEC Exports to the United States

Negotiations on the Transatlantic Trade and Investment Partnership may lead to the creation of the largest free trade area in the world. Free access to commodity markets may contribute to an increase in mutual trade of negotiating partners.

The purpose of this chapter is to discuss the changes that may occur in the structure of Polish exports to the US and to compare these exports with the exports from selected Central and Eastern European countries. The main analysis covers the years 2010–2014. In the initial section of this chapter, taking into consideration the changes occurring in the trade exchange of Poland and other Central and Eastern European countries following their accession to the European Union, the period of under study was extended to the years 2004–2014.

1. Consequences of the free trade area

As defined by Balassa (1973), free trade areas (FTAs) are institutionalized forms of international economic integration. In the classical approach, their formation involves liberalization of tariff barriers to bilateral trade and applies to commerce in ready-made industrial products, raw materials, food, and – to a lesser extent – parts, subassemblies, and components. It implies a growth in horizontal connections and generates advantages based on comparative cost differences. Today, the scope of such agreements increasingly goes beyond commodity trade and also covers other areas of economic integration, facilitating the free flow of capital and services, access to public procurement opportunities, and intellectual property rights protection, as well as regulatory issues related to sanitary and phytosanitary requirements and other trade barriers. When it covers the factors of production as well, vertical connections are created within international corporations, where an important role is played by cost differences between individual branches of transnational enterprises (Bożyk 2005).

FTAs are usually studied in terms of their impact on third parties (Kozielski 2014). The European Union has 28 members and, accordingly, any agreement it contracts with its strategic partner, the United States, will not only have repercussions for third parties, but will also affect the mutual relations between the member states. Any change in the conditions that govern access to the market can have a varying impact on their export and import volumes, trade structure, and respective shares in mutual trade (Sapir 1992). Alongside classical trade creation and trade diversion effects, outcomes may include trade expansion, cost decrease, flawed specialization, trade distortion, and allocation effect. While their impact is often less pronounced in FTAs than in customs unions, it can show greater short-term efficiency (Wysokińska, Witkowska 1999). The liberalization of trade within a free trade zone boosts connections between the entities involved, which often increases competition in the market, accelerates technological progress, modernizes production, and induces a rise in quality (Misala 2009). When economies open for international trade, creating e.g. FTAs, consequences can be observed already during the process of liberalization (Machlup 1986). Benefits may stem from differences in manufacturing technology, different factors of production, or a specialization in goods that bring a comparative advantage; they can also be connected to the changes in relative prices that occur as a result of opening (Czarny 2013).

Removal of trade barriers should intensify mutual trade and help to exploit increasing returns to scale in production. In addition, FTAs not only cement relations between the countries involved in cooperation but also generate benefits connected to liberalized trade flows (Mucha-Leszko 2012).

It is often argued in the literature of the subject that because FTAs eliminate trade barriers between members and do not increase them with respect to third parties, their effects are not limited to FTAs: they also increase the welfare of both member states and third parties (Żołądkiewicz 2007).

The following section offers an analysis of the structural relationships and similarities between Central and Eastern European countries (with Poland among them) in terms of their exports to the US market.

2. Central and Eastern European countries exports to the United States in 2004–2014

Potential outcomes of the TTIP will be linked to the participation of Central and Eastern European countries in trade with the United States.

Table 1. Share of CEE countries in the US exports in 2004–2014 (in %)

Country	2004	2007	2010	2014
	CEECs share in the US exports			
Bulgaria	0.02	0.03	0.01	0.02
Croatia	0.02	0.02	0.02	0.02
Czech Republic	0.10	0.11	0.11	0.14
Estonia	0.02	0.02	0.01	0.02
Hungary	0.14	0.11	0.10	0.11
Latvia	0.01	0.03	0.03	0.03
Lithuania	0.04	0.06	0.05	0.04
Poland	0.11	0.27	0.23	0.23
Romania	0.06	0.06	0.06	0.06
Slovakia	0.02	0.06	0.02	0.03
Slovenia	0.02	0.03	0.03	0.02

Source: WITS and own calculations, accessed: 10 November 2015.

Countries entering the EU in 2004 do not play a major role in exports with the United States. Among the studied group, the greatest shares were reported for Poland, Hungary, the Czech Republic, and, a little lower, for Romania. Relations with the US market significantly increased, especially for Polish exports, in 2014 as compared to 2004 (Table 1).

Table 2. Commodity structure of Polish exports to the US in 2004–2014 (in %)

Products grouped by stages of processing	2004	2007	2010	2014
Capital goods	28.03	35.89	43.38	45.44
Consumer goods	39.39	45.08	33.40	37.58
Intermediate goods	29.93	17.10	19.77	13.71
Raw materials	1.65	1.24	3.09	2.83

Source: WITS, accessed 10 November 2015.

Commodities classified as capital and consumer goods were the two most important categories in the exports between Poland and the United States. In 2004–2014, the importance of Polish capital products on the US market grew. The process was especially noticeable for commodities used in the production of other goods, which may be taken as evidence of Polish manufacturing relations with entities in the United States. The studied period witnessed a slight decrease in the share shown in consumer goods exported to the US (by ca. 2 pp. relative to 2004 and 7 pp. relative to 2007). Even greater changes were observed for the group of intermediate goods, which share decreased by ca. 16 pp. between 2004 and 2014. Raw materials never played an important role in exports between Poland and the US (Table 2). The changes observed in the structure of Polish exports to the US market indicate that it is beginning to resemble that of highly developed countries.

The next section focuses on a comparative analysis of the structure of trade between Poland and the US against the background of Central and Eastern European countries, using one of the methods of hierarchical cluster analysis, i.e. the Ward's method[1]. 16 commodity bundles were distinguished in the structure of imports and exports based on official HS classifications[2].

Table 3. Structure of exports of CEE countries to the United States in 2010 and 2014.

2010	2014
Cluster 1: {Bulgaria, Poland}	Cluster 1: {Bulgaria}
Cluster 2: {Croatia}	Cluster 2: {Croatia}
Cluster 3: {Czech Rep., Romania, Slovenia}	Cluster 3: {Czech Rep., Romania, Slovenia}
Cluster 4: {Estonia, Lithuania}	Cluster 4: {Estonia, Lithuania}
Cluster 5: {Latvia}	Cluster 5: {Latvia}
Cluster 6: {Slovakia}	Cluster 6: {Poland, Hungary}
Cluster 7: {Hungary}	Cluster 7: {Slovakia}

Source: WITS and own calculations, accessed 10 November 2015.

1 J. H. Ward Jr. suggested a general agglomerative hierarchical clustering procedure, where the criterion for choosing the pairs of clusters to merge at each step is based on the optimal value of an objective algorithm which reflects the researcher's purpose. At the initial step, the structure of exports of each CEE country to the US is a single cluster. At each subsequent step, this method finds the pair of clusters that leads to a minimum increase in the total within-cluster variance after merging. Detailed information on this method can be found in Shalizi (2009), Murtagh, Legendre (2011).

2 These groups are based on sector classification for the Harmonized System product nomenclature: Animal (sections 01–05); Vegetable (sections 06–15); Food Products (sections 16–24); Minerals (sections 25–26); Fuels (section 27); Chemicals

There are few similarities between the commodity structures of exports of CEE countries to the United States. Poland was not a one-element cluster either in 2010 or in 2014. In 2010, the structure of Polish exports to the United States resembled that of Bulgaria. It stood apart from other countries studied due to its relatively high share of agricultural products. Alongside Poland and Bulgaria, two-element clusters were observed in the case of Estonia and Lithuania. Nearly ¾ of total exports to the US dealt with commodities bracketed under fuels. Over the studied period, no important changes occurred in the structure of Czech exports, which resembled those of Slovenia and Romania, and were distinguished from other countries by the relatively large share of chemical products, which in Romania accounted for ca. 10% of total exports (18% in the case of Slovenia), and various industrial products. At least every third commodity sold to the USA was bracketed under electrical machines and devices. Transportation equipment originating in the three countries, on the other hand, was rarely exported to the Unites States (4–8% share).

In 2014, the structure of Polish exports to the US began to resemble Hungarian sales in terms of the importance of individual commodity bundles. Agricultural products declined in importance, even though Poland continued to deliver more (8% of exports to the US) than any other country in the group, except Bulgaria (20% share). The most important commodity bundle for Poland and Hungary were electrical machines and devices, followed by transportation equipment. Both for Hungary and in Poland, chemical products and synthetic materials had a relatively low share, accounting for ca. 6–8% of total exports to the US (tab. 3).

An analysis was also performed of the similarity between the export structure of individual Eastern and Central European countries and the import structure of the US. The figure for each commodity bundle was calculated using the Canberra metric[3].

(sections 28–38); Plastic or Rubber (sections 39–40); Hides and Skins (sections 41–43); Wood (sections 44–49); Textiles and Clothing (sections 50–63); Footwear (sections 64–67); Stone and Glass (sections 68–71); Metals (sections 72–83); Machineries and Electric (sections 84–85); Transportation (sections 86–89); Miscellaneous (sections 90–99).

3 The analysis used one of the indicators of structural similarity, i.e. *the Canberra metric*, calculated from the formula: $d_{il} = \frac{1}{m}\sum_{j=1}^{m}\frac{|q_{ij} - q_{lj}|}{|q_{ij} + q_{lj}|}$ where: d_{ij} – similarity indicator for the export structure of commodity bundle *j* from country *i*; *q* – structural indicator, *i*, *l* – countries, m – number of commodity bundles. The metric takes values from 0 to 1. The closer it is to 0, the more similarities exist between the two compared structures (Zeliaś (ed.) 1988)

Table 4. Comparison of the export structure of CEE countries[4] and US import structure in 2010 and 2014

Product group	BG	HR	CZ	EE	LT	LV	PL	RO	SK	SI	HU
2010											
Goods grouped in stages of processing											
Capital goods	0.128	0.337	0.251	0.488	0.730	0.055	0.190	0.179	0.031	0.027	0.396
Consumer goods	0.163	0.318	0.096	0.421	0.422	0.256	0.008	0.280	0.323	0.110	0.221
Intermediate goods	0.017	0.130	0.171	0.525	0.134	0.073	0.142	0.422	0.445	0.250	0.289
Raw materials	0.052	0.960	0.896	0.811	0.955	0.661	0.689	0.940	0.976	0.878	0.907
Products grouped in major HS sectors											
Agricultural and processed food products	0.523	0.637	0.739	0.680	0.381	0.872	0.312	0.558	0.952	0.549	0.544
Mineral products	0.463	0.918	0.936	0.801	0.800	0.851	0.670	0.775	0.674	0.967	0.863
Industrial products	0.441	0.654	0.327	0.651	0.688	0.372	0.342	0.504	0.401	0.387	0.364
All products	0.459	0.684	0.480	0.675	0.644	0.526	0.377	0.548	0.538	0.490	0.460
2014											
Goods grouped in stages of processing											
Capital goods	0.021	0.163	0.266	0.242	0.745	0.033	0.171	0.134	0.182	0.037	0.276
Consumer goods	0.044	0.275	0.138	0.356	0.446	0.142	0.051	0.230	0.362	0.114	0.052
Intermediate goods	0.281	0.028	0.075	0.403	0.278	0.027	0.057	0.324	0.501	0.156	0.519
Raw materials	0.145	0.926	0.898	0.705	0.989	0.537	0.665	0.889	0.979	0.945	0.903

4 Codes used for the countries: Bulgaria – BG; Croatia – HR; Czech Republic – CZ; Estonia – EE; Hungary – HU; Latvia – LV; Lithuania – LT; Poland – PL; Romania – RO; Slovakia – SK; Slovenia – SI.

Product group	BG	HR	CZ	EE	LT	LV	PL	RO	SK	SI	HU
Products grouped in major HS sectors											
Agricultural and processed food products	0.524	0.686	0.752	0.798	0.261	0.764	0.318	0.475	0.929	0.750	0.653
Mineral products	0.915	0.825	0.991	0.811	0.831	0.799	0.515	0.999	0.737	1.000	0.964
Industrial products	0.434	0.641	0.362	0.571	0.651	0.441	0.298	0.315	0.434	0.362	0.442
All products	0.511	0.672	0.513	0.644	0.600	0.546	0.329	0.431	0.565	0.515	0.547

Source: WITS and own calculations, accessed 10 November 2015.

The high level of data aggregation for the structure of CEE exports and US imports shed light only on the similarities between commodities classified in terms of stages of processing and major HS bundles[5]. In 2010, the greatest similarities existed between the structures of commodities classified as capital and intermediate goods. For both these categories, a similarity was reported for both CEE exports and US imports for: Bulgaria, the Czech Republic, Latvia, Poland, and Slovenia. Romania and Slovakia, present in the first group, were replaced by Croatia and Lithuania in the second. In the group of consumer goods, American imports were more closely resembled by the structure of exports from six countries (Bulgaria, the Czech Republic, Latvia, Poland, Slovenia, and Hungary). The greatest diversity was observed for raw materials, whose resources largely depend on natural conditions. The results for 2014 indicated an increase in the similarity between the structure of exports from the studied countries and US imports. Capital goods were the only commodity bundle that showed high variability. Except for raw materials, the structure of Polish exports in the remaining three commodity bundles was quite similar to US imports. The classification in terms of major HS bundles revealed high variability among the structures and commodity groups compared (Table 4).

With the ongoing negotiations in mind, the next section focuses on the access conditions of CEE commodities to the US market.

5 Agricultural and processed food products encompasses sections 01–24; Mineral products – section 25–27 and Industrial products cover sections 28–99.

3. The TTIP and the exports of Poland and other CEE countries to the United States

Once the TTIP enters into force, the greatest FTA in the world will be created, going well beyond commodity trade liberalization; there might also occur a change in the current balance of power (Czarny, Menkes Śledziewska 2014). In terms of market access, the 11th round of negotiations proposed the liberalization of 97 percent of all tariff lines (European Commission 2015). In comparison, duty-free trade applies to 98 percent of tariff lines under the NAFTA agreement. Customs duties are maintained for certain agricultural products (products of animal origin and processed foods) exported by Mexico and Canada to the US. A similar level of market access (liberalization of 98.7% of duties within 5 years) was negotiated under a free trade agreement between the European Union and South Korea.

Dietrich et al. (2014) evaluated the trade openness of EU and US markets by comparing average customs duties in individual sectors and for selected commodity bundles. With a view to showing potential effects of these regulations, a comparative analysis was performed of the tariff barriers that limit the access of commodity bundles from Poland and other CEE countries to the US market. To do so, the following figures were included: the number of commodities by tariff lines on the level of 6-digit HS codes, the proportions of US imports delivered from the studied group in 2010 and 2014 on which duties were and were not levied, and the average customs duties in 2014. Data from Poland was compared with figures from individual CEE countries to enable their relative ranking.

Table 5. Customs duties levied on US imports from Poland compared with other CEE countries in 2010–2014, according to their stages of processing (in %)

Product group	2010			2014				
	Total tariff lines	Dutiable tariff lines share (%)	Duty free tariff lines share (%)	Total tariff lines	Dutiable tariff lines share (%)	Duty free tariff lines share (%)	Average duty rate (%)	Weighted average duty rate (%)
Higher ranking countries								
All products	–	LV	CZ, SK, SI, HU	–	CZ, EE, SK, SI	CZ, EE,SK, SI, HU	CZ, SI*,	EE, LV,
Capital goods	CZ	BG, EE, LT, LV,	BG, EE, LT, LV	CZ	BG, HR, EE, LT, LV, RO, SK, SI, HU	BG, HR, EE, LT, LV, RO, SK, SI, HU	BG, HR, EE, LT, LV, RO, SK, SI, HU	BG, EE, LV,

Product group	2010			2014				
	Total tariff lines	Dutiable tariff lines share (%)	Duty free tariff lines share (%)	Total tariff lines	Dutiable tariff lines share (%)	Duty free tariff lines share (%)	Average duty rate (%)	Weighted average duty rate (%)
Consumer goods	–		CZ	–	–	CZ, SI, HU	CZ	LV, SK, SI, HU
Intermediate goods	CZ	EE, LT, LV, RO, SI	CZ, EE, LT, LV, RO, SI	–	EE, LT, LV, RO, SI	CZ, EE, LT, LV, RO, SK, SI	HR, EE, SI	BG, HR, CZ, RO, SK
Raw materials	–	BG, HR, CZ, EE, RO, SI, HU	BG, HR, CZ, EE, LT, LV, RO, SK, SI, HU	–	BG, CZ, EE, RO, SI, HU	BG, HR, CZ, EE, SK, SI, HU	HR, CZ, EE, LV, RO, SK, SI	EE, LV
Poland								
All products	4639		33.15	5773	51.24	42.80	3.27	1.15
Capital goods	1009		52.03	1425	37.61	62.18	1.07	0.59
Consumer goods	2322		23.69	2672	60.33	30.39	5.02	2.24
Intermediate goods	1120		35.54	1330	48.95	47.74	2.68	0.99
Raw materials	139		41.01	139	31.65	43.88	2.25	0.75
Lower-ranking countries								
All products	BG, HR, CZ, EE, LT, LV, RO, SK, SI, HU		BG, HR, EE, LT, LV, RO	BG, HR, CZ, EE, LT, LV, RO, SK, SI, HU	BG, HR, LT, LV, RO, HU	BG, HR, LT, LV, RO	BG, HR, EE, LT, LV, RO, SK, HU	BG, HR, CZ, LT, RO, SK, SI, HU
Capital goods	BG, HR, EE, LT, LV, RO, SK,SI, HU		HR, CZ, RO, SK, SI, HU	BG, HR, EE, LT, LV, RO, SK,SI, HU	CZ	CZ	CZ	HR, CZ, LT, RO, SK,SI, HU
Consumer goods	BG, HR, CZ, EE, LT, LV, RO, SK, SI, HU		BG, HR, EE, LT, LV, RO, SK, SI, HU	BG, HR, CZ, EE, LT, LV, RO, SK, SI, HU	BG, HR, CZ, EE, LT, LV, RO, SK, SI, HU	BG, HR, EE, LT, LV, RO, SK	BG, HR, EE, LT, LV, RO, SK, SI, HU	BG, HR, CZ, EE, LT, RO,

Product group	2010			2014				
	Total tariff lines	Dutiable tariff lines share (%)	Duty free tariff lines share (%)	Total tariff lines	Dutiable tariff lines share (%)	Duty free tariff lines share (%)	Average duty rate (%)	Weighted average duty rate (%)
Intermediate goods	BG, HR, EE, LT, LV, RO, SK, SI, HU		BG, HR, SK, HU	BG, HR, EE, LT, LV, RO, SK, SI, HU	BG, HR, CZ, SK, HU	BG, HR, HU	BG, CZ, LT, LV, RO, SK, HU	EE, LT, LV, SI, HU
Raw materials	BG, HR, CZ, EE, LT, LA, RO, SK, SI, HU		–	BG, HR, CZ, EE, LT, LV, RO, SK, SI, HU	HR, LT, LV, SK,	LT, LV, RO	BG, LT, HU	BG, HR, CZ, LT, RO, SK, SI, HU

[*] – Customs duty rate is at the same level as for Polish goods
Source: WITS, accessed 10 November 2015.

In Poland and in other CEE countries, an increase was observed in tariff lines exported to the United States over the studied period. Except for intermediate and capital goods (in 2010), Poland exported the largest volumes of goods classified at the level of 6-digit HS codes to the US out of all countries in the studied region. In 2014, customs duties were levied on as much as half of all exports from CEE countries to the US. The situation of Polish exports on the US market deteriorated. Goods charged with duties, except consumer goods, had a greater share in Polish exports than in at least half of the studied CEE countries. The structure of exports of the studied countries also saw an increase in the importance of goods for which duties had already been liberalized. For lower-ranking countries, the customs rate was higher than that for Polish goods. A different situation was noticed in case of higher-ranking countries for which the customs rate was lower than in case of goods from Poland. Moreover, that group of countries had a higher participation of goods not covered by customs in export to USA both in comparison to Poland and countries with positions inferior in relation to our country (Table 5).

Intermediate and consumer goods exported to the US were most frequently charged with customs duties. The average rate for Polish exports was relatively low compared with other CEE countries; the same was true for the Czech Republic, Estonia, Slovakia, Slovenia, and Hungary. In all studied countries, the highest duty-free trade indicator was reported for capital goods. Estonia, Slovakia, and the Czech Republic also had a high share of duty-free raw materials. However, it should be noted that these products were not the largest group of exports[6].

The following section focuses on ten commodity bundles with the highest share in exports to the US (based on HS classifications) originated from five CEE countries (the Czech Republic, Poland, Romania, Slovakia, and Hungary).

Table 6. Product groups with the largest share in the exports from selected CEE countries to the US[7], including customs duty rates in 2014.

Czech Republic			Poland			Romania			Slovakia			Hungary		
HS Section	share (%)	Duty rate (%)	HS Section	share (%)	Duty rate (%)	HS Sec-tion	share (%)	Duty rate (%)	HS Section	share (%)	Duty rate (%)	HS Section	share (%)	Duty rate (%)
84	27.17	0.6	**84**	24.30	0.6	**84**	26.83	0.6	**87**	54.84	1.8	**84**	27.25	0.6
85	17.60	0.7	**85**	11.11	0.7	**73**	17.52	1.1	**84**	11.47	0.6	**85**	26.99	0.7
73	10.43	1.1	**94**	8.99	1.1	**85**	8.38	0.7	**40**	9.84	1.8	**87**	24.67	1.8
87	5.92	1.8	**27**	8.32	0.3	**40**	7.55	1.8	**85**	7.71	0.7	**90**	5.92	1.5
40	4.62	1.8	**89**	6.69	0.2	**31**	5.62	0.0	**94**	3.63	1.1	**40**	2.37	1.8
90	3.89	1.5	**88**	5.59	0.0	**99**	5.57	–	**73**	1.86	1.1	**68**	1.53	1.5
30	3.11	0.1	**90**	4.64	1.5	**87**	4.41	1.8	**72**	1.47	0.2	**29**	1.27	2.8

6 http://wits.worldbank.org, [accessed 20 November 2015].

7 HS section notes in table 6: 27 – Mineral fuels, mineral oils and products of their distillation; bituminous substances; mineral waxes; 29 – Organic chemicals; 30 – Pharmaceutical products; 31 – Fertilisers; 39 – Plastics and articles thereof; 40 – Rubber and articles thereof; 62 – Articles of apparel and clothing accessories, not knitted or crocheted; 64 – Footwear, gaiters and the like; parts of such articles; 68 – Articles of stone, plaster, cement, asbestos, mica or similar materials; 69 – Ceramic products; 70 – Glass and glassware; 72 – Iron and steel; 73 – Articles of iron or steel; 84 – Nuclear reactors, boilers, machinery and mechanical appliances; parts thereof; 85 – Electrical machinery and equipment and parts thereof; sound recorders and reproducers, television image and sound recorders and reproducers, and parts and accessories of such articles; 87 – Vehicles other than railway or tramway rolling-stock, and parts and accessories thereof; 88 – Aircraft, spacecraft, and parts thereof; 89 – Ships, boats and floating structures; 90 – Optical, photographic, cinematographic, measuring, checking, precision, medical or surgical instruments and apparatus; parts and accessories thereof; 94 – Furniture; bedding, mattresses, mattress supports, cushions and similar stuffed furnishings; lamps and lighting fittings, not elsewhere specified or included; illuminated signs, illuminated nameplates and the like; prefabricated buildings; 95 – Toys, games and sports requisites; parts and accessories thereof; 99 – Works of Art, Collectors' pieces – reserved for special uses.

Czech Republic			Poland			Romania			Slovakia			Hungary		
HS Section	share (%)	Duty rate (%)	HS Section	share (%)	Duty rate (%)	HS Sec-tion	share (%)	Duty rate (%)	HS Section	share (%)	Duty rate (%)	HS Section	share (%)	Duty rate (%)
88	2.85	0.0	**39**	2.50	4.4	**90**	3.65	1.5	**90**	1.30	1.5	**69**	1.15	6.5
72	2.59	0.2	**73**	2.34	1.1	**94**	3.23	1.1	**64**	1.03	12.2	**94**	1.11	1.1
39	2.52	4.4	**87**	2.09	1.8	**62**	2.79	10.8	**70**	0.75	4.0	**95**	1.08	0.7
Together: 80.70%			**Together: 76.57%**			**Together: 85.53%**			**Together: 93.89%**			**Together: 93.33%**		

Source: ITC Trade Map and own calculations, accessed 15 November 2015.

Within the group of ten top commodity bundles, exports showed a high degree of concentration, especially in Slovakia (more than half were bracketed under the automotive industry) and Hungary (the three most important groups: nuclear reactors, boilers, mechanical machines and devices; electrical machines and devices; and automotive industry products together accounted for more than 75 percent of the total value of products delivered to the US). This suggests that the countries narrowly specialize in particular commodity bundles sold to the US market. Greater diversity can be observed in the exports from Poland, the Czech Republic, and Romania. CEE exports to the US characteristically include at least five common commodity bundles with relatively low average customs duties (in the Czech Republic, Poland, Romania, and Hungary, they exceed four percent for one relatively unimportant bundle, and in Slovakia – for two) (Table 6). Table 7 shows commodity bundles with the greatest customs duties.

Table 7. The share of the 10 commodity bundles with the highest customs duty rates in the exports from selected CEE countries to the US in 2014

HS Section	Customs duty rate (%)	Product share in export to USA (%)				
		Czech Rep.	Poland	Romania	Slovakia	Hungary
24 Tobacco and manufactured tobacco substitutes	29.9	00.00	0.00	0.03	0.00	0.01
17 Sugars and sugar confectionery	18.8	0.10	0.27	0.00	0.01	0.04
04 Dairy produce; birds eggs; natural honey; edible products of animal origin, not elsewhere specified or included	16.9	0.01	0.20	0.24	0.00	0.02

HS Section	Customs duty rate (%)	Product share in export to USA (%)				
		Czech Rep.	Poland	Romania	Slovakia	Hungary
61 Articles of apparel and clothing accessories, knitted or crocheted	14.4	0.02	0.12	0.55	0.15	0.20
64 Footwear, gaiters and the like; parts of such articles	12.2	0.09	0.16	0.38	1.03	0.20
60 Knitted or crocheted fabrics	11.1	0.00	0.00	0.00	0.05	0.00
62 Articles of apparel and clothing accessories, not knitted or crocheted	10.8	0,04	0.36	2.79	0.18	0.15
54 Man-made filaments	9.9	0.01	0.04	0.11	0.12	0.08
21 Miscellaneous edible preparations	9.8	0.14	0.33	0.07	0.00	0.01
55 Man-made staple fibres	8.5	0.00	0.00	0.09	0.00	0.00
The share of the 10 commodity groups in exports to the US		0.40	1.49	4.26	1.55	0.72

Source: ITC Trade Map and own calculations, accessed 15 November 2015.

The share of commodities from the most protected US industries is low (the highest for Romania, the lowest for the Czech Republic). The analysis shows that abolishing customs duties even for those commodity bundles will not significantly stimulate trade, and, as a consequence, is unlikely to cause changes in the structure of exports from Poland and other CEE countries to the US (Table 7).

Conclusions

The creation of a FTA between the European Union and the United States will not significantly affect the structure of Polish and CEE exports to the US. These countries are not an important trade partner for USA, except for Poland which participation in export to that country has doubled in 2014 in comparison to 2004. In case of other countries, there were no significant changes.

In 2010, the structure of Polish exports (based on sixteen commodity bundles distinguished according to HS classification) was similar to that of Bulgaria; in 2014, it most closely resembled that of Hungary.

In Poland and other CEE countries, exports to the US, as measured by tariff lines, increased in 2014, compared with 2010. In 2014, customs duties were levied on at least half of all goods exported to the US.

Polish and CEE exports to the US showed a very high level of concentration in commodity bundles with low customs duty rates. High-duty goods accounted for only 1.5 percent of total Polish exports. In the context of the TTIP, it should be kept in mind that national markets are much better protected by non-tariff barriers which limit and restrict market access, mostly of the regulatory and administrative kind. Their harmonization and reduction may contribute to stimulating the exports from Poland and other CEE countries to the United States.

References

Balassa B., 1973, The Theory of Economic Integration, George Allen and Unwin Ltd., London.

Bożyk P., 2005, Tendencje w europejskiej współpracy gospodarczej, in: J. Misala (ed.), Perspektywy europejskiej współpracy gospodarczej. Teoria i praktyka, Wyd. Politechniki Radomskiej, Radom.

Czarny E., J. Menkes, K. Śledziewska, 2014, Umowa o Partnerstwie Handlowo-Inwestycyjnym między Stanami Zjednoczonymi i Unią Europejską jako narzędzie międzynarodowej współpracy gospodarczej, „International Business and Global Economy", no. 33, Wyd. Uniwersytetu Gdańskiego, Gdańsk, pp. 201–204.

Czarny E., 2013, Regionalne ugrupowania integracyjne w gospodarce światowej, PWE, Warszawa.

Dietrich V., F. Hungerland, J. Quitzau, C. Sonnberg, J. Puckelwald, H. Voepel, A. Wolf, 2014, Free Trade, Strategy 2030 – Wealth and Life in the Next Generation, no. 20, Hamburg Institute of International Economics and Brenberg.

ITC Trade Map, http://www.trademap.org/Bilateral.aspx, accessed: 15 November 2015.

Kozielski P., 2014, Australia a Transatlantyckie Partnerstwo Handlowe i Inwestycyjne, Wyd. Uniwersytetu Ekonomicznego w Katowicach, Studia Ekonomiczne, no. 184, Katowice.

Machlup F., 1986, Integracja gospodarcza – narodziny i rozwój idei, PWN, Warszawa.

Misala J., 2001, Zarys teoretycznych podstaw międzynarodowej integracji gospodarczej, in: J. Misala (ed.), Proces integracji gospodarczej Polski z krajami członkowskimi Unii Europejskiej w świetle teorii, Politechnika Radomska, Radom.

Misala J., 2009, Historia rozwoju teorii i polityki konkurencyjności międzynarodowej, SGH, Warszawa.

Mucha-Leszko B., 2012, Korzyści międzynarodowej integracji gospodarczej a osiągnięcia i problemy Unii Europejskiej, in: W. Bieńkowski, S. I. Bukowski, G. Olszewska (eds.) Przyszłość integracji europejskiej – konkurencyjność i rynki, CeDeWu.pl, Warszawa.

Murtagh F., P. Legendre, 2011, Ward's Hierarchical Clustering Method: Clustering Criterion and Agglomerative Algorithm, https://arxiv.org/pdf/1111.6285.pdf, accessed 20 November 2015.

Report of the Eleventh Round of Negotiations for the Transatlantic Trade and Investment Partnership, Miami, 19–23 October, 2015; European Commission, http://trade.ec.europa.eu/doclib/docs/2015/november/tradoc_153935.pdf, accessed 25 November 2015.

Sapir A., 1992, Regional Integration in Europe, "Economic Papers", No. 94, Commission of the European Communities, Directorate-General for Economic and Financial Affairs, September.

Shalizi C., Distances between Clustering, Hierarchical Clustering', http://www.stat.cmu.edu/~cshalizi/350/lectures/08/lecture-08.pdf, accessed 20 November 2015.

WITS, http://wits.worldbank.org, accessed 10 November 2015.

Wysokińska Z., J. Witkowska, 1999, Integracja europejska. Rozwój rynków, WN PWN, Warszawa, Łódź.

Zeliaś A. (ed.), 1988, Metody statystyki międzynarodowe, PWE, Warszawa.

Żołądkiewicz K., 2007, Integracja ekonomiczna Australii i Nowej Zelandii jako przykład współczesnych procesów integracyjnych, Wyd. Uniwersytetu Gdańskiego, Gdańsk.

Andrzej P. Sikora (The Energy Studies Institute and AGH University of Science and Technology), Stanisław Cios (Ministry of Foreign Affairs), Marcin Krupa (The Energy Studies Institute), Adam Szurlej (AGH University of Science and Technology), Rafał Jarosz (Ministry of Foreign Affairs)

Chapter 11. The potential impact of the Transatlantic Trade and Investment Partnership on crude oil and distillates' trade between the US and the EU, with implications for Poland

There is a growing interest in the potential economic, political and social impact of the Transatlantic Trade and Investment Partnership. However, in-depth studies on these issues are still very few (e.g. Benes 2015; Rademaekers, Slingerland, Bressand, Felbermayr, Törnmarck 2015). The purpose of this chapter is to focus on the oil sector. We try to answer the question – what will be the dynamics of the oil sector in the US and how will it affect future trade pattern with the EU? We also discuss some other aspects related to the oil trade, i.e. refined products. We present a synthesis of parts of an unpublished report prepared by the Institute of Energy Studies in Warsaw in August 2015 for the Ministry of Foreign Affairs of Poland, on the potential impact of the TTIP on the energy sector in the EU and Poland.

1. Methodological remarks

Crude oil is not a homogeneous commodity. There are several brands of oil and their classification is usually based on two most important parameters. The first one is density, based on the American Petroleum Institute scale (API specific gravity): light (> 33 API), medium (28–33 API) and heavy (< 28 API). The second parameter is sulphur content (measured per mass): sweet (< 0.5%), medium (0.5–2.0%) and sour (>2,0%).

The higher the API gravity (the lighter is the oil) and the lower the sulphur content, the more valuable the crude. From a technical point of view any lighter or sweeter oil may serve as a substitute for the heavier and more sour types. However, from an economic point of view this may not be feasible. It is easier to produce more gasoline from light oil, but if there is an abundance of gasoline on the market then the oversupply of light oil cannot be used optimally. Therefore, projecting trends on the basis of aggregate data (net imports and exports of oil) may lead to false conclusions and the analysis must include various types of oil in trade.

The US is treated here together with Canada, while Norway is included in the analysis of the situation in the EU. Both Canada and Norway have a major impact on the oil markets in the US and the EU. Canadian oil will even enable US exports of distillates and to a certain extent also of crude oil.

We assume that – regardless of the TTIP – the US government will liberalize exports of oil[1]. However, the final solution will probably still involve some administrative procedures, perhaps resembling the ones for the LNG.

For crude oil we used data and projections of the US Energy Information Administration, International Energy Agency (especially World Energy Outlook 2014, WEO 2014) and IHS (however, there are no such data for distillates). The projections differ and we used data, which we considered more realistic and applicable. Part of the data was transformed in a model at the disposal of the Institute of Energy Studies in Warsaw.

2. The situation on EU and US markets

Most of the oil produced in Europe (the North Sea and Norway) is light with low sulphur content. EU oil production and consumption are steadily dropping (Table 1). So are imports, currently ca. 500 Mt, with most of the oil coming from Norway (in 2014–12,6 percent). These trends are expected to continue.

Table 1. Crude oil imports, exports and consumption in the EU, 2000–2020 (Mt)

	2000	2005	2010	2015	2020
Production	164	127	93	60	81
Imports	608	632	569	518	480
Exports	108	69	50	36	30
Consumption	663	684	612	542	531

Sources: Eurostat, IHS

The situation in the EU oil refining sector is currently determined by the following factors: the drop in oil consumption (a result of the economic crises and development of renewables), production (due to depletion of resources) and

1 On December 18th, 2015, President B. Obama signed a bill lifting the ban on oil exports.

competitiveness of the industry, in particular refineries (due to high price of energy). The refineries are undergoing a transformation – some plants have been closed (over 30 of them in the years 2009–2014, with a capacity of ca. 120 Mt), some restructured to produce biofuels, some are used as storage facilities. There are no symptoms indicating that this trend will be reversed. The demand for fuels is met by rising imports, mainly from the Arab Gulf countries.

The situation is different in the US (Table 2). Oil consumption is on the rise, with the exception of the recession years 2008–2009. Since 2010, due to the light tight oil production boom, imports have dropped by ca. 100 Mt. They will continue to drop or will level out, in spite of the growing consumption and the envisaged growth of exports (over 100 Mt by the end of the decade). In the US, a process similar to the one in the EU led to the closure of ca. 80 Mt. worth of refining capacity. In this case this is due to the substitution of imports of heavy oil by light US oil.

US refineries use mainly heavy grades of oil, including these imported from Canada and Venezuela. Unconventional oil, which is expected to form over 50 percent of the domestic production in the coming years, is light. As a result there is a high possibility of a strong oversupply of light oil on the North American market, further pushing down the price of oil both on this market and the global one.

Table 2. Crude oil imports, exports and consumption in the US, 2000–2020 (Mt)

		2000	2005	2010	2015	2020
Production	**Total**	295	262	275	472	593
	Unconventional	*3*	*11*	*35*	*218*	*334*
Imports		460	511	467	364	365
Exports		1	2	2	20	119
Consumption		764	771	746	814	832

Sources: EIA and IHS.

3. EU and US crude oil trade

Until recently small amounts of crude oil were exported from the EU to the USA. These exports will be gradually phased out. Since 2017 the trend most likely will be reversed, initially in the order of 15–17 Mtoe (an amount used by a medium sized refinery, like in Płock in Poland) (Figure 1).

Figure 1. Balance of oil trade between USA and EU countries, 2010–2040

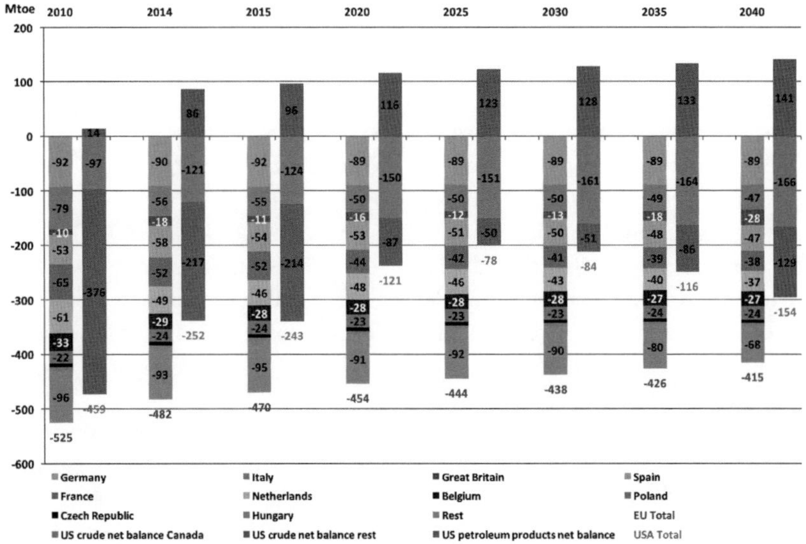

Source: The Energy Studies Institute model.

The US will remain an importer of oil, but exports will continue to rise, according to various projections and forecasts (EIA and IHS). Exports of US crude oil to Europe may start soon after lifting the ban (Figure 2)[2]. The envisaged exports will be dominated by light and sweet oil, which together will constitute ca. 90–100 percent of the exported oil. After 2020 one should expect also larger quantities (10–16 Mtoe) of sour types, both light and medium. Heavy and intermediate sour types probably will not be exported. This will be compensated by supplies from Canada of heavy and sour types.

The supply of light and sweet oils from the US and sour from Canada to a certain extent meets the import demand in the EU (Figure 3). However, European imports are still dominated (with a 60–65 percent share, total 250–280 Mtoe) by light and medium sour types mainly from Russia, Kazakhstan and the Arab Gulf

2 It took only 5 days for the Vitol Group, after lifting of the ban, to announce the first contract for exports of oil from Texas to Switzerland on December 23rd, 2015.

countries[3]. The share of light types imported mainly from Africa (Libya, Algeria, Nigeria and Angola) and the Caspian region, constitutes less than a third of the import needs (130–150 Mtoe) (Figure 4). European refineries never processed heavy (API < 22–23) and sour types, since they lack installations[4] enabling upgrading heavy oil feedstocks. Without investments the total demand for heavy types should not surpass the current level of 33–35 Mtoe, of which ca. 8–10 Mtoe can be imported from Canada.

Figure 2. Structure of projected exports of US and Canadian crude oil

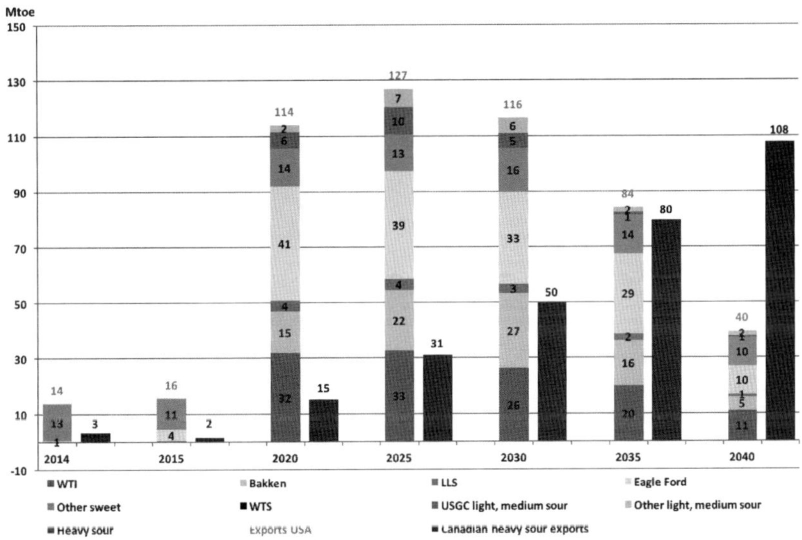

Source: The Energy Studies Institute model.

3 This is mainly due to demand for intermediate refined oil products, which from an economic point of view, are best produced from medium sour types.

4 Like cokers ROSE (Residual Oil Supercritical Extraction) or IGCC (Integrated Gasification Combined-Cycle).

Figure 3. Projected oil trade between the US and the EU (including Norway)

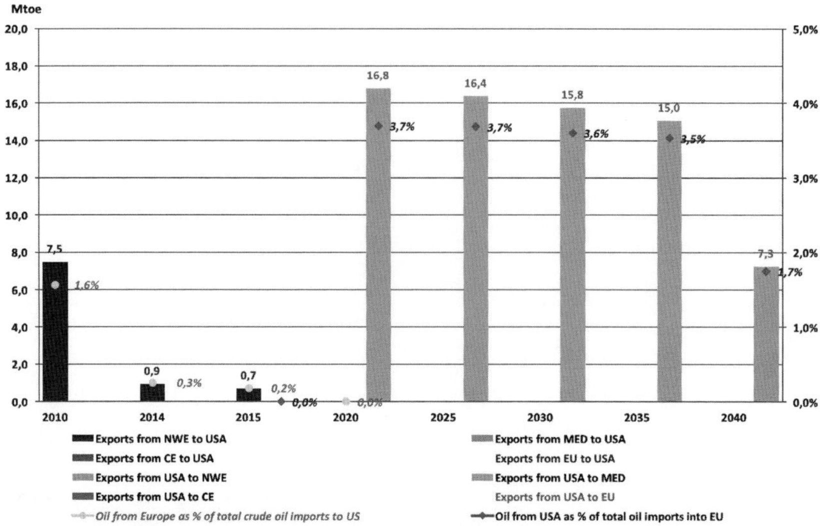

NWE – North West Europe; MED – Mediterranean Region; CE – Central Europe (including Poland)
Source: The Energy Studies Institute model.

Figure 4. Structure of projected European imports of crude oil

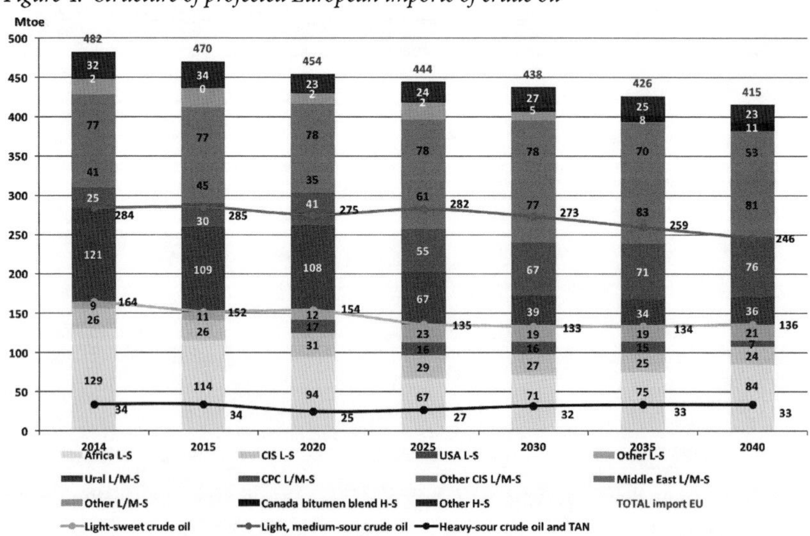

L-S light sweet; L/M-S light medium sour; M-S medium/heavy sour; TAN – highly sour
Source: The Energy Studies Institute model.

The largest number of substitutes for European oil imports are in the light sweet types (Figure 4). In the case of medium light and medium sour types, which have the largest potential in Europe; US export possibilities are small. On the other hand, heavy and sour types, with big export potential from North America, are in small demand in Western Europe, where such types are not usually processed.

Logistical costs from the US (mainly Gulf of Mexico) to Europe may have an impact on the oil trade. Transport costs are normally included in the CIF price, which is common for oil from the Arab Gulf, Africa and CIS countries. This is not the case with US oil, which is usually quoted as loco USGC (Gulf of Mexico). In order to compare the prices, it is necessary to add transportation costs across the Atlantic, which currently are not projected. Therefore, we compared them with projections of delivery costs from the Arab Gulf to the ARA region[5] (a comparable distance), which in the projected period amount to slightly more than 1 USD/b. The results of our analysis indicate that the export types of US oil (light and sweet) are attractive from an economic point of view. Eagle Ford oil (the largest projected volume) and the benchmark WTI are all the time cheaper than all the other types, while Bakken oil until 2020, and LLS until ca. 2025.

Medium light and medium sour are represented by WTS oil. Its price projected until 2020 appears to be much more attractive than any other type among its substitutes, while with respect to main competitors, Urals and oil from the Arab Gulf countries, respectively until 2025 and 2035. Only after 2035 imports of medium sour/light oil from the USA may become uneconomic.

A price analysis in the last group of medium heavy (API < 30), heavy (API < 22) and sour types is more difficult, because only Mars Blend, Poseidon and Southern Green Canyon are similar to oils from the Arab Gulf countries. Other oils from North America are much heavier and more difficult to process for most refineries in Europe. Nevertheless all types of oil from the US and Canada appear to have a more attractive price than their counterparts from the Arab Gulf countries.

The price difference varies and usually becomes smaller with time. Currently US oils are 3–9 USD/bbl cheaper than their counterparts, but with time it will be reduced to 0.5–1 USD/bbl. However, for a refinery processing 100 Mbbl/y[6], just one USD cheaper input implies 100 million USD of profit. Therefore potential profits may be large.

---

5 Amsterdam, Rotterdam, Antwerp.

6 This is slightly less than the amount of oil processed by PKN Orlen in Płock.

4. EU-US trade in refined products

In principle refined products are standardized in the EU and the US. Minor technical differences[7] should not have any major impact on their trade.

Gasoline was the main distillate exported from the EU to the US. The US traditionally had a deficit of gasoline, which to a large extent was met by imports from the EU (Figure 5). High gasoline production in the EU is expected to be maintained. However, due to oversupply of light oil in the US, the situation on the market will become balanced or even an oversupply of gasoline will appear. European refineries may need to look for new markets for their gasoline, if they want to continue the production.

Figure 5. Gasoline balance in the US and the EU

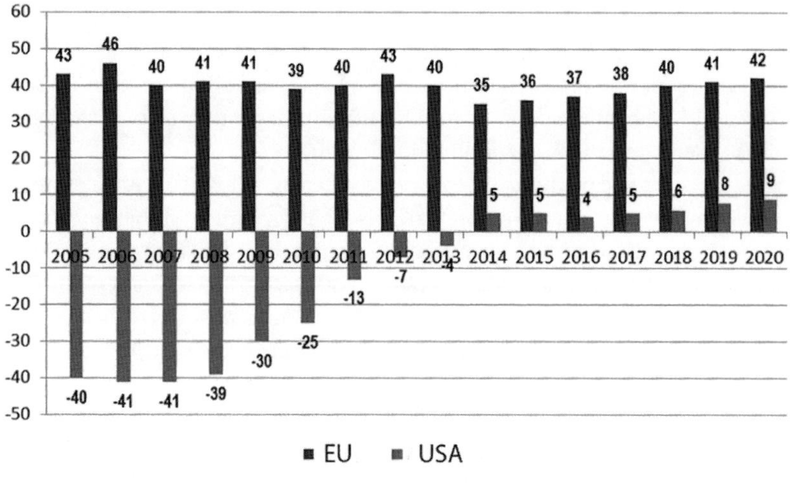

Source: Own calculation on the basis of IHS Energy data (August 2014).

The consumption of medium fuels (diesel and heating oil) has dropped in the EU and the US, as a result of the economic crisis. Traditionally EU had a deficit of diesel fuel, which was imported, e.g. from Russia and Belarus. Should US fuels become competitive and the relations with Russia strained, than we may expect a flow from the US to the European market (Figure 6).

7 For example, in the US sulfur content in diesel oil cannot exceed 15 ppm, while in the EU – 10 ppm.

Figure 6. Medium distillates' balance in the US and the EU

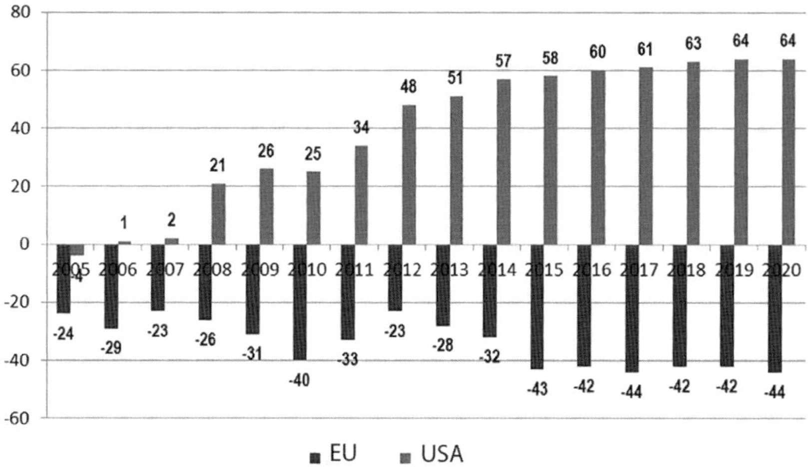

Source: Own calculation on the basis of IHS Energy data (August 2014).

As for naphtha, both markets are balanced and we do not envisage any major flows between them. Neither will jet fuel trade be affected. Europe needs over a dozen billion tons annually, but imports are not from the US, which has a balanced market and therefore will not become a significant exporter.

As for heavy fuels, we envisage a drop in their consumption due to environmental restrictions. There are no prospects for increased trade between the EU and the US.

5. Potential flow of oil and refined products between the USA and the EU

A change in the volume of oil exported to the EU from North America, above the projected volumes, can take place only with more favourable prices for comparable types of oil. The second condition is the availability of adequate types of oil for exports from the US or Canada[8], as well as larger, or at least equal comparable projected volume of imported types of oil, serving as a substitute. In such a situation we may foresee an additional potential volume related to the development of trade relations between both sides, as a result of the TTIP. This potential volume is

8 We assume that there will be no shift of additional volumes of oil from domestic use to exports.

not a direct result of the elimination of duties[9] but rather a shift of exports destined for more privileged markets (like Latin America), to the largest non-tariff market, i.e. EU after signing of the TTIP.

In the most optimistic scenario, the potential exports of oil from the USA to the EU may reach in the peak period (2025) even over 100 Mtoe, what may constitute ca. 23 percent of the total demand of EU refineries for imported crude oil (Figure 7). According to our estimates in 2020 and 2030 the maximum potential should be ca. 70 Mtoe (fifteen percent of EU's imports) and in 2040 a drop to ca. 21 Mtoe (five percent). In such a scenario, in 2020–2030 the USA could become at least equally important as Russia, Kazakhstan, the Arab Gulf countries (jointly) or African countries (also jointly).

Figure 7. Projection of potential oil exports from the US and Canada to the EU, after signing of TTIP

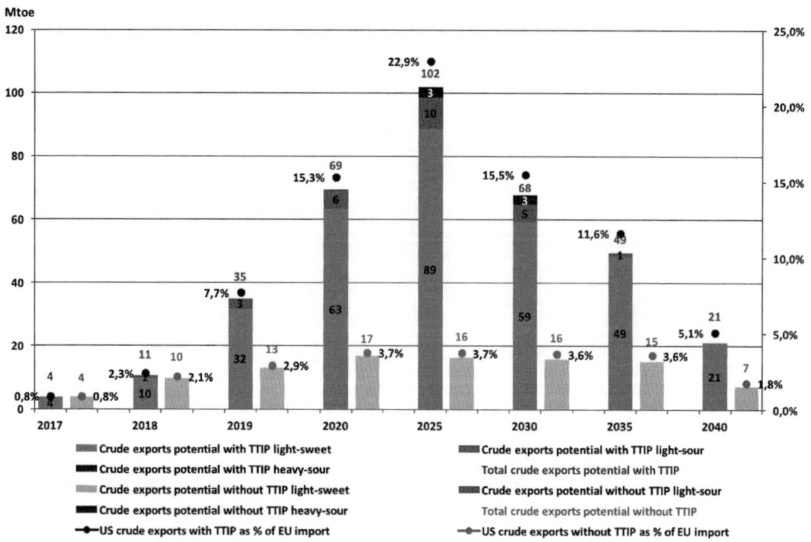

Source: The Energy Studies Institute model.

9 The current EU import duty for crude oil is 0%. For refined products it is in the range 0.7–4.7%. The US import duty for crude oil is also 0%, while for various refined products it is in the range 0–10.5 c/bbl. Details: Commission Implementing Regulation (EU) No 1101/2014 of 16 October 2014 amending Annex I to Council Regulation (EEC) No 2658/87 (Official Journal of the European Union, L312); US International Trade Commission: Harmonized Tariff Schedule of the US (2015).

The EU will remain a net importer of refined products, in particular intermediate distillates, jet fuel and LPG, while the USA will become their major exporter, in particular diesel oil, and to a lesser extent LPG and naphtha. The EU net deficit will constitute only 20–25 percent of the US surplus, but EU will not be able to absorb even this amount, due to imports from third countries. In this respect the future trend will strengthen complementarity between the EU and the USA.

The potential for collision of interests lies in the gasoline. The US market, which traditionally showed a deficit, will become balanced and in ten to twenty years may even offer gasoline for exports. This will be a threat to EU refineries, for which the US market was an important export destination. It may even speed up closure of some further refineries in the EU.

Light and sweet US oil would flow mainly to West Europe. Due to the small volume of exportable medium sour and sour oil types the potential for US trade with Poland is limited. Sweet oil constitutes just a few percent of the total crude oil processed in the Polish refineries in Płock and Gdańsk. In view of the possible drop in supply of Russian Urals oil (as an effect of the sanctions and lack of investments in the upstream sector) in medium and long term there might arise a need to increase imports from other countries, perhaps also from North America. Currently Russian oil constitutes over 90 percent of all oil processed in the Polish refineries.

We estimate that in the period 2015–2040 the potential profits of US exporters, resulting from the lifting of duties for distillates, are much larger than of EU exporters. US exporters' profits would total 16 123 m USD (13 659 m – LPG, 2 472 m – heavy heating oil), while EU's – 2 371 m USD (1 910 m – gasoline, 390 m – jet fuel, 50 m – heavy heating oil). The TTIP will not generate a substantial new flow of distillates, since the current prices and duties already render such trade profitable. We envisage some flow of jet fuel (19.6 Mtoe) and heavy heating oil (6.7 Mtoe) from the EU, and heavy heating oil (70 Mtoe) from the USA. However, lifting of the duties will increase the profits. Since the duties are much higher in the EU (usually in the range 3.5–4.7 percent *ad valorem*), than in the US (0,052–0,52 USD/bbl, which is 0.1–0.5 percent at the current price), then US exporters' profits would be larger. Should competition pressure reduce the price, then some of the benefits would be shared by consumers, in this case mainly in Europe.

Due to the small volume of exportable medium sour and sour oil types (not heavy ones) the potential for US trade with Poland is limited (at most ca. 1.5 Mt). Sweet oil constitutes at most only ten percent of the total crude oil processed in the Polish refineries in Płock and Gdańsk (in 2014–24.2 Mt). It is usually bought on spot markets in small quantities. These refineries can work on US light oil, but this isn't economic.

However, in view of a possible drop in the supply of Russian oil (as an effect of sanctions and lack of investments in the upstream sector) in the medium and long terms there might arise a need to increase imports from other countries, perhaps also from North America. Currently Polish refineries use mainly Russian oil (in 2014–91 percent). There are no indications that the domestic production of crude oil in Poland (in 2014–0.95 Mt) will increase in the foreseeable future.

Potential imports of cheaper light oil to Western Europe do not constitute an important challenge for Polish refineries. Currently ca. 80–90 percent of domestically produced distillates are destined for the domestic market. Imports are mainly from refineries in the neighboring countries (Belarus, Slovakia, Germany, Czech Republic and Lithuania), which all process the same Russian oil.

Conclusions

Most of the presented scenarios will take place regardless of the TTIP. As a result of the shale revolution all important international benchmarks in the oil sector are set by US companies and the situation on the US market. This has a positive impact on the stability on international oil markets, reduction of speculation and uncertainty, which were common features on the oil markets in recent years.

Even if this potential is not fully used, imports of oil from the US will increase diversification and security for the EU, contributing to the goals of the Energy Union. The potential impact could consist of some substitution of EU's imports from third countries (a general principle of all free-trade-areas). A positive effect would be greater competition on the European market, implying increased pressure to lower the price for consumers. Due to the current European duty regime, US exporters of distillates stand to gain more than European exporters. The TTIP should not have any major negative impact on the EU oil sector, since the EU and US economies show more complementarity than the competition.

References

Benes K. J., 2015, Considerations for the treatment of Energy in the US-EU Transatlantic Trade and Investment Partnership The Lugar Center, GMF, Columbia SIPA Center on Global Energy Policy

Rademaekers K., S. Slingerland, A. Bressand, G. Felbermayr, K. Törnmarck, 2015, TTIP impacts on European energy markets and manufacturing industries. European Parliament

The Energy Studies Institute, http://www.en.ise.com.pl/.

World Energy Outlook, 2014.

Honorata Nyga-Łukaszewska (Warsaw School of Economics)

Chapter 12. Energy in the Transatlantic Trade and Investment Partnership – the Domestic Perspective

Energy became one of the most fiercely discussed topics in TTIP negotiations. Much of the ongoing discussion about energy issues in the TTIP focuses either on the conditions for gains in liberalized energy trade at the regional level, or on the way the topic will be dealt with in the agreement. There are several interesting standpoints analyzing this issue among which particularly worth mentioning are the efforts of Benes (2015) and Natali, Egenhofer, Molnar (2015).

Due to the regional nature of this bilateral agreement, conditions for possible gains are depicted on an aggregated level. Conversely, this chapter focuses on the perspective of a single EU member state – Poland. The analysis includes Polish determinants for possible gains from the standpoint of the primary energy mix. Such a study allows identifying possible areas of benefits – in terms of demand and supply – for Poland in the future. Forecasts referring to the future energy consumption trends in Poland come from the analysis supporting draft of the *Polish Energy Policy 2050*. The analysis concentrates only on the raw materials perspective as possible trade in energy technologies seems to require deeper research on an industry/company level. The quantitative data used in the study come from the BP Statistical Review of World Energy 2015, whereas the qualitative data come from the renowned Polish academia centres.

1. The primary energy mix

Polish energy situation stems from its primary energy mix. Primary energy – in keeping with the terminology of the International Energy Agency (IEA 2005) – refers to energy captured from primary energy resources. That includes on the one hand fossil fuels such as: crude oil, hard coal, and natural gas, and on the other renewables such as solar, wind or water energy.

Figure 1. Primary energy consumption in Poland by fuel type 2014 (in Mtoe)[1]

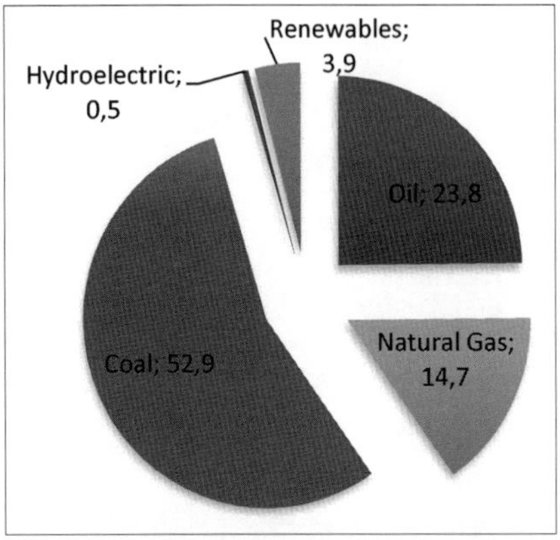

Source: own work based on the BP Statistical Review of World Energy 2015.

Poland consumes around 100 Mtoe primary energy yearly (95.7 Mtoe – 2014, BP 2015). According to the latest forecasts prepared by the Polish Ministry of Economy (Ministerstwo Gospodarki 2015a), Poland will continue to use that amount of energy each year until 2030. However, two decades later, Poland will reduce its energy consumption by fifteen percent, making energy demand and economic growth trends disentangle. Achieving such an ambitious goal by the year 2050 will be possible thanks to the energy conservation process. This refers especially to building insulation processes, further development of low-energy consuming household appliances and introduction of hybrid cars.

The current primary energy mix of Poland has not changed substantially for the last fifteen years. Strong fossil fuel dominance is accompanied by a relatively meagre share of renewables (See figure 1). Among the former, the most important role is played by domestically abundant resources. This is why coal – both hard and lignite – has more than a fifty-percent share in the primary energy balance. The dominant position of coal is inherently connected to the tradition of the mining and coal industry in Poland. Several efforts undertaken in the mid-1990's directed this industry into the path of greater efficiency and profitability. Ongoing discussion on the future of different Polish coal mines includes their further restructuring. The logic and economic sense behind the continuous process of investments in the coal industry in the carbon-constrained world, pertains to the role this resource plays in the creation of the Polish energy

1 Mtoe – Million tonnes of oil equivalent – a unit of energy.

security. At the end of 2014 nearly 80 percent[2] of electricity production was based on coal generation (both hard coal and lignite). According to the latest forecasts prepared by the Polish Ministry of Economy (Ministerstwo Gospodarki 2015a) the fundamental position of coal will change by 2050, reducing by half the current yearly coal demand from ca. 52 Mtoe. All of this will be possible due to energy conservation processes, broader use of natural gas and nuclear power plant development.

Another significant fossil fuel present in the Polish energy mix is crude oil. Even though there is no oil-based electricity generation, this hydrocarbon plays a role in the transport sector. Current oil consumption amounts to 25% of the primary energy balance. According to the forecasts prepared by the Polish Ministry of Economy (Ministerstwo Gospodarki 2015a) demand for oil from the transport services will keep oil consumption at the same levels (around 25 Mtoe) until 2030. However, popularization of hybrid vehicles by 2050 will reduce it to 21.5 Mtoe/year.

Natural gas is the last hydrocarbon present in the Polish primary energy mix. Its role since the last fifteen years has remained unchanged. Gas consumption is focused primarily in households and industry sectors, respectively for cooking and chemical production purposes. Recently, more and more attention has gained the idea of gas-based electricity production. Nevertheless, its share in the global electricity production is low – two percent at the end of 2015[3]. This is going to change by 2050 – according to the forecasts prepared by the Polish Ministry of Economy (Ministerstwo Gospodarki 2015a). At that time gas-fired power plants are expected to deliver nearly ten percent of the Polish electricity production. Surging natural gas consumption results from the increasing share of renewables in electricity generation. Natural gas acts as a backup fuel for wind turbines.

Currently, renewables are modestly represented in the Polish primary energy mix. With 4.4 Mtoe of yearly consumption, they account for a five-percent share in the mix. According to the latest forecasts of the Polish Ministry of Economy (Ministerstwo Gospodarki 2015a) this is going to change by 2030. At that time, renewables are expected to achieve a fifteen-percent share in the primary energy balance. Such a change will be possible thanks to popularization of photovoltaic and wind technologies. Development of renewable energy with zero marginal

2 Energy Market Agency, http://www.rynek-energii-elektrycznej.cire.pl/st,33,207,tr,75,0,0,0,0,0,podstawowe-dane.html

3 Energy Market Agency, http://www.rynek-energii-elektrycznej.cire.pl/st,33,207,tr,75,0,0,0,0,0,podstawowe-dane.html

cost of production will change the market position of traditional technologies. Combining that with rising fees for emissions in the EU ETS will change the economic balance of individual investments in renewables.

Even though the current primary energy mix does not allow for nuclear electricity generation, by 2025 it is going to change, as the Polish Ministry of Economy forecasts (Ministerstwo Gospodarki 2015a). At that time the nuclear share in electricity generation will amount to two percent, and by 2050 it will increase to twenty percent.

2. Coal in the Polish energy policy

Abundant domestic hard coal and lignite resources make these fuels the primary energy sources in the Polish energy policy. In 2014 the coal deposits held the R/P ratio of 40[4]. It means that with 2014 levels of production existing coal deposits would be sufficient for the next 40 years. Estimation of coal reservoirs includes only known and geologically proven basins (BP 2015).

Polish production of hard coal and lignite gradually decreases. In 2000 Poland produced more than 70 Mtoe of coal and in 2014 only 55 Mtoe (Figure 2). Lignite and hard coal are the main resources used for electricity and heat generation on the Polish energy market. According to the latest forecasts of the Polish Ministry of Economy (Ministerstwo Gospodarki 2015a) the share of coal in satisfying the demand for primary energy will decrease from the current 42 percent to 28 percent in 2050. This trend will occur as a result of depletion of lignite deposits and a drop in the coal-fired power plant profitability with an increase in the price of carbon emission allowances. Lignite will be substituted primarily by nuclear fuel as a substantial part of currently operated deposits will deplete by 2023. For further details see: Tajduś, Czaja, Kasztelewicz (2010).

Abundant domestic coal base combined with strict pan-European and worldwide carbon emission standards encouraged Poland to undertake several efforts aimed at using coal in a cleaner way. Polish technical universities (such as AGH in Cracow) and other public institutions (such as Main Mining Institute-GIG) have been conducting research on so-called clean coal technologies (abbreviated as CCT). CCTs have become one of the priorities for the Polish energy policy. Therefore, it is estimated that, within next ten to fifteen years, this technology will allow broader use of domestic coal reserves which will be safer for the atmosphere (Wnukowski 2014; Ministerstwo Gospodarki 2015b).

---

4 R/P ratio is Resources to Production ratio.

Figure 2. Coal production and consumption in Poland 2000–2014 (in Mtoe)

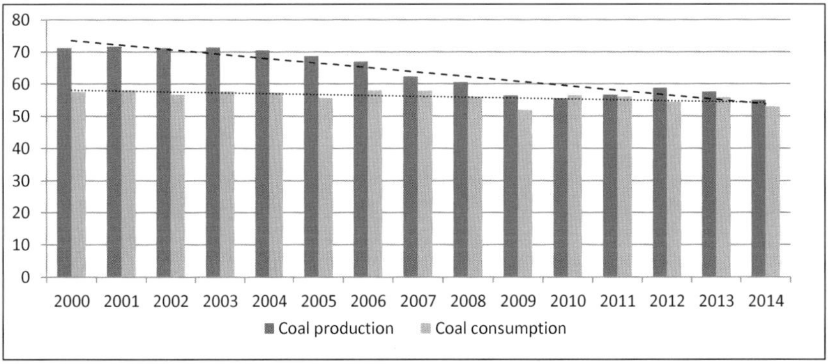

Dashed lines indicate linear trend lines. The upper one: trend line for coal production. The lower one: trend line for coal consumption.
Source: own work based on the BP Statistical Review of World Energy 2015.

Even though between 1966–1978 Poland was one of the most important coal producers and exporters with a twenty-percent share in the global coal export, in 2008 the country became for the first time a net importer of coal. Reasons for this situation are lying in the period between 2006 and 2007, when insufficient domestic supply encouraged local consumers to look for different suppliers abroad. Between 2004 and 2013 already thirteen percent of imported coal came from the USA (Stala-Szlugaj 2015).

3. Hydrocarbons in the Polish energy policy

Despite the fact that in solid fossil fuels Poland has the ability to meet its domestic energy needs, the use of hydrocarbons poses many different challenges for the country. Polish reserves of crude oil are so small that in international statistics they are not included. According to the latest available estimates of the Polish Geological Service, at the end of 2014, Poland held crude oil reserves of 23 m tonnes (Szuflicki, Malon, Tymiński 2015). With the current (2014) production level domestic crude oil reserves will meet Polish demand for the next 26 years (own estimates based on: Szuflicki, Malon, Tymiński 2015).

Domestic production of crude oil (ca. 918 500 tonnes – 2014) meets only a small part (ca. 4.5 percent – 2014) of the internal demand (Szuflicki, Malon, Tymiński 2015). Therefore, the majority of crude oil comes from abroad. Imported fuel is domestically processed and refined into products such as diesel fuel or gasoline (POPIHN 2014). According to the energy policy forecast prepared by the Polish Ministry of Economy (Ministerstwo Gospodarki 2015b) the future goals in the crude oil sector are: deeper diversification of supply and decrease in the energy-intensity of the transport sector.

Figure 3. Crude oil consumption in Poland 2000–2014 (in million tonnes)

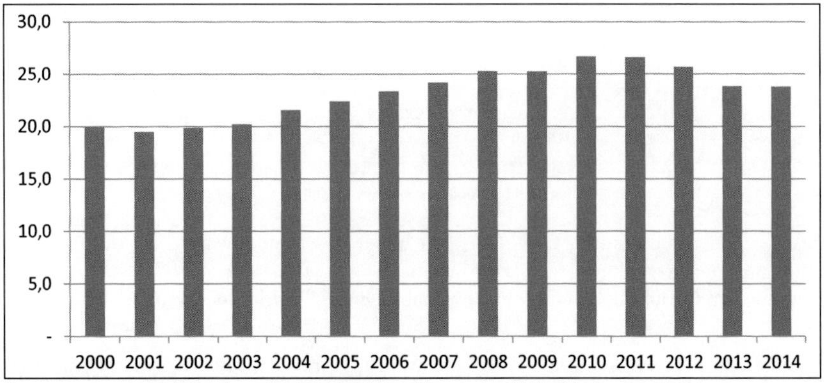

Source: own work based on the BP Statistical Review of World Energy 2015.

Similar observations pertain to natural gas production and consumption patterns. Domestic production of this resource, even though higher in the absolute sense (4 bcm – 2014) and relative values (25 percent of the demand in 2014), still is not sufficient to meet the demand. Production of natural gas from home deposits remains unchanged since the beginning of the 21st century. Expectations connected with prospection of the unconventional gas reservoirs have not so far brought any substantial commercial gas volumes to the market. Nevertheless, according to the Polish Ministry of Economy (Ministerstwo Gospodarki 2015b) further prospection of unconventional gas will proceed in the future.

Figure 4. Natural gas production and consumption in Poland 2000–2014 (in bcm)[5]

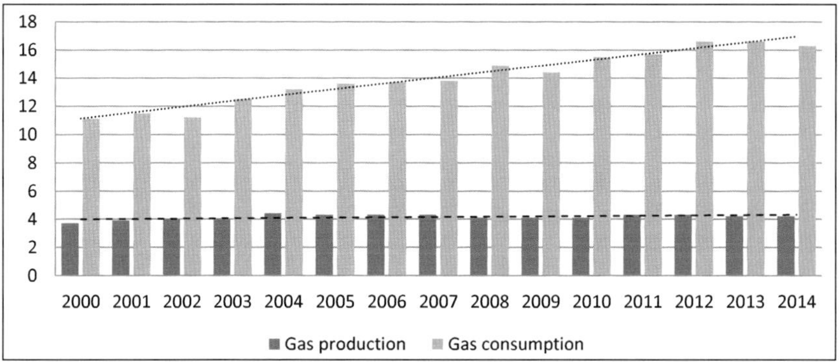

Dashed lines indicate linear trend lines. The upper one: trend line for natural gas consumption. The lower one: trend line for natural gas production.
Source: own work based on the BP Statistical Review of World Energy 2015.

Similar to crude oil market forecasts, the Polish Ministry of Economy (Ministerstwo Gospodarki 2015b) hopes for deeper diversification of supply on the natural gas market in the future. The launching of the LNG terminal certainly makes this goal feasible. The facility will be working with initial regasification capacity of 5 bcm/year with the possibility of extending it to 7.5 bcm/year (Polskie LNG 2015).

4. The role of renewables and the possibility of introducing nuclear energy into the Polish energy policy

The gradual increase of renewables in the Polish energy mix stems from the European obligations such as *inter alia*: EU Directive 2009/28/EC, introducing a binding target for Poland to increase the share of renewable energy in the gross final energy consumption with a set of indicative intermediary targets (IEA 2011). Among the most frequently used renewables in the Polish primary energy mix are, respectively, energy from: biomass, water, bioethanol, biodiesel (IEO 2007). Renewables are used for heat generation, electricity production or as an input to traditional fuels in the transport sector. In electricity production, biomass use prevails. The recently passed bill on renewables will make production of electricity from renewables by prosumers even easier (Odnawialne źródła energii 2015).

5 Bcm – billion cubic metres, unit of energy.

Figure 5. Renewables share in the electricity production in Poland 2013

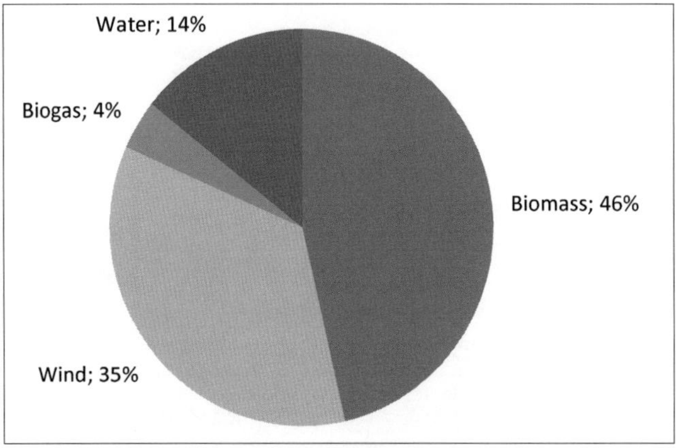

Source: own work based on the: GUS (2013).

Since the TTIP has not entered into force yet, it is justified to analyze the role of the nuclear energy in the future Polish energy mix. The projected launching date has been set for 2025. The detailed roadmap indicates several milestones that are to be achieved before that time (See table 1). Currently the project is in its the second stage. The first phase ended with establishing the regulatory framework vital for the operational stages of the project. Currently there is an ongoing debate on the possible options of locating the facility. The short-list includes three spots in the northern Poland[6].

The rationale behind introducing nuclear energy into the Polish energy mix include energy sector challenges. Among them the most important ones are: ageing power-generation assets in Polish electric power engineering system; inadequate development of the fuels and energy manufacturing, transmission and transportation infrastructure and environmental obligations. Additionally the nuclear power plant project responds positively to the necessity to ensure long-lasting and reliable supplies of electricity with stable pricing mechanisms (Ministerstwo Gospodarki 2014).

6 For further details see: Elektrownia jądrowa.pl, Available at: http://www.elektrownia-jadrowa.pl/Lokalizacja-elektrowni-jadrowej-w-Polsce-2.html. Accessed on: 28th December 2015.

Table 1. Schedule of developing nuclear power plants in Poland

Stage	Description
Stage I till 31.12.2013	Creation of institutional foundations for the development of nuclear energy sector; adoption and entry into force of legislation necessary for the development and operation of nuclear power plant
Stage II 01.01.2014–31.12.2016	Determination of the location and concluding a contract on the technology for the first nuclear power plant
Stage III 01.01.2017–31.12.2018	Preparations of the technical project and obtaining all required by law decisions and opinions
Stage IV 01.01.2019–31.12.2024	Obtaining the building permit, built and connection to the network the first block first nuclear power plant. Initializing the built of other units /nuclear power plants
Stage V 01.01.2025–31.12.2030	Continuation and commencement of construction of the other blocks /power plants. Completion of construction of the first nuclear power plant. Completion of construction of the second nuclear power plant is planned for 2035.

Source: own work based on the information of Ministry of Energy. Available from: http://www.mg.gov.pl/Energetyka+jadrowa. Accessed on: 28th December 2015.

Conclusions

Due to Poland's reliance on domestic coal reserves in electricity production and the role of its mining industry, it would be difficult to completely shift towards imported resources. What seems plausible, however, based on current coal supply structure, is an increased import of coal in the short term from the partner country of a preferential trade agreement as a result of a trade diversion effect. Nevertheless, the closer the agreement conclusion will be to the completion of the nuclear power plant, the more the incentives for increased coal import will recede. This is why in the long term nuclear power plant commissioning excludes coal import.

In contrast, a positive effect from the preferential trade agreement will be observed in case of hydrocarbons. The available technical infrastructure allows importing of gas and oil from different sources. Again, increased import might happen as a result of a trade diversion effect. In the long term, any successful development of the domestic unconventional gas resources might decrease the need for imported gas volumes. A surge in gas consumption might also be driven by the increased use of renewables (especially wind and solar). In this way, natural gas will be a complementary resource to renewables.

This is all true providing that price mechanisms act in favour of the Polish energy market. However, once price competitiveness of other regions geographically closer to the exporting market becomes higher than that of Poland, a preferential trade agreement will not lure those trade flows anymore. Recognizing the price as a limitation of the above analysis, it is indicated as the next research step for other studies.

References

Benes K., 2015, Considerations for the treatment of energy in the US–EU Transatlantic Trade And Investment Partnership, Columbia University in the City of New YorkThe Lugar Center, GMF, Columbia SIPA Center on Global Energy Policy.

BP, 2015, BP Statistical Review of World Energy.

Elektrownia jądrowa.pl, http://www.elektrownia-jadrowa.pl/Lokalizacja-elektrowni-jadrowej-w-Polsce-2.html; accessed on: 28th December 2015

Energy Market Agency, http://www.rynek-energii-elektrycznej.cire.pl/st,33,207,tr,75,0,0,0,0,0,podstawowe-dane.html, accessed on: 28th December 2015.

GUS, 2013, Energia ze źródeł odnawialnych w 2013 roku, Warszawa.

IEA, 2005, Energy Statistics Manual, Paris.

IEA, 2011, Energy Policies of IEA Countries – Poland 2011 Review, Paris.

IEO, 2007, Możliwości wykorzystania odnawialnych źródeł energii w Polsce do roku 2020, Warszawa.

Ministerstwo Energii, http://www.mg.gov.pl/Energetyka+jadrowa, accessed on: 28th December 2015.

Ministerstwo Gospodarki, 2014, Polish Nuclear Power Programme, 2014.

Ministerstwo Gospodarki, 2015a, Wnioski z analiz prognostycznych na potrzeby Polityki energetycznej Polski do 2050 roku, 2015.

Ministerstwo Gospodarki, 2015b, Projekt Polityki energetycznej Polski do 2050 roku, 2015.

Natali P., Ch. Egenhofer, G. Molnar, 2015, Energising the TTIP: Political economy of the trade policy rationale, CEPS Special Report No. 113.

Olkuski T., Zależność Polski w zakresie importu węgla kamiennego, Gospodarka Surowcami Mineralnymi, Tom 29, Zeszyt 3/2013, pp. 115–130.

Odnawialne źródła energii, Ustawa o OZE – taryfy gwarantowane dla prosumentów, http://www.odnawialnezrodlaenergii.pl/oze-aktualnosci/item/1469-ustawa-o-oze-taryfy-gwarantowane-dla-prosumentow, accessed on: 28th December 2015.

Polskie LNG, http://www.polskielng.pl/en/lng/lng-terminal-in-poland/, accessed on: 28th December 2014.

POPIHN, 2014, Przemysł i handel naftowy 2013.

Szuflicki M., A. Malon, M. Tymiński, 2015, Bilans zasobów i złóż kopalin w Polsce wg stanu na 31 grudnia 2014, PIG-PIB, Warszawa.

Stala-Szlugaj K., 2015, Import węgla kamiennego do Polski, http://www.sitg.pl/dopobrania/aktualnosci/gdjref03.pdf., accessed on: 28th December 2015.

Tajduś A., P. Czaja, Z. Kasztelewicz, 2010, Stan obecny i strategia rozwoju branży węgla brunatnego w i połowie XXI wieku w Polsce, „Górnictwo i Geologia", Tom 5, Zeszyt 3, pp. 137–167.

Wnukowski D., 2014, Clean Coal Technologies: Green Shoots for Poland's Energy Sector, "Bulletin PISM", No. 36 (631), 18 March 2014.

Anna Odrobina (Cracow University of Economics)

Chapter 13. The European Union as the United States' Partner in Research and Development Cooperation

International cooperation has already become a permanent element of the contemporary global economy, taking the form of various sorts of cooperation between companies, institutions, universities, private and public organisations or countries (UNCTAD 2002). Currently, fact that entities compete with one another on the international market and cooperate in certain areas of their activity, is no longer surprising. One such area is research and development, which is highly capital-intensive, time-consuming, and above all risky. For these reasons, R&D cooperation allows reducing costs, shortening research time and sharing risk with partners. At the same time cooperation (pooling the knowledge, competence and experience of the cooperating entities) enables transfer and diffusion of information, access to information (including complementary ideas), gaining tacit knowledge, and the emergence of technological synergy effects (Hagedoorn, Lundan 2001; Farell 2006; Contractor et al. 2011; Belderbos, Gilsing, Jacob 2011).

It is obvious that various US and EU entities, since they are traditional global R&D centres, cooperate with one another to a significant extent in the research and development arena. However, since the 1990s clear changes in the global R&D sphere, marked with internationalisation and decentralisation, may be observed. As a result of this, new countries from outside the Triad have emerged and aspire to play an increasingly important role in global R&D (UNCTAD 2005a; 2005b; 2011; Kehal, Singh 2006; Lu, Chen 2012). Consequently, the positions of the United States and the European Union have changed, and the question arises as to whether intensive R&D cooperation among these partners will remain at the existing level and whether the EU is still an attractive partner for the US in this field.

The aim of this chapter[1] is to analyze the importance of the EU for the US in R&D cooperation, as well as indicate trends and identify the factors affecting this cooperation. The discussion begins with determining the R&D potential of the European Union and the US against the backdrop of the global situation. Further on, mutual R&D investment projects as well as patent and scientific cooperation among the entities in question are analysed. It is worth pointing out here that a description of all manifestations and results of R&D cooperation should be considered impossible due to frequent phenomena and cooperation results which are elusive to international statistics. For this reason, and given the above limitations, this paper focuses on an analysis of those aspects of R&D cooperation which have already been quantified, yet in a very modest way.

1. R&D potential of the EU and US

The United States and the European Union are traditionally centres of global R&D, but the former has always been the clear leader. In 2013 global research and development outlays in the US amounted to approx. USD 460 billion, which accounted for 2.7 percent of the GDP. In the EU it was USD 340 billion, i.e. 1.9 percent of the GDP. These figures themselves prove that there is a significant difference between the leader and the EU; while at the same time there are various other deficits in the research and development activity in the European Union. First of all, one problem is insufficient involvement of businesses in R&D implementation, as in the EU they represent just 63 percent of R&D investment projects, whereas in the US – 71 percent. Furthermore, in the European Union R&D is excessively financed from public funds (34 percent of the gross domestic expenditure on R&D), whereas in the USA it is limited to a quarter. The EU's weakness is also manifested in the insufficient financing of R&D by the business sector (54 percent of the gross domestic expenditure on R&D), as compared to 61 percent of US enterprises (OECD 2015a).

However, one of the EU's strengths is the fact that in a ranking of the top 1,000 global TNCs with the greatest R&D outlays there are many EU corporations with total R&D investment of EUR 151 billion in 2013. There are even more TNCs from the USA in this ranking, and their outlays in 2013 amounted to EUR 178 billion (European Commission 2014a). Nevertheless, the world's strongest R&D companies come from the USA and EU, and this fact may constitute a favourable premise for the development of R&D cooperation between companies.

1 The project was financed from funds allocated to the Faculty of Economics and International Relations at the Cracow University of Economics, within the framework of the grants for the maintenance of research capacity.

Figure 1. Global R&D

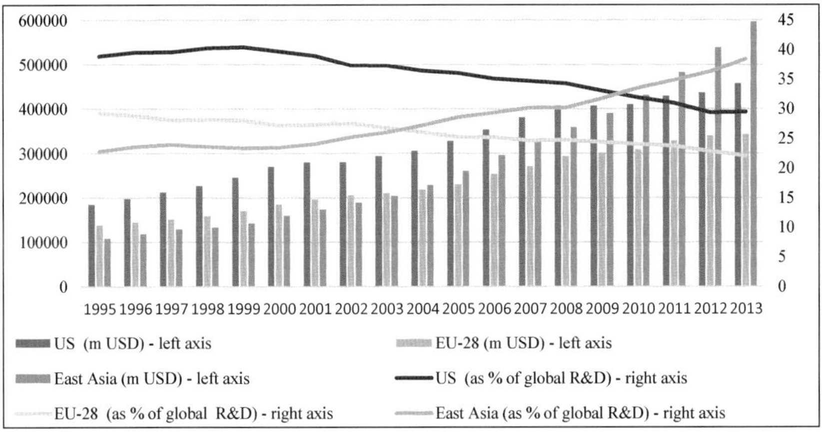

Source: own calculations based on OECD (2015a).

Analysing the US and EU's R&D potential, one should also clarify the global situation (presented in Figure 1): currently East Asia is the global R&D centre (China, Japan, South Korea, Singapore and Taiwan). Since 1990s until the end of the 20th century there was a stable situation in terms of the shares of the main centres, i.e. the US, with over 40 percent of the global R&D, was the leader, followed by the EU with slightly less than 30 percent. At that time Japan was the only Asian country that was a significant global player (for decades it followed the US in rankings of countries with the most invested in R&D). The beginning of the 21st century saw major changes in global R&D, spurred by dynamic growth in the Chinese R&D sector, which by 2009 grew to occupy the second place behind the US. At the same time, South Korea started to invest in R&D intensively, thus the 'Asian centre' was created, and in 2004 it outpaced the EU-28 and in 2010 the US in terms of R&D value. Since then it has been strengthening its position as the global leader, conducting approx. 40 percent of global R&D. Consequently, the US share in global R&D dropped to approx. 30 percent and that of the EU-28 dropped to approx. 22 percent (Figure 1).

Such a change in the structure of global R&D suggests that both the USA and the European Union will react to the creation of the Asian centre by directing cooperation towards it. Such a reaction seems obvious, but a question arises as to whether the increased interest in R&D cooperation with East Asia will take place at the cost of the traditionally strong cooperation at the US-EU level – or parallel to it.

2. Mutual R&D investment

One of the manifestations of the process of R&D internationalisation is the fact that transnational corporations place their research and development units abroad, as they face growing competition and acceleration of technological process, and, consequently, try to create their technological advantage on the basis of internal and external sources of knowledge, launching a transfer of knowledge and cooperation (OECD 2008, Chesbrough 2003, Pilat et al. 2009). The impetus for conducting R&D in the network of foreign TNC units is the willingness to take advantage of knowledge and technologies in the international environment by placing R&D units in locations with attractive resources of knowledge, technologies and talent, as well as a concentration of companies and institutions whose resources a given corporation wants to acquire (Ietto-Gillies 2012, UNCTAD 2005c, Barton 2007). Due to the fact that the largest TNCs come from the countries of the Triad, and the biggest resources of knowledge, technologies and talent are also located in the Triad, in principle R&D investment flows take place within the Triad. It has to be pointed out, however, that since the late 1990s corporations have also started to create their R&D units in developing countries, and have been particularly active in China, India, Singapore, Brazil and Russia (OECD 2008).

TNCs from the US are strongly involved in conducting R&D investment projects outside their home country, implementing over USD 40 billion worth of R&D outlays in their foreign units (Table 1). Up until 2009 US corporations placed over 80 percent of their R&D investment projects in the EU-27. However, since 2010 the EU-27's share of the US TNCs' investment projects dropped, and in 2012 amounted to 68.2 percent. In absolute terms a clear downward trend in US TNCs' involvement in the European Union is visible, and the drop in the EU-27's share proves that other locations have become increasingly important to US corporations.

Table 1. R&D of US TNCs abroad

	2008	2009	2010	2011	2012
World total (m USD)	41699	39205	39887	44684	44610
EU-27 (m EUR)	25130	23435	22046	24706	23772
EU-27 (m USD)*	36941	32574	29321	34341	30428
EU-27 as a % of the world	88.6	83.1	73.5	76.9	68.2

* converted at the ECB exchange rate
Source: own calculations based on OECD (2015b).

In general, US companies implement approx. 85 percent of R&D outlays in the US, and the main direction of placing R&D abroad are the developed countries, yet also increased involvement in developing countries has been observed (UNCTAD 2010). In 2012, US TNCs invested in R&D approx. USD 2 billion in China and India each. Meanwhile, in the European Union, Germany (EUR 8 billion), UK (EUR 6.5 billion), Belgium (EUR 2.5 billion), and France (EUR 2 billion) attracted the biggest R&D investments carried out by US corporations. EUR 1.5 billion was invested in Ireland and Netherlands each (OECD 2015b). This means that the remaining 21 EU countries accounted for merely EUR 1.8 billion and shows that TNCs from the USA are interested in conducting R&D only in the strongest economies of the EU-27, which have a recognised knowledge potential and at the same time are home countries of important corporations in terms of R&D.

Table 2. R&D of foreign TNCs in the US

	2008	2009	2010	2011	2012
World total (m USD)	40727	40425	42360	45177	47994
From EU-27 (m EUR)	23210	20921	22008	24330	27342
From EU-27 (m USD)*	34119	29080	29271	33819	34998
EU-27 as a % of the world	83.8	71.9	69.1	74.9	72.9

*converted at the ECB exchange rate
Source: as for Table 1.

Due to the strength of the US economy and its companies it is obvious that in the US R&D investments of foreign corporations are located, and its volume is continuously on the rise – in 2012 foreign TNCs implemented USD 48 billion worth of R&D (Table 2). It needs to be pointed out that the most important investors here include corporations from the EU-27, whose share in 2008 amounted to 83.8 percent, and in the following years it was at a lower level, reaching 72.9 percent (EUR 27.3 billion) in 2012. In nominal terms, the involvement of EU TNCs increased from 2009, which means that it is corporations from outside the EU-27 that intensified their R&D investment in the US.

It is also worth mentioning that in 2010 the biggest R&D investment in the USA was made by TNCs from the UK (EUR 8.3 billion), France (EUR 6.5 billion) and Germany (EUR 5.8 billion). In addition, Italian (EUR 2.3 billion), Irish (EUR 2.2. billion) and Dutch (EUR 1.9 billion) corporations were active. The remaining 21 countries of the EU-27 accounted for as little as EUR 0.3 billion of the R&D investment in the US (OECD 2015b). Despite the fact that TNCs from the European Union are the largest foreign R&D investor in the USA, in fact only the strongest corporations from a small group of EU countries create their R&D units on the US market, thus opening up opportunities for cooperation with partners from the USA.

3. Patent cooperation

Applying for a patent is one way of showing that positive results of research and development activity have been achieved and new technological solutions created, which in turn gain the protection of intellectual property laws. Due to the fact that certain inventions are a result of cooperation between various entities – at both the domestic and international level, we deal with joint applications of the cooperating companies. The analysis concerns patent applications with foreign co-inventors using two patent types; these are European patents granted by the European Patent Office (EPO) as well as international patents, which comply with the Patent Cooperation Treaty (PCT) international procedure.

Each year more than one hundred thousand patent applications are submitted to the EPO, in 1999 this figure reached 111.3 thousand, whereas in 2011 it was 134.3 thousand. The largest number of applications is submitted by entities from the EU, which accounted for 44–47% of all applications in the years 1999–2011. The second most active group consists of inventors from the USA, who accounted for approx. 30 percent of the applications, but this share has been steadily decreasing (in 2011 it was 26 percent). One can notice that in the years 1999–2011 more and more entities from outside the EU and US submitted patents to the EPO (in 1999 this group accounted for 25.3 thousand applications and by 2011 the number had increased to 39.7 thousand) (OECD 2015c).

In the years 1999–2011 among patent applications from the US just fifteen percent were applications submitted with a foreign co-inventor, and the number of such applications kept increasing until 2006 (5.2 thousand). In the years 2007–2009, the global financial crisis weakened the activity of US inventors, though later the number of such applications kept increasing to reach the level of 5,170 in 2011 (Figure 2). The biggest number of patents submitted to the EPO by US entities in cooperation with foreign partners is with EU partners, but the share of these EU partner applications clearly and regularly dropped from 64.5 percent in 1999 to 54.6 percent in 2011, and a sharp drop was recorded in the years 2007–2010 (Figure 2). This means that inventors from the USA cooperate more intensively with partners from third countries. Also cooperation with Japanese partners for patents submitted to the EPO is, in fact, insignificant and shows a downward trend – from 346 in 1999 to 222 in 2011 (OECD 2015c). Unfortunately, the data does not cover the remaining countries, but one may conclude that this patent cooperation concerns co-inventors from outside the countries of the Triad.

Figure 2. US patent applications to the EPO with foreign co-inventors

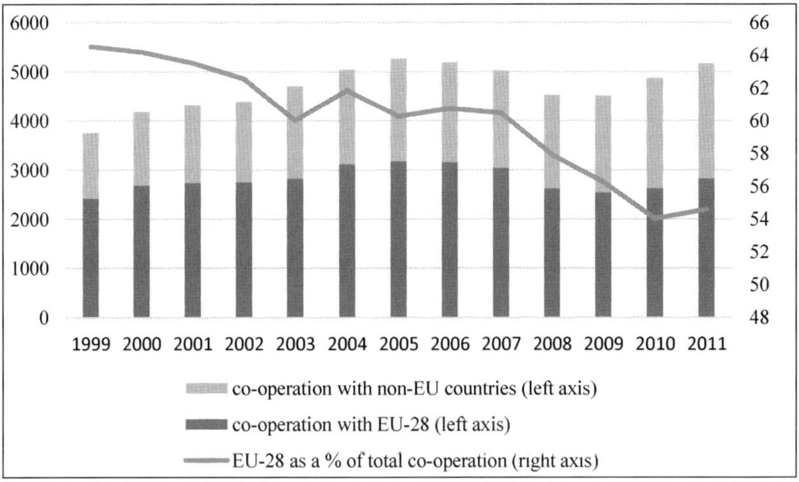

Source: own study and calculations based on OECD (2015c).

Figure 3. EU-28 patent applications to the EPO with foreign co-inventors

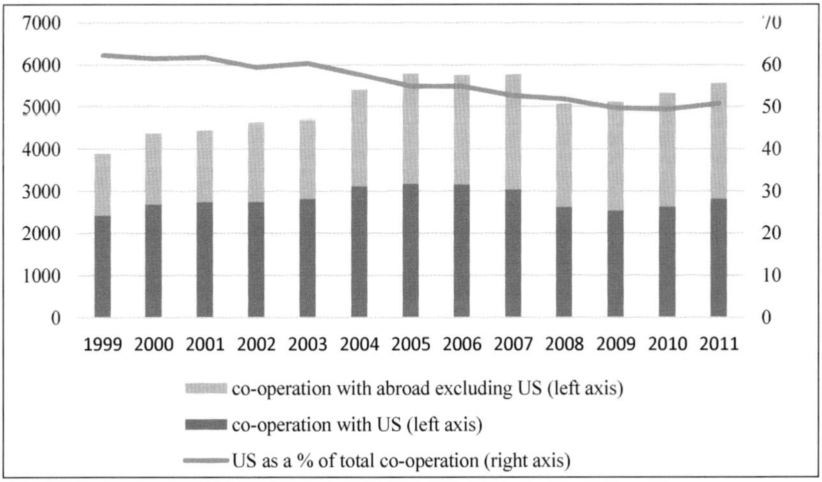

Source: as for Figure 2.

Patent applications in cooperation with foreign inventors account for 7.5–9.3 percent of all applications from the EU to the EPO. The number of applications increased from 3.9 thousand in 1999 to 5.6 thousand in 2011 with small decreases in the years 2008–2009, although the most were submitted in the period 2005–2007, i.e. 5.8 thousand each year. (Figure 3). As is the case with the US, for the EU the most important partner for cooperation on inventions was the US, but the corresponding share of patents submitted together with US partners decreased from 62.2 percent (1999) to 50.8 percent (2011), and in the years 2009–2010 it was slightly below 50 percent. As the US share in EU patent cooperation in the EPO decreased, and patents in cooperation with Japanese partners represent an insignificant share (from 211 to 345 depending on the year), the numbers imply broader patent cooperation of entities from the EU with partners from outside the Triad. It has to be pointed out, however, that the biggest share of patents submitted by the EU results from intra-community cooperation (from 56 to as much as 67 percent).

Figure 4. US patent applications filed under the PCT with foreign co-inventors

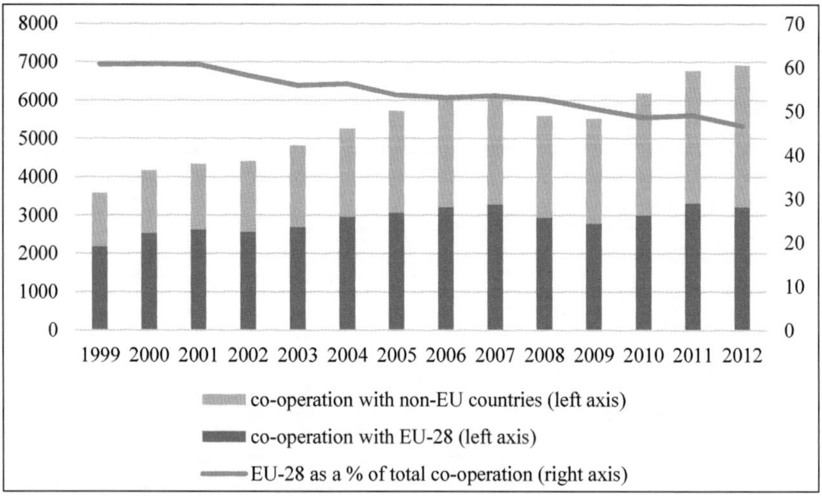

Source: as for Figure 2.

Figure 5. EU-28 patent applications filed under the PCT with foreign co-inventors

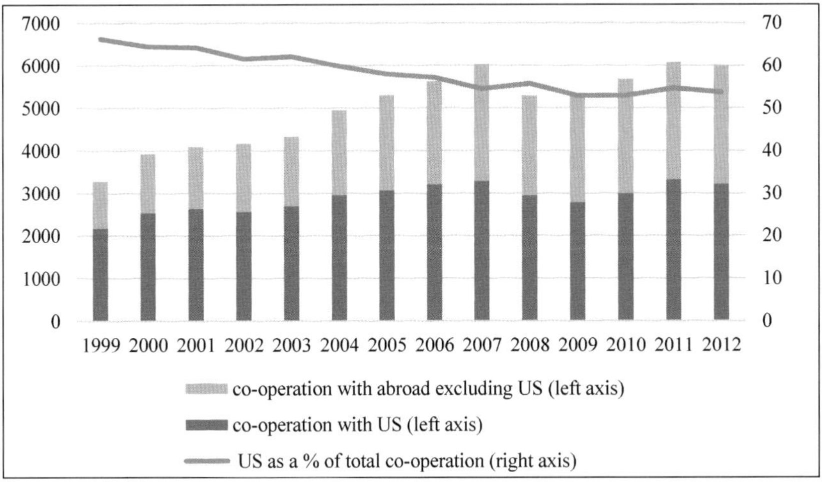

Source: as for Figure 2.

In the case of international PCT patents, the number of applications increased in the years 1999–2012 2.2 times – from 88.8 to 194.1 thousand. The number of patent applications resulting from international cooperation was at the level of around 7 percent throughout that period. Analysing PCT patent applications involving international cooperation, one can conclude that the US submitted slightly more patents of this kind than the EU (Figures 4 and 5). In both groups the number of applications nearly doubled in the years 1999–2012. Both in regard to the US and EU the greatest number of PCT patents result from cooperation between US and EU inventors, but the mutual share was regularly on the decrease. In the case of patents based on international cooperation and submitted by the US, the EU share exceeded 60.7 percent in 1999 and dropped to 46.6 percent in 2012. On the other hand, PCT patents based on cooperation with US inventors submitted by the EU accounted for 66.2 percent of all EU patent cooperation in 1999 and over the years decreased to 53.7 percent by 2012; however, in the case of PCT patent cooperation internal cooperation takes place as well, but at a lower level than cooperation with the USA (OECD 2015c).

In terms of patent cooperation, the European Union remains the main partner of the United States, but its share of patent applications to the EPO and PCT with foreign co-inventors is on the decrease, despite insignificant changes (in absolute terms), of the number of joint US-EU patent applications. This means that the US is directing its R&D and patent cooperation towards other countries outside the

EU. A similar situation is typical of EU patent cooperation, but cooperation with internal partners plays an important role here as well.

4. Scientific cooperation

Scientific cooperation between the EU and US has been developing for the past few decades. Although it is impossible to represent exhaustively the various forms of cooperation between scientists, one can indicate certain areas in which specific data are available. Scientific cooperation is manifested, for example, in joint publications. In the years 2007–2011, the biggest share of joint publications was edited by co-authors from the EU-27 and US (Table 3). Out of the 3.1 million publications by EU authors, as many as 9.9 percent were co-authored by researchers from the US. Out of the 2.7 million US publications approx. 11.4 percent were edited by co-authors from the EU-27. In fact, no other regions have such strong cooperation bonds in this area as the EU and the USA. For the sake of comparison, joint publications with Chinese authors account for merely 2.6 percent of US and 1.5 percent of EU publications. Furthermore, the EU and US are unquestionable global leaders in terms of the absolute number of publications.

Table 3. Share of joint publications with third countries in the years 2007–2011

	EU 27	US	China	Russia
Total number of publications (millions)	3.1	2.7	0.9	0.2
% of joint publications with:				
UE-27	100	11.4	4.9	19.7
US	9.9	100	7.4	7.9
China	1.5	2.6	100	1.5
Russia	1.0	0.5	0.3	100

Source: Kucera, Vondrak, Frank 2013.

An important element of cooperation amongst scientific milieus is also researchers' mobility in order to attend conferences, symposia, project meetings and conduct research or academic lectures at cooperating foreign universities. In this respect, researchers from the US lead the way, which might be characterised by their most active foreign mobility: they participated in the nine largest flows of academics in 1996–2013 (OECD 2015d). Most of such mobility takes place between the US and UK: in the years 1996–2013 approx. 23 thousand British scientists travelled to the US, whereas approx. eighteen thousand Americans travelled in the opposite direction. During the same period approx. thirteen thousand German researchers went to US universities, whereas Germany hosted approx. eleven thousand US researchers. The United States was also an important destination for scientists from France (approx. 8 thousand), Italy (approx. five thousand), Spain (approx. four thousand), the Netherlands (approx. four thousand), and Sweden (approx. 2 thousand). At the same time, these countries played host to the following numbers of US researchers respectively: approx. six thousand, three thousand, three thousand, two thousand and two thousand. Thus one may note that the mobility of researchers between the EU and US in the years 1996–2013 was indeed significant.

However, it is also worth mentioning that other destinations apart from the European Union were also attractive for American scientists. Due to the geographical and linguistic proximity, the exchange between the US and Canada is quickly developing (approx. 18 thousand Canadians and approx. fourteen thousand Americans). Researchers from the US also eagerly choose Asian destinations: China (approx. eighteen thousand Americans and approx. fourteen thousand Chinese), India (approx. eleven thousand Indians and eight thousand Americans), Japan (approx. eight thousand Japanese and seven thousand American scientists) and South Korea (approx. eight thousand Americans and approx. five thousand Koreans). Another important destination for American researchers (approx. seven thousand) was Australia (approx. six thousand). Back in Europe, approx. four thousand scientists from the US went to Switzerland, whereas approx. three thousand Swiss citizens moved in the opposite direction. During this time there was also significant mobility of researchers between the US (approx. two thousand) and Israel (approx. four thousand).

The data presented above show that in the case of US researchers destinations other than within the EU, in particular Asian ones, are more important for research cooperation – apart from two of the EU countries (UK and Germany). Though it is generally a characteristic of the mutual mobility of scientists that a greater number travel from abroad to the US than the other way around, in the case of mobility between the USA and China, Australia, Korea or Switzerland the situation is reversed: more US scientists travelled to those countries than scientists from those countries to the US. This demonstrates that the level of US researchers' interest in cooperating with the scientists of these four economies is exceptionally high.

It is worth pointing out that the scientific cooperation between the EU and US takes place on the basis of the Agreement for Scientific and Technological Cooperation of 1998, which is renewed every five years. The Euratom-US Agreement on combined energy research was signed in 2000 (European Commission 2014b). Other agreements supporting R&D cooperation between the US and EU include BILAT USA 2.0 (aimed at coordination and dialogue in research, innovation and technological cooperation) and EURAXESS (links to a US database, which was established in 2007, with the task of promoting the creation of scientific cooperation networks between the EU and USA) (Gnamus 2011).

Furthermore, US researchers are very active in EU research programmes. For instance, within the 7th Framework Programme 514 participants from the US received subsidies totalling EUR 82 million as part of 410 grants, with 6.3 thousand Americans sending in grant applications. Additionally, during the first 17 months of the Horizon Programme over 1,000 US researchers applied for grants worth a total of EUR 143 million[2]. It seems that EU research programmes, due to significant funds for their implementation, create an opportunity to attract the attention of US entities to R&D cooperation financed by the EU.

Conclusions

To sum up the above analysis, one may conclude that the EU still remains the most important R&D cooperation partner for the US, although its position is becoming weaker. One of the reasons for this loss of attractiveness for cooperation with the leader of global R&D is definitely a drop in the EU importance in research and development activity in the global economy.

Despite the fact that R&D cooperation between the US and EU remains at a similar level with no significant decreases in nominal values observed, both partners are turning in other directions for cooperation – in particular towards East Asia, which is currently the strongest global R&D centre. To a significant extent, this phenomenon can be seen in a smaller mutual share in R&D investment projects or patent cooperation. Although scientific cooperation between the US and EU, in particular in the field of joint publication, is still quite high, non-EU destinations attract the most US researchers – with only the UK and Germany at the top of this group within the EU.

Another reason for the European Union's weakening role as an R&D cooperation partner of the US is that in reality the intensive cooperation concerns as few as seven EU countries, with Germany, the UK and France at the forefront, and remaining member states of marginal importance to the R&D cooperation with

2 http://ec.europa.eu/research/iscp/index.cfm?lg=en&pg=usa#news

the United States. This results from their poor R&D potential, and consequently, lack of involvement in cooperation with partners from the US.

References

Barton J. H., 2007, New Trends in Technology Transfer. Implications for National and International Policy, ICTSD Geneva.

Belderbos R., V. Gilsing, J. Jacob, 2011, Technology alliances in emerging economies: Persistence and interrelations in European firms' alliance formation, Maastricht, UNU-MERIT.

Chesbrough H., 2003, The era of open innovation, "Sloan Management Review", nr 44(3).

Contractor F. J. et al., 2011, Global Outsourcing and Offshoring: An Integrated Approach to Theory and Corporate Strategy, New York: Cambridge University Press.

European Commission, 2014a, R&D ranking of the world top 2500 companies. http://iri.jrc.ec.europa.eu/scoreboard14.html, accessed 24 September 2015.

European Commission, 2014b, Roadmaps for international cooperation. European Union SWD(2014)276, Brussels.

Farrell D. (ed.), 2006, Offshoring. Understanding the Emerging Global Labor Market, McKinsey & Company, Boston.

Gnamus A., 2011, Report on S&T Cooperation between Europe and the United States of America: European Union, Luxembourg

Hagedoorn J., S. Lundan, 2001, Strategic Technology Alliances: Trends and Patterns Since the Early Eighties, Maastricht University, Maastricht.

Ietto-Gillies G., 2012, Transnational Corporations and International Production: Concepts, Theories and Effects, Edward Elgar Publishing, Northampton.

Kehal H. S., V .P Singh, 2006, Outsourcing and Offshoring In the 21st Century: a socio-economic perspective. Hershey London Melbourne Singapore: Idea Group Publishing.

Kucera Z., T. Vondrak, D. Frank, 2013, R&D collaboration of EU countries with partners beyond the EU group, "Ergo", April. pp. 9–16.

Lu L. Y. Y., T. M. Chen, 2012, Technology Strategy of R&D Internationalization: An Empirical Study from a Developing Country, in: F. Betz (ed.), Creating and Managing a Technology Economy. Singapore: World Scientific Publishing. pp. 81–108.

OECD, 2008, The Internationalisation of business R&D, Evidence, Impacts and implications, OECD Publishing, Paris.

OECD, 2015a, MSTI database, <http://han.uek.krakow.pl/han/oecd/stats.oecd.org/BrandedView.aspx?oecd_bv_id=strd-data-en&doi=data-00182-en> accessed 22 November 2015.

OECD, 2015b, Statistics on Measuring Globalisation. <http://han.uek.krakow.pl/han/oecd/www.oecd-ilibrary.org/finance-and-investment/data/activity-of-multinationals-in-manufacturing_glob-man-data-en> accessed 22 November 2015.

OECD, 2015c, Patent statistics, http://han.uek.krakow.pl/han/oecd/stats.oecd.org/BrandedView.aspx?oecd_bv_id=patent-data-en&doi=data-00507-en> accessed 22 November 2015.

OECD, 2015d, OECD Science, Technology and Industry Scoreboard 2015. Innovations for Growth and Society, OECD Publishing, Paris.

Pilat D. et al, 2009, The development of global innovation networks and the transfer of knowledge, in: C. A. Primo Braga (ed.), Innovation and Growth: Chasing a Moving Frontier, OECD, Paris.

UNCTAD, 2002, Partnerships and Networking in Science and Technology for Development, United Nations, New York and Geneva.

UNCTAD, 2005a, Globalization of R&D and developing countries, United Nations, New York and Geneva.

UNCTAD, 2005b, The impact of FDI on development: globalization of R&D by transnational corporations and implications for developing countries, UNCTAD, Geneva.

UNCTAD, 2005c, World Investment Report. Transnational corporations and the Internationalization of R&D, United Nations, New York and Geneva.

UNCTAD, 2010, Foreign direct investment, the transfer and diffusion of technology, and sustainable development, United Nations, Geneva.

UNCTAD, 2011, Foreign direct investment, the transfer and diffusion of technology, and sustainable development, UNCTAD, Geneva.

<http://ec.europa.eu/research/iscp/index.cfm?lg=en&pg=usa#news> accessed 25 November 2015.

Sylwia Talar (University of Economics in Katowice)

Chapter 14. Trade in ICT Services Between the EU and the US in the Context of the TTIP

The creation and development of the internet and its related technologies (Information and Communication Technologies – ICT) have brought about profound changes in the way business is conducted and have created a new sector of economy – the ICT sector. A great deal of research has confirmed the essential impact of the use of ICT on innovation, total factor productivity growth and economic growth as a result. A comprehensive review of the literature pointing out the economic effects of ICT in various areas and at different levels includes the works of Atkinson and McKay (2007) and Katz (2012). Considering the crucial importance of the ICT sector for the economy, individual countries take measures to develop and increase the use of new technologies. International cooperation in ICT and trade in products of this sector, particularly services, have also growth dynamically. According to the WTO (2015), the share of ICT services in total commercial services trade in 2014 was 9.3 percent, and turnover in computer and information services was the most rapidly growing among not only all sectors of services, but also all groups of goods, reaching an average annual growth rate of eighteen percent in the years 1995 to 2014. In these circumstances, the competitiveness of the economy is primarily determined by the level of its inclusion in the processes of creation, trade and usage of ICT. Further to the above, the level of development and innovativeness of ICT services, along with their availability, including their prices and the scope of use, have far-reaching impact on the economy in general. In consequence, the strategic nature of this sector should be recognized in development policy and the focus should be on facilitating its development, drawing also on international cooperation. The Transatlantic Trade and Investment Partnership (TTIP) may be a source of such opportunities for the EU.

The digital revolution, including the development of the internet, has been pioneered by the US, which has maintained its leading position in numerous areas, withstanding growing competition from other countries. For example, China has recorded the greatest increase in ICT-related specialization (the revealed technological advantage based on patent applications) since the late 1990s and became the second most specialized ICT economy in the years 2010–2013 (OECD 2011, 2015). The EU has also taken part in the technological race. Comparing

Scandinavian and southern European countries (like Italy or Spain), the considerable internal differentiation of EU states in terms of ICT development can be observed. However, the EU is an organization of highly integrated states with a single market since 1993. Furthermore, the EU has been setting supranational economic development programs (the Lisbon strategy, Europe 2020) since 2000. This is an argument for treating the EU as a single economic entity which has been acting on the international arena as such, undertaking negotiations with the US to conclude the TTIP.

The EU as a whole has been struggling with the problem of reducing the competitive gap relative to the US. At that point, the EU should take all opportunities to improve the terms of cooperation with the US aiming at developing its own ICT service sector. The very sector of ICT services is not considered separately in the TTIP negotiations and therefore the most important issues pertaining to it are within such parts of the planned agreement as access to the services market, regulatory cooperation in the ICT sector, and regulations relating to intellectual property rights (European Commission 2015).

The main purpose of this chapter is to assess the position of the EU in the trade in ICT services with the US and to specify the directions of possible impact of the planned TTIP on the development of this sector in the EU. It was assumed that low competitiveness of the EU relative to the US results in its unfavourable position in the bilateral trade in ICT services, and the specific character of this sector requires a multifaceted approach to creating favourable conditions for its development. The first section assumes the methodological issues of international statistics of trade in ICT services. The second section contains a comparative analysis of the integrated data. The third section provides suggestions for directions of the EU to develop its ICT sector in reference to the TTIP under negotiations and is complemented by literature reviews. The final section presents the conclusions.

1. The issues of statistics on trade in ICT services

An analysis of bilateral trade in ICT services involves a series of difficulties resulting from the need to define the very sector of ICT services and also to access detailed data. Another issue which affects the statistics on trade in services (including ICT services) is the ability of cross-border provision of services in different ways. There are four modes of supply defined in GATS (WTO 2010):

1) cross-border supply,
2) consumption abroad,

3) commercial presence,
4) presence of natural persons.

The main source of data on international trade in services is balance of payments statistics (BOP), which covers (to some extent) only three of the four above-mentioned modes (i.e. 1, 2 and 4). The information for services supplied by foreign affiliates (commercial presence – mode 3) can be captured in Foreign Affiliates Statistics (FATS).

For the purposes of this analysis, the sector of ICT services was defined on the basis of international standards for trade in services statistics. The latest, sixth edition of the IMF "Balance of Payments and International Investment Position Manual Sixth Edition (BPM6)" and the 2010 edition of the UN's "Manual on Statistics of International Trade in Services (MSITS 2010)", introduced a new classification of commercial services, which included a category of "telecommunications, computer and information technology" services (hereinafter called ICT services). This group includes many services items such as (EU 2012, BEA 2014, WTO 2015):

- telecommunications services – the broadcast or transmission of sound, image and data or other information by electronic means (without the value of information),
- computer services – services related to hardware and software, as well as data processing, including, but not limited to sales and licenses to use of customized, non-customized software with a periodic license fee (with the exception of non-customized packaged software with a license for perpetual use – included in goods), software downloaded on the internet, fees and subscriptions for online gaming, downloading of applications by end users, hosting services, consultancy and trainings in these areas,
- information services – comprise the services of news agencies, database, web search portals and others (without software and audiovisual content).

This group of ICT services does not include charges for the use of intellectual property rights to computer software (licenses to reproduce or/and distribute general use software). These are in a separate category under BPM6 classification, and are analyzed here as such.

Taking into account all modes of supply (mode 1, 2, 3, 4) and the related data sources (BOP and FATS), as well as the scope of the ICT service sector under BPM6 classification, the analysis of trade in ICT service between the EU and the US covers: ICT services flows based on BOP, charges for the use of intellectual property for computer software (IP-CS) also based on BOP and available FATS data. This scope of analysis is feasible (and with limitations) only on the basis of data from national sources. The only international database providing comparable and consistent data on bilateral trade and across numerous sectors of services is the Trade in Services Database (TSD) (Francois, Pindyuk 2013). However, the TSD data is not based on BPM6, includes mode 1 and 2 only and is available just until 2011 (updated in February 2015) (World Bank 2015). So the data from TSD is used in addition to this analysis.

2. Position of the EU in the ICT service trade with the US

US statistics (Bureau of Economic Analysis – BEA) based on BPM6 provide trade data for 2006–2014 in USD, whereas the EU (Eurostat) publishes data in EUR for 2010–2014. The Eurostat (2015) database neither shows data on bilateral trade in IP-CS with the US, nor total EU turnover aggregates in this category. Table 1 presents the most important indicators on bilateral trade in ICT service on the basis of BOP from available domestic sources.

Table 1. Trade in ICT and IP-CS services (BOP) between the EU and the US, 2006–2014, by sources (Eurostat and BEA)

Category	2006	2007	2008	2009	2010	2011	2012	2013	2014
Eurostat									
EU ICT services exports to the US (millions of EUR)	:	:	:	:	13056	14051	16769	17828	19103
EU ICT services imports from the US (millions of EUR)	:	:	:	:	13007	13018	15056	16337	12043
EU ICT services balance (millions of EUR)	**:**	**:**	**:**	**:**	**49**	**1033**	**1712**	**1492**	**7060**
Coverage ratio	:	:	:	:	1.00	1.08	1.11	1.09	1.59
BEA									
US ICT services exports to the EU (millions of USD)	7066	8843	10193	9567	9631	10219	11279	11986	11789
US ICT services imports from the EU (millions of USD)	7922	7602	8122	8496	9283	8302	6982	7387	7109
US ICT services balance (millions of USD)	**-856**	**1241**	**2071**	**1071**	**348**	**1917**	**4297**	**4599**	**4680**

Category	2006	2007	2008	2009	2010	2011	2012	2013	2014
Coverage ratio	0.89	1.16	1.25	1.13	1.04	1.23	1.62	1.62	1.66
IP-CS exports from the US to the EU (millions of USD)	8182	15424	17186	16177	12847	13991	14158	15430	16123
IP-CS imports to the US from the EU (millions of USD)	2175	3797	4223	4238	:	3721	4084	4118	4415
Balance for IP-CS **(millions of USD)**	**6007**	**11627**	**12963**	**11939**	:	**10270**	**10074**	**11312**	**11708**
Ratio of IP-CS balance to ICT balance	:	9.4	6.3	11.1	:	5.4	2.3	2.5	2.5

: Data is not available.
Source: Eurostat (2015); BEA (2015), own compilation.

The EU and the US domestic statistics on trade in ICT services show very different figures. Both economies have reported a surplus in bilateral trade, regardless of the differences in the currencies in which the data is provided. Thus, it is not possible to draw any conclusions in this regard. Some discrepancies in statistics of international trade in services are already recognized. The causes for this are largely explained by the WTO (2015). However, even if this inadequacy is taken into account, the data reviewed here are puzzling, since the trends are opposite, the statistics are based on international standards (BPM6 and MSITS 2010) and provided by major economies in the world, that can be expected to be of high quality.

Due to considerable discrepancies in the data from domestic sources, TSD data is also taken into account (Table 2).

Table 2. EU-US trade in ICT services[1] (BOP), 2000–2011, based on TSD (millions of USD)

Year	Imports	Exports	Balance
2000	4911	3384	-1527
2001	4670	3482	-1188
2002	5110	3624	-1487
2003	6504	5877	-627
2004	6444	5849	-595
2005	6320	6219	-101
2006	7893	6174	-1719

Year	Imports	Exports	Balance
2007	8604	6601	-2004
2008	9327	6283	-3043
2009	13045	8887	-4159
2010	13497	9777	-3720
2011	9069	10302	1233

[1] ICT services classification by BOP: 247 3.2 – telecommunications services and 262 7 – computer and information services.
Source: TSD (World Bank 2015).

Using the TSD figures (Table 2), the EU's deficit instead of surplus in trade in ICT services should be approved. However, in the last year under review there was a positive trade balance. This may mean that 2011 is a breakthrough year and the surplus will be further maintained, and this would be broadly in line with figures in table 1.

Data on trade in IP-CS between the US and the EU (Table 1) indicates that this category is more important to the trade balance in the sector of ICT services. The positive balance in IP-CS trade for the US exceeded at least twice its trade balance declared in ICT services and the value remained at a similar level throughout almost the whole period considered, while the relation between them has been dropping. These results confirm the studies carried out on the largest global companies, which display the dominance of American companies in the ICT services suppliers group, and the software leaders in particular. PwC (2014) data shows that there were 67 US companies and only 17 companies from the EU among the 100 largest global software companies ranked by software revenue in 2012.

Despite applicable guidelines and frameworks, the data on services supplied by foreign affiliates (FATS) is still provided at a very limited level, both in terms of scope and disaggregation. Bilateral trade data based on FATS are available for the US only. The comparison of the US trade turnover in total and ICT services is carried out to describe the importance of trade in ICT services supplied by commercial presence. There are also calculations to assess US trade with the EU in ICT services by this mode.

Table 3. US services trade flows, by source of data (BOP and FATS[1]), 2012–2013 (millions of USD)

No.	Category	2012	2013	2012	2013	2012	2013
		Exports		Imports		Balance	
1.	Total services – BOP	656411	687894	452013	463700	204398	224194
2.	Total services – FATS	1285947	1320875	813285	878471	472662	442404
3.	Ratio of 2 to 1	**2.0**	**1.9**	**1.8**	**1.9**	**2.3**	**2.0**
4.	ICT services – BOP	32510	35035	32779	33812	-269	1223
5.	ICT services[2] – FATS	257874	263976	95903	137338	161971	126638
6.	Ratio of 5 to 4	**7.9**	**7.5**	**2.9**	**4.1**	–	**103.5**
7.	ICT services to the EU4[3] – BOP	11279	11986	6982	7387	4297	4599
8.	ICT services [2] to the EU4[3] – FATS	153220	121010	60563	62867	92657	58143
9.	Ratio of 8 to 7	**13.6**	**10.1**	**8.7**	**8.5**	**21.6**	**12.6**

[1] FATS – export means the supply of services to non-residents by US majority-owned foreign affiliates and import is the supply of services to US residents by the US affiliates of foreign multinational enterprises.
[2] The ICT services in FATS are classified here as information industry (including activities such as publishing, telecommunications, data processing, hosting) and computer systems design and related services (as a part of professional, scientific and technical services industry).
[3] Data is only available for France, Germany, the Netherlands and the UK.
Source: BEA (2015), own compilation.

Data presented in table 3 for the years 2012 and 2013 shows that US exports of ICT services by commercial presence (FATS) is close to eight times higher than the exports of ICT services supplied by the three remaining modes (BOP). It follows from the above that trade in ICT services largely depends on direct commercial presence on foreign markets, much more than total trade in services, for which the dominance of turnover generated by foreign affiliates is around twice the size of BOP. The available data refers to four EU states only. The US supplies over ten times more ICT services to the EU4 market by direct commercial presence than by any other modes, and imports over eight times more by this mode. Therefore, considering the total amount of ICT service trade between the EU and the US by all modes of supply, the matter of an accurate assessment of mutual turnover and the balance on the basis of BOPs themselves is not that important in identifying the net trade position. According to American data (BEA), the US has reached a large surplus with the EU4 in ICT services supplied by foreign affiliates. Due to the short, two-year analysis period, determined by the availability of relevant data, conclusions on trends in these relations cannot be drawn. It can be however claimed that the current and past conditions, including the technological development, have not increased the cross-border tradability of ICT services so much.

In summary, the total value of trade in ICT services between the US and the EU (as well as the balance of this trade) depends primarily on services supplied by foreign affiliates (commercial presence – mode 3 under GATT definition), second, on trade in intellectual property for computer software (IP-CS) as a separate category of services and to the least extend on broad group of ICT services supplied by the three remaining modes (i.e. cross-border, consumption abroad and presence of natural persons).

3. Conditions for the development of the ICT service sector in the EU in the context of the TTIP

The structure of trade in ICT services between the EU and the US defined in the conclusion of the above section allows to state that regulatory framework is crucial for making full use of reciprocal market access and thus creating conditions for the development of the ICT services sector, as it determines conditions for the activity of multinationals. Issues related to the protection of intellectual property for computer software must be considered of secondary importance. Direct trade policy measures which shape access to the services market (e.g. cross-border supply) are least important.

Considering the development of the ICT services sector, which is particularly significant to the economy in general, regulatory aspects require special attention. Furthermore, new challenges related to them must be profoundly analyzed. In this case, the liberalization (reduction or elimination of regulatory barriers) can have no effect on the growth of competition. The need to differentiate between liberalization and competition has been pointed out by Lim and De Meester (2014). The EU should not undertake the traditional approach in this area (i.e. minimise the regulatory burdens), instead it is desirable to implement a regulatory mechanism of high quality and efficiency.

The protection of intellectual property for software is a very important issue, but it is not a subject of TTIP negotiations. However, this issue is raising considerable controversies. The most commonly cited justifications for such protection, as claimed by Fisher (1989), have to be scientifically substantiated. Arguments opposing the protection of proprietary rights to software are often relied on the standpoint of Stallman, the founder of the Free Software Foundation. He is one of the most prominent opponents of the current approach to intellectual property, who uses software licenses for the opposite purpose – to maintain software use free of charge. He claims that the terminology regarding protection of intellectual property is deliberately overcomplicated and distorted. The negative aspects of protection of intellectual property, particularly those related to the ICT sector, are described by Kinsella (2010), who uses IBM as the example. IBM held about 40–50 thousand live patents in 2008. According to the data provided and having regard also to the high patenting costs, most benefits of this system are drawn by the largest companies.

Khan (2005) admits that the democratic, egalitarian US patent system is an important contributor to the high level of innovation and economic development of this country. The EU patent system is not as effective. The differences in the size of software patenting between European and American companies are explained, to a certain extent, by Guntersdorfer (2003) who points to certain nuances in the approach to this issue on both sides of the Atlantic (e.g. in the US only the inventor may claim for a patent, while the EU has a first-to-file system; applying for a patent in the EU automatically entails publication but it is not necessarily in the US; there are differences due to the application process or granted rights). The advantages of the US in software patenting are discussed at some length by Moetteli (2005), who underlines the clearness of the rules governing the patentability of software (as well business methods) in the US and confusing European patent law in regards to software technology. However, it may not be claimed that the EU should change its patent system, making it more competitive in relation to the US, but should consider profound policy shift, taking into account the adverse effects of software patenting on the rest of the economy. It is however not possible in the context of the current scope of the TTIP. It follows from the above that the TTIP will not alter the existing situation in this field.

The latter issue related to trade in services, particularly the cross-border trade, is relatively well recognized and discussed in numerous studies. Liberalization of tariff and non-tariff barriers to trade in services is expected to stimulate price reductions and improvement in quality of service as the direct result of boosting competition. Assuming that ICT services are inputs not only to exports, as it is generally in case of services (Francois, Woerz 2008), but also to the development and competitiveness of all other sectors of the economy, the results of research pointing to the positive effects of the growth of services imports should be particularly applied in improving the conditions for the development of the ICT sector. Furthermore, Li, Greenaway and Hine (2003) proves the significant positive impact of the imports of services on economic growth in developed countries with its simultaneous negative effect on developing economies. It is therefore justified for the EU to strive for the liberalization of trade with the US, even if the current deficit is to be maintained or widened. However, such measures could prove to be insufficient to achieve the expected effect. The recommendations given by Mattoo and Hoekman (2013) to the developing countries on the creation of a mechanism for promoting pro-competitive national regulatory reforms with international cooperation in this matter are now also relevant to the sector of ICT services in developed countries. Transparency, dialogue and cooperation between regulatory bodies are most needed due to the unique nature of this sector and, in particular, the presence of network effects, a very broad range of stakeholders and an unspecified approach to ICT services sector regulations. This can be seen for example in EU attempts to implement the Services Directive and to complete the Digital Single Market. The unfinished creation of a fully functioning single market for services leads to a question about the main drivers of EU development based on widespread usage of ICT services, one that is also put forward by Hegemejer, Michałek and Michałek (2010) in the context of their research results indicating greater impact of internal EU liberalization on Polish trade in services in comparison to possible effect of liberalization under the Doha Development Round.

Conclusions

An analysis of the trade in ICT services between the EU and the US is tied to a series of methodological and technical issues affecting the quality of data. Comparing the data from national sources, it can be claimed that the ICT services trade statistics are a severe and widespread problem restricting detailed analyses of bilateral service relations.

The primary analysis of trade in ICT services between the EU and the US was based on the latest classification of services (BMP6) and included: ICT services basing on BOP, charges for the use of intellectual property for computer software (IP-CS) basing on BOP and available FATS data. The data are derived from national sources and, to a limited extent, from the Trade in Services Database (TSD). Considering the imperfection of these statistics, it can be claimed that the EU is characterized by a trade deficit in ICT service with the US, which confirms the expectations under the general assessment of competitiveness of the EU in relation to the US.

The potential effect of the TTIP on improving the development of the ICT services sector in the EU is relatively limited due to the absence of references to intellectual property of computer software. It is in the interest of the EU to liberalize ICT services trade supplied by mode 1, 2 and 4, and to increase the import of these services, which can be easiest to achieve in the TTIP negotiations. However, such actions, without implementing any changes in other areas, may prove insufficient to achieve any benefits. It is difficult to refer to regulatory aspects of access to the ICT services market for foreign companies within the scope of this study. This is so because of the need to thoroughly analyze the challenges related to regulations in this new sector, which induces further analyses in this field.

References

Atkinson R. D., A. S. McKay, 2007, Digital Prosperity – Understanding the Economic Benefits of the Information Technology Revolution, The Information Technology and Innovation Foundation Report.

BEA, 2014, US International Economic Accounts: Concepts and Methods <http://www.bea.gov/international/pdf/concepts-methods/ONE%20PDF%20-%20IEA%20Concepts%20Methods.pdf> accessed 12 November 2015.

BEA, 2015, International Services <http://www.bea.gov/iTable/iTable.cfm?reqid=62&step=1#reqid=62&step=9&isuri=1&6210=4> accessed 12 November 2015.

EU, 2012, Commission Regulation (EU), No 555/2012 of 22 June 2012, "Official Journal of the European Union", L166/22, <http://eur-lex.europa.eu/LexUriServ/LexUriServ.do?uri=OJ:L:2012:166:0022:0066:EN:PDF> accessed 12 November 2015.

European Commission, 2015, EU Negotiating Texts in TTIP <http://trade.ec.europa.eu/doclib/press/index.cfm?id=1230&serie=866&langId=en> accessed 20 November 2015.

Eurostat, 2015, International Trade in Services (since 2010) (BPM6) [bop_its6_det], <http://appsso.eurostat.ec.europa.eu/nui/show.do> accessed 15 November 2015.

Fisher F. D., 1989, 'The Electronic Lumberyard and Builders' Rights: Technology, Copyrights, Patents, and Academe, "Change", Vol. 21, No. 3, 12–21.

Francois J., O. Pindyuk, 2013, Consolidated Data on International Trade in Services v8.9, IIDE Discussion Papers, 20130101, Institue for International and Development Economics.

Francois J., J. Woerz, 2008, Producer Services, Manufacturing Linkages, and Trade, "Journal of Industry, Competition and Trade", Vol. 8, Issue 3, 199–229.

Guntersdorfer M., 2003, Software Patent Law: United States and Europe Compared, 2 Duke Law & Technology Review.

Hagemejer J., J.J. Michałek, T. Michałek, 2010, Implications of the Doha Round negotiations in services for Poland, "Bank i Kredyt", Vol. 41, No. 1.

Katz R., 2012, Impact of Broadband on the Economy: Research to Date and Policy Issues, Broadband Series, ITU, Geneva.

Khan B. Z., 2005, The Democratization of Invention: Patents and Copyrights in American Economic Development, 1790–1920, Cambridge University Press, New York.

Kinsella S., 2010, Ideas Are Free: The Case Against Intellectual Property, "Mises Daily", Mises Institute https://mises.org/library/ideas-are-free-case-against-intellectual-property, accessed 30 November 2015.

Li X., D. Greenaway, R.C. Hine, 2003, Imports of Services and Economic Growth: a Dynamic Panel Approach, SETI – Sustainable Growth, Employment Creation and Technological Integration in the European Knowledge-Based Economy.

Lim A. H., B. De Meester (eds.), 2014, WTO Domestic Regulation and Services Trade Putting Principles into Practice, WTO, Geneva.

Mattoo A., B. Hoekman, 2013, Liberalizing Trade in Services: Lessons From Regional and WTO Negotiations, "International Negotiation", 01/2013.

Moetteli J., 2005, The Patentability of Software in the US and Europe, Presented at St. Gallen, Switzerland, October 28.

OECD, 2002, Measuring the Information Economy, OECD, Paris.

OECD, 2011, Science, Technology and Industry Scoreboard 2011, OECD, Paris.

PwC, 2014, PwC Global 100 Software Leaders, <http://www.pwc.com/gx/en/technology/publications/global-software-100-leaders/assets/pwc-global-100-software-leaders-2014.pdf> accessed 22 November 2015.

Spinello R. A., H. T. Tavani (eds.), 2005, Intellectual Property Rights in a Networked World: Theory and Practice, Information Science Publishing.

World Bank, 2015, Trade in Services Database (TSD) http://data.worldbank.org/data-catalog/trade-in-services, accessed 15 November 2015.

WTO, 2010, Measuring Trade in Services, A training module produced by WTO/OMC, WTO, Geneva.

WTO, 2015, International Trade Statistics 2015, WTO, Geneva.

Zimny Z., P. Mallampally, 2003, Internationalization of Services: Are the Modes Changing?, in: M. Miozzo, I. Miles (ed.s), Internationalization, Technology and Services, Edward Elgar, UK.

Katarzyna Byszek (Warsaw School of Economics)

Chapter 15. Concerns over the TTIP Regarding Public Health

This chapter presents concerns regarding the conclusion of the Transatlantic Trade and Investment Partnership in the field of public health. The concerns arise from addressing regulatory differences between the parties, particularly with regard to registering and marketing pharmaceuticals and assuring food safety and carrying out appropriate policies and practices in the EU member states with their right to regulate when necessary. The chapter also briefly presents controversies that have emerged over the negotiations of the treaty in the field of public health, including accusations of a lack of transparency during the consultation process as well as the European Commission's effort to ensure transparency and mitigate the concerns. As an agreement between the US and the EU, the TTIP will require the convergence of different legal systems and the terms for doing that to be negotiated, which inevitably will result in laws being changed. This complex issue has brought about concerns and difficulties similar to those which attend the harmonisation of laws between EU Member States.

1. The link between the TTIP and public health

The free trade agreement between the European Union and the United States includes three components: market access, regulatory cooperation and rules. They are aimed at facilitating economic growth, providing regulatory cohesion and establishing international standards (European Commission 2014a). The proposed the TTIP is said to be the most complex FTA ever to be pursued, and is also the most ambitious.

There is an established link between GDP growth and improved population health; however, it is vital to determine whether the manner in which wealth is utilised will have a positive or negative effect on the standards of living and health conditions (Khan, Pallot, Taylor, Kanavos 2015). The impact on health may be a result of implementing provisions on both goods and services, particularly pharmaceuticals, food and chemicals, and healthcare services. The TTIP is divided into a number of chapters, including ones dedicated to trade in goods, trade in services, investor protection, intellectual property, regulatory cooperation and some industries (e.g. pharmaceutical).

To protect the health of their citizens, the EU member states have established regulations, whose scope and complexity depend on the approach the state takes to intervening in the market. Khan, Pallot, Taylor, Kanavos (2015) observe that the social market model of the economy takes a significantly more active approach to regulatory measures than does its free market economy counterpart. Most European countries are based on a social economy model, with healthcare financed (or co-financed) from public funds (OECD 2012). Protecting citizens' health entails not only providing access to medical procedures and medicines but also preventing the occurrence of diseases and accidents by establishing safety standards, including on food safety.

2. Regulatory cooperation

An essential component of the TTIP is regulatory cooperation. According to Weiss, Middleton and Schrecker (2015), 80 percent of the TTIP's claimed benefits in terms of economic growth are derived from regulatory harmonisation and the elimination of non-tariff barriers.

The European Commission presented principles of regulatory cooperation such as the right to regulate and regulators' independence, and further stated that the TTIP would establish ways for regulators to work together closely on particular areas, swap information, and consult each other (European Commission 2015b).

Ensuring regulatory cohesion will come down to bringing US and EU regulations in line by decreasing or eliminating non-tariff barriers. It is crucial to understand the differences in the approaches of policymakers and regulators to regulate the affairs in the US and EU. The debate on approaches to regulations seeks a conciliatory solution to deal with differences in laws resulting from applying the precautionary principle in the EU regulations and approaches to risk assessment and risk management in the US. The precautionary principle is enshrined in EU law and allows regulators to take measures when there is a risk to public health or other common good even though insufficient scientific evidence exists to definitively prove causation or negative effects (Rose-Ackerman 2013).

According to the Council of the EU's *Directives for the negotiation on the Transatlantic Trade and Investment Partnership between the European Union and the United States of America* (2013), the precautionary principle is to be applied only to the extent necessary to protect human, animal, or plant life or health, and developed in a transparent manner, without undue delay. The use of the word 'necessary', as with the exceptions clauses of GATT and GATS, implies an intention to impose restrictive conditions on the exercise of the precautionary principle (von Schomberg 2012). If it is not possible to present a scientific link between the government's intervention and its purpose, the link would be presumed not to exist. When applying the precautionary approach, where the presumption may often be the other way around – the inability or failure to make the link does not bring about the presumption that intervention does not lead to achieving its purpose. Some interventions are a matter of 'common sense'. Sometimes the measures to be taken are obvious and therefore they have not been the subject of extensive scientific inquiry (Curtis, Reynolds 2015).

The essential difference between the EU and US approaches to regulations comes down to the general conclusion that, when applying the precautionary principle (as the EU does), a company must prove to the state that there is sufficient evidence to claim that a product is not harmful before it is introduced onto the market. A risk-assessment approach, however, would require a state to prove that a certain level of harm will occur and cannot be reduced if it wants to bar imports of hazardous products (Myers 2000).

Curtis and Reynolds (2015) are concerned that the unclear but extensive influence of the Regulatory Cooperation Body (RCB), currently proposed within the framework of the TTIP, will internalise an unbalanced approach to regulations. To change laws which have been passed by legislators (parliaments) with a public mandate is to ignore not only the legislature but also the people who have chosen its members. This is probably why the TTIP has received so much public attention. The EU member states have developed social schemes and regulations protecting workers' rights and a variety of safety regulations, including food safety. On the other hand, the drive toward minimum necessary regulations and a free market economy have always been the decisive arguments for lawmakers in the US. Thus, according to Andrei (2015), any FTA between the EU and US, which by definition involves eliminating barriers, will inevitably see the European side of the equation yield to the *'American way of doing things'*.

EU-US collaboration on regulations raises a number of questions: for which areas do the EU and US regulations provide similarly high levels of protection? Can they be compatible? In which areas will different regulations apply? Is there a rule-maker and rule-taker? Final answers to these very important questions remain unknown, leaving room for doubts and concerns.

3. The most common concerns over the TTIP with respect to health

Many non-govermental organisations, associations and academics have expressed their concerns over the influence of the TTIP on people's health. They include Health Action International, European Public Health Alliance, Friends of the Earth Europe, The European Consumer Organisation (Bureau Européen des Unions de Consommateurs), Oxfam International, Center for International Environmental Law (CIEL), Corporate Europe Observatory, People's NHS, Patients4NHS, International Federation of Medical Students Associations, The Standing Committee of European Doctors, as well as researchers from the London School of Economics, National University of Ireland, the University of Michigan, Royal College of Nursing and The Faculty of Public Health in the United Kingdom and many others. The impact of the TTIP on the large category of health will be felt across multiple industries, and on both goods and services, particularly pharmaceuticals, food safety and healthcare. Chapters of the TTIP which relate to health issues incorporate the following areas.

3.1. Trade in services

Many have suggested that drafted provisions in the TTIP regarding the removal of restrictions from the supply of services may have a negative impact on public services in Europe, particularly in the healthcare sector. Opening the market up to private healthcare providers in the interests of market liberalisation and competition may also lead to an increasing loss of government control over quality and its accountability in this area (Curtis, Reynolds 2015). Liberalisation in the healthcare sector may result in lowering standards in order to reduce costs and maximise profits and possibly care of a poorer quality (Kaucher 2013). It may also negatively impact the employment terms and conditions medical staff currently receive or would potentially receive (Hamilton 2015). The sector is crucial for the labour market, a fact acknowledged by the European Commission and borne out by the numbers: in 2010 in Europe, 17 million people were employed in the health sector, accounting for 8% of jobs in EU territory at that time (European Commission 2012, p. 2).

While the mechanisms of liberalisation are potentially quite expansive, the TTIP will contain an option for States to exempt public services from the provisions of the agreement. The question is whether EU Member States have provided for sufficient room to manoeuvre in the final TTIP wording to exempt public health services from the requirements of market access and national treatment (Siles-Brügge 2014).

3.2. Dispute resolution – Investor-State Dispute Settlement (ISDS)

Numerous concerns have been expressed over the inclusion of provisions on Investor-State Dispute Settlement (ISDS) in the TTIP. According to facts and figures highlighted at the United Nations Conference on Trade and Development in February 2015, investors continue to use the ISDS mechanism and claimants initiated 42 known cases in 2014. Additionally, the relative share of cases against developed countries increased in 2014 (from 28% to 40%). Amounts claimed by investors range from USD 8 million to about USD 2.5 billion; however, as UNCTAD's IIA Team has emphasised, information is scant and most international investment agreements allow for fully confidential arbitration, so the actual figures could be higher.

Many are of opinion that ISDS strengthens the ability of multinational corporations to press legal challenges against public health regulations (Bennet 2014), giving the example of tobacco companies currently employing ISDS to challenge tobacco control regulations in Australia (Gleeson and Friel 2013). The analysis of Australian cases would seem to cast doubt on the claim that ISDS represents a faster means of resolving disputes than the domestic courts. Japan Tobacco International challenged the Australian government's tobacco plain packaging legislation before the domestic court and it took less than a year for the Australian High Court to give its final ruling. An identical claim raised by Phillip Morris regarding the same regulations through investment arbitration (Hong Kong-Australia BIT) has taken over 4 years and remains unresolved.

The costs of arbitration awards can be disproportionately high, representing a significant drain on public funds as billions of USD are sought for damages. Adding to the expense, the state sometimes must cover the costs of litigation even when it wins the case (Poulsen, Bonnitcha, Yackee 2015). On the other hand, the cost of litigation (defending) can be a strong incentive for governments to settle a case and pay off investors even when a claim has little chance of succeeding (Tietje, Beatens 2014). Concerns over potentially significant expenditure from the state budget due to ISDS are particularly common in countries with high concentrations of foreign investment, such as Ireland (Curtis, Reynolds 2015). ISDS is considered to be harmful because it can be used to challenge regulations adopted in the democratic legislative process (Jarman 2014). Another concern is that ISDS would be dominated by law firms and arbitrators operating without transparency and with few or no restrictions on conflicts of interest (Van Harten 2014).

3.3. Pharmaceuticals

Many organisations, including the European Public Health Alliance, Oxfam and Health Action International, have expressed concerns over provisions in the TTIP that apply to pharmaceuticals, as provisions on intellectual property have also been included.

The *Directives* of 2013 included information that the agreement will reflect the importance of intellectual property, provide enhanced protection and will be built upon the Trade-Related Aspects of Intellectual Property Rights (TRIPS). TRIPS has bolstered the international protection of patents by narrowing the scope for differentiation within national patent policies. It has also influenced access to life-saving pharmaceuticals primarily in developing countries, especially those lacking pharmaceutical manufacturing capacities, though also in the EU and US (Correa 2002). An expansion of IPR protection will have an impact on the price and availability of medicines (El Said 2010). Advances in medical technologies and treatments may be prohibitively expensive for people in developed countries and the cost of treatment does not seem to be justified by production costs, especially when companies are supported in their research by subsidies from public funds.

Another concern, expressed by both the European Consumer Organisation (French name: Bureau Européen des Unions de Consommateurs, BEUC) and Health Action International (HAI) Europe, relates to the definition of commercial confidentiality. If reports from clinical trials on safety, adverse effects and adverse reactions are classified as confidential, public access to important information would be restricted. This would run counter to the aim of Clinical Trials Regulation EU No. 536/2014 to improve greater transparency in conducting clinical trials and providing information on their outcomes.

Concerns over pharmaceuticals with respect to intellectual property are also linked to pharmaceutical companies' use of ISDS to protect their profits from changing laws on administering patent rights. A dispute between Eli Lilly and Canada is an example of how companies seek to employ ISDS (Eli Lilly and Company v. the Government of Canada, UNCITRAL, ICSID Case No. UNCT/14/2).

3.4. Food and chemicals

There are myriad concerns over TTIP provisions relating to food and chemicals, which will also have an impact on public health. Regulations regarding these areas are an important element of the agreement as its aim is to facilitate market access and ensure recognition of equivalence or mutual recognition of those regulations pertaining in both parties' jurisdictions. The Center for International Environmental Law stresses that there are significant differences in regulations governing food, beverages and chemicals, all of which are less regulated in the US (Smith, Azoulay, Tuncak 2015). This could be explained by the existence of fundamentally different approaches to safety (see Section 1 of this chapter).

According to Weiss, Middleton, and Schrecker (2015), the European Commission is promoting Sanitary and Phytosanitary Standards-plus (SPS-plus), which go far beyond the regime which has been already used to challenge the EU regulations regarding hormone-treated meat for human consumption. The researchers are also of the opinion that the TTIP may give multinational corporations an opportunity to claim that currently binding regulations in Europe are 'unnecessarily restrictive'. This, according to the UK Faculty of Public Health (2014), may prove an essential issue in the light of measures taken or planned by the countries to prevent obesity, diabetes and heart disease by reducing consumption of food with high amounts of sugar and/or salt and providing detailed information on foods (required labelling). Khan, Pallot, Taylor and Kanavos (2015) indicate that whether imports of chlorine-treated chicken from the US would be allowable in the EU would be based on the assumption that mutual recognition of standards is agreed in TTIP. However, findings from the study conducted in the food sector for the European Parliament suggests that regulatory convergence will result in lowering standards in the EU in some areas (Risks and Opportunities… 2014). In addition, Curtis and Reynolds (2015) note that there are very significant differences between the US Toxic Substances Control Act and the EU's REACH regulations (the Regulation on Registration, Evaluation, Authorisation and Restriction of Chemicals).

Another concern has been raised by the BEUC over hazardous substances used in American cosmetics but banned in the EU. According to the BEUC, the EU has forbidden 1377 chemicals and regulated another 250 ingredients while the US has banned approximately 11 substances at the federal level. The organisation also emphasised that labelling requirements pose a threat to consumer health and gave the example of listing ingredients that are suspected allergens. CIEL also stresses the risks which broadly defining 'trade secrets', as is done in the US, poses to health and safety. It gives the example of protecting information such as the identity and percentage of ingredients (Smith, Azoulay, Tuncak 2015, p. 18).

Conclusions

The TTIP is surely more than just another free trade agreement as all its elements go beyond traditional trade arrangements. Based on the analysis of the materials gathered for this research, two main reasons for the concerns that have been expressed come to light: first, the lack of transparency that has characterised negotiations from the outset, and, second, the awareness of differences between the EU and US in regulation-related issues.

The way this treaty is being negotiated and consulted has raised a variety of doubts, including those of the EU Ombudsman and members of European governments. Many organisations, particularly the European Health Alliance, argue that transnational corporations have had frequent opportunities to lobby the EU Trade Department about the treaty while the same opportunities have not been afforded trade unions or civil society groups. Indeed, of the 560 meetings that the Trade Department held in preparation for negotiations, 520 were with business lobbyists and only 26 (4%) with public interest groups (e.g. Patients4NHS, Corporate Europe). Others expressed their opinion that the public is not well informed about the TTIP (e.g Bernd Lange for the Parliament Magazine, October 2014). Many organisations, including Oxfam, were calling for the negotiating texts and documents submitted by the EU and US to be made public, so concerned people and organisations could find out about the proposals given. Dr David Suppan, of the Institute for Agriculture and Trade Policy, indicated that the European Commission decided to publish in January 2015 drafts of texts being negotiated because Wiki-Leads had published several chapters of the TTIP (Suppan 2015).

Because the European Commission (DG Trade) strives to ensure that the TTIP consultation and negotiating processes are transparent, the Commission's website contains a significant amount of information about the agreement. The EC also takes under consideration concerns expressed during consultations. It has published facts and myths about the TTIP, the EU's negotiating texts and factsheets with explanations about each chapter of the agreement. Written in plain language, the documents make it possible to understand the scope and framework of complex regulatory issues mixed with economic jargon. DG Trade holds meetings and public hearings with businesses, consumer bodies, trade unions, and environmental and health groups. A TTIP Advisory Group of 16 outside experts representing the interests of these groups has been set up and has held several public consultations. The EC also enabled members of the European Parliament to read other documents that remain confidential. The questions are: do they understand the language well enough to read the documents with full comprehension, and therefore do they know the context and assess the impact of the proposals?

The main areas of the negotiations are regulatory convergence, cooperation and harmonisation. Hence those are the concerns this chapter has addressed. The broad and not very well defined 'technical barriers to trade', which essentially are domestic rules and regulations, have been prompted by the drive for trade liberalisation. Many of these 'barriers'/regulations have evolved from consultations and legislative debates. Their foundation may be the conception of the social economy or the application of social criteria that are not included in economic analysis. If regulatory harmonisation does not take under consideration the social value of regulations, there is a risk that the public interest, and public health in particular, will be damaged.

Concerns about the outcome of negotiations would seem inevitable as a few decide on the future of the many; there is, moreover, the question of trust in protecting the welfare of citizens. Finally, if changing regulations is at the heart of the TTIP, there will always be the question of who is changing the laws, how, and why. These questions are also discussed among the EU Member States when the European Commission proposes new regulations.

References

Andrei S., 2015, Resisting TTIP: Dissecting the popular resentment toward the world's most ambitious free trade agreement, Economic Affairs. Available at: http://bit.ly/1IIx728 accessed 30 November 2015.

Bennet N., 2014, Health concerns raised over EU-US trade deal, "The Lancet", Vol 384, Issue 9946, pp. 843–844. Congressional Research Service, http://bit.ly/1XpVavb, accessed 10 December 2015.

Bloemen S., T. Mellema, 2014, Trading Away Access to Medicines – Revisited, Joint Agency Briefing Paper. Oxford: HAI Europe and Oxfam International, http://bit.ly/1×5hJTk, accessed 30 November 2015.

Bureau Européen des Unions de Consommateurs (BEUC) press statement of July 15, 2015, http://bit.ly/25Y8zQe, accessed 30 November 2015.

Correa C., 2002, Implications of the Doha Declaration on the TRIPS Agreement and Public Health, Health Economics and Drugs, EDM Series No. 12, Essential Drugs and Medicines Policy, World Health Organisation, WHO/EDM/PAR/2002.3, http://bit.ly/25Y8zQe, accessed 30 November 2015.

Council of European Union, 2013, Directives for the negotiation on the Transatlantic Trade and Investment Partnership between the European Union and the United States of America, http://bit.ly/1vOSUxF, accessed 30 November 2015.

Curtis J., R. Reynolds, 2015, TTIP, ISDS and the Implications for Irish Public Health Policy. A Report for the Irish Cancer Society.

Driesen D., 2013, Cost-Benefit Analysis and the Precautionary Principle: Can they be Reconciled?, "Michigan State Law Review", 2013, Vol. 2013 Issue 3, pp. 771–772.

El Said M., 2010, Public Health Related TRIPS-plus Provisions in Bilateral Trade Agreements: A Policy Guide for Negotiators and Implementers in the WHO

Eastern Mediterranean Region World Health Organization and International Centre for Trade and Sustainable Development, http://bit.ly/1XpWoXb, accessed 30 November 2015.

European Commission, 2012, Staff Working Document on an Action Plan for the EU Health Workforce, SWD(2012) 93 final, Strasbourg, p. 2.

European Commission, 2014a, Investment Protection and Investor-State Dispute Settlement (ISDS) in EU agreements, http://bit.ly/1fo6AFD, accessed 30 November 2015.

European Commission, 2014b, The Transatlantic Trade and Investment Partnership – TTIP explained, http://bit.ly/1jRJQ6h, accessed 30 November 2015.

European Commission, 2015a, Commission Staff Working Document: Report – online public consultation on investment protection and investor-to-state dispute settlement (ISDS) in the Transatlantic Trade and Investment Partnership Agreement, http://bit.ly/1u249WJ, accessed 30 November 2015.

European Commission, 2015b, Factsheet on regulatory cooperation, http://bit.ly/1ScJHYT, accessed 30 November 2015.

European Public Health Alliance (EPHA) Position, 2015, How to include Public Health into the EU Trade Policy Strategy?, http://bit.ly/1XpWqON, accessed 30 November 2015.

Gleeson D., S. Friel, 2013, Emerging threats to public health from regional trade agreements, "Lancet", Volume 381, No. 9876, pp. 1507–1509, http://bit.ly/1Q5uSw1, accessed 30 November 2015.

Goyens M., 2014, How will TTIP affect the health of Europeans?, http://bit.ly/1sGN9W7, accessed 30 November 2015.

Hamilton M., 2015, The Transatlantic Trade and Investment Partnership (TTIP): What RCN members need to know, http://bit.ly/1VZMA5j, accessed 30 November 2015.

Health Action International (HAI) Europe and Oxfam, 2014, Trading away access to medicines – revisited. How the European trade agenda continues to undermine access to medicines, Joint Agency Briefing Paper, http://bit.ly/25Y9gct, accessed 30 November 2015.

Health Action International (HAI), Universities Allied for Essential Medicines, Stop AIDS brochure, http://bit.ly/1rqwBAs, accessed 30 November 2015.

Horel S., 2015, A Toxic Affair: How the Chemical Lobby Blocked Action on Hormone Disrupting Chemicals, Corporate Europe Observatory, Brussels, http://bit.ly/1PwDqLH, accessed 30 November 2015.

Jarman H., 2014, Public health and the Transatlantic Trade and Investment Partnership, "European Journal of Public Health", Vol. 24, No. 2, p. 181. Published by Oxford University Press on behalf of the European Public Health Association, http://bit.ly/1U9YrZP, accessed 30 November 2015.

Johnson R., 2014, The US-EU Beef Hormone Dispute, Congressional Research Service, Washington, DC, http://bit.ly/1S5R2IU, accessed 30 November 2015.

Kaucher L., 2013, The real force behind the NHS Act: The EU-US trade agreement, Open Democracy, http://bit.ly/1Uk5l0Y, accessed 30 November 2015.

Khan U., R. Pallot, D. Taylor, P. Kanavos, 2015, Transatlantic Trade and Investment Partnership: international trade law, health systems and public health. The London School of Economics and Political Science, Modus Europe, London, UK.

Myers N., 2000, Debating the Precautionary Principle, Science and Environmental Health Network, http://www.sehn.org/ppdebate.html, accessed 30 November 2015.

Organisation for Economic Co-operation and Development, 2012, Financing of health care, in Health at a Glance: Europe 2012, OECD Publishing, http://dx.doi.org/10.1787/9789264183896–56-en, accessed 30 November 2015.

Poulsen L., J. Bonnitcha, J. Yackee, 2015, Transatlantic Investment Treaty Protection. Paper No. 3 in the CEPS-CTR Project on "TTIP in the Balance" and CEPS Special Report No. 102, https://www.ceps.eu/system/files/SR102_ISDS.pdf, accessed 30 November 2015.

Risks and Opportunities for the EU Agri-Food Sector in a Possible EU-US Trade Agreement, 2014, DG for Internal Policies, Policy Department B: Structural and Cohesion Policies, , accessed 30 November 2015.

Rose-Ackerman S., 2013, Precaution, Proportionality, and Cost/Benefit Analysis: False Analogies, "European Journal of Risk Regulation", Volume 4, Issue 2, pp. 281–286.

Siles-Brügge G., 2014, 'Race to the bottom' or setting global standards? Assessing the regulatory impact of the Transatlantic Trade and Investment Partnership (TTIP), accessed 30 November 2015.

Smith E., D. Azoulay, B. Tuncak, 2015, Lower Common Denominator: How the proposed EU-US trade deal threatens to lower standards of protection from toxic chemicals, Center For International Environmental Law.

Suppan S., 2015, Food Import Re-Inspection and the "High Standards" of 21st Century Trade Agreements, http://bit.ly/23bUMk5, accessed 30 November 2015.

Tietje C., F. Baetens, 2014, The Impact of Investor-State-Dispute Settlement (ISDS) in the Transatlantic Trade and Investment Partnership, Study prepared for the Minister for Foreign Trade and Development Cooperation, Ministry of Foreign Affairs, The Netherlands.

UK Faculty of Public Health, 2014, Start Well, Live Better: A Manifesto for the Public's Health, http://bit.ly/1xTtwp2, accessed 30 November 2015.

United Nations Conference on Trade and Development, 2014, Trade and Development Report 2014: global governance and policy space for development, United Nations, New York, http://bit.ly/1Bu3MTZ, accessed 30 November 2015.

United Nations Conference on Trade and Development, 2015, *Recent Trends in IIAS and ISDS*, Issues Note 1, UNCTAD, New York, *http://bit.ly/1B6f44w*, accessed 30 November 2015.

Van Harten G., 2014, Why Arbitrators Not Judges? Comments on the European Commission's Approach to Investor-State Arbitration in TTIP and CETA, Osgoode Hall Law School, York University, Toronto, http://bit.ly/1tZOelD, accessed 30 November 2015.

von Schomberg R., 2012, The Precautionary Principle: Its Use Within Hard and Soft Law, "European Journal of Risk Regulation", Issue 2, pp. 147–156.

Weiss M., 2015, Trading Health? UK Faculty of Public Health Policy Report on the Transatlantic Trade and Investment Partnership. London: Faculty of Public Health, http://bit.ly/1EgZilk, accessed 30 November 2015.

Weiss M., J. Middleton, T. Schrecker, 2014, Warning: TTIP could be hazardous to your health, "Journal of Public Health", Volume 37, Issue 3, pp. 367–369.

World Trade Organisation, 2001, Doha WTO Ministerial: Declaration on the TRIPS agreement and public health http://bit.ly/IXJa04, accessed 30 November 2015.

Paweł Folfas (Warsaw School of Economics)

Chapter 16. Regions in the United States and European Union in the 21st Century – Wealth of Citizens, Convergence Processes and Spatial Dependencies

The forthcoming Transatlantic Trade and Investment Partnership may become a crucial element in post-crisis world economics and politics; consequently, it is worth scrutinising the economic performance of the United States and European Union. The chapter is aimed at answering the question whether absolute income (GDP *per capita*) beta-convergence existed for regions of the United States[1] (US counties) and the EU-28[2] (NUTS 3) during the period 2000–2011[3].

The research[4] is based on econometric models, namely, on the spatial lagged (SLM), spatial error (SEM) and Durbin spatial models, which seem to be better specifications of convergence than the ordinary least squares (OLS) model. Detailed information concerning the applied econometric tools is included in Section 1, while Section 2 contains estimation results.

1. Methodology and data

Since in this chapter absolute income beta-convergence among regions is investigated, I used the following equation proposed by Baumol (1986):

$$(1/n)\ln(y_{i,1}/y_{i,0}) = \alpha + \beta \ln y_{i,0} + \varepsilon_i, \tag{1}$$

1 For studies on convergence among US regions, see, e.g.: Genc et al. (2011), Higgins et al. (2006) and Rey et al. (1999).

2 For studies on convergence among EU regions, see, e.g.: Mikulić et al. (2013), Misiak, Jabłoński (2013), Paas et al. (2007) and Supińska (2013).

3 During the period 2000–2011 the European Union obviously did not consist of 28 Member States, but these 28 states had been integrating with each other since the early 1990s (because of participation in various RTAs and support via pre-accession EU funds).

4 The project is funded by the National Science Centre of Poland based on decision No. DEC-2013/11/B/HS4/02126.

where $y_{i,0}$ and $y_{i,1}$ correspond to the GDP *per capita* of region i at the initial and final year, respectively, and n is the number of years in the analysed period. Whenever a negative and statistically significant relation was found between the initial GDP *per capita* level and the corresponding growth rate, we could assume the presence of absolute income beta-convergence (variable $y_{i,0}$ is statistically significant and the parameter β is negative, thus the annual speed of convergence equals: $[-\ln(1 + n\beta)]/n$).

Convergence equations can be estimated by ordinary or non-linear least squares (OLS or NLS) methods; however, they do not include the possible spatial dependencies between regions. Instead, I used spatial estimation techniques, namely, the spatial lagged model (SLM) and spatial error model (SEM). I also implemented the following estimation procedure. First, I checked the existence of spatial dependencies by use of a statistical test (e.g., Moran test, Lagrange multiplier test). Second, if the tests showed spatial dependencies, I introduced a special spatial component to the equation—matrix $\boldsymbol{W}$—which reflects the spatial relations between the analysed regions. More precisely, it shows how pairs of regions relate to each other. I applied a common border matrix (a binary matrix with values equalling "1" when the regions are neighbours and "0" otherwise). Third, I estimated the SLM and SEM and compared their quality using information criteria and results of previous statistical tests (Kopczewska 2006, pp. 123–142).

Spatial lagged model includes external spillover as a result of economic growth in other regions (namely neighbouring regions). In SLM, spatial dependence is introduced to the equation through a spatially lagged dependent variable. Matrix $\boldsymbol{W}$ in this type of model is included together with the spatial lag of the dependent variable, as presented in equation (2):

$$y_i = \beta_i \boldsymbol{X}_i + \rho \boldsymbol{W} y_j + u_i \qquad u \sim \mathrm{IIDN}(0,1), \tag{2}$$

where y_i and y_j correspond to the dependent variable in region i and in neighbouring regions j, respectively, and $\boldsymbol{X}$ is the set of independent variables. The Rho-parameter (ρ) is the spatial coefficient and is used to assess the existence and strength of spatial relations. If it is significant, a dependent variable is explained not only by the domestic determinants but also by factors stemming from external (neighbouring) regions. However, spillover may result from many other factors not captured by the SLM model. To incorporate the effect of unknown sources of spillover, I use the spatial error model. In this model, spillover becomes a part of the error term component and spatial dependency is revealed in error terms, i.e., the error terms are correlated and show spatial covariance.

In spatial error models, matrix W is introduced to the error term equation, as shown in equation (3):

$$y_i = \beta_i X_i + u_i, \text{ where } \qquad u_i = \lambda W u_i + \varepsilon_i \qquad \varepsilon_i \sim \text{IIDN}(0,1), \tag{3}$$

where Wu_i is the spatial lagged error term, ε_i is the random error term of the model, and λ is a coefficient introduced to satisfy the random error terms assumption. This assumption shows to what extent shocks in neighbouring regions are transferred to the analysed region (Kopczewska 2006, pp. 132–133).

Finally, spatial Durbin models were estimated. These models include both spatial lag and error and therefore are probably the most universal spatial econometric tools.

The samples analysed contained 3,130 US regions (all US counties and county equivalents[5], apart from those without neighbouring regions on land) and 1,252 NUTS 3[6] regions belonging to the 28 EU Member States (all NUTS 3 regions except for those without neighbouring regions on land). The selection of regions was made to compare similar areas (see Fig. 1). In addition, the average number of neighbouring regions for each region in the United States and in the European Union is similar as well at 5.85 and 5.13, respectively. Data concerning GDP *per capita* are extracted from BEA [<http://bea.gov/> accessed 13 June 2015] and Eurostat [Eurostat <http://ec.europa.eu/eurostat> accessed 13 June 2015] databases, respectively.

---

5 In the United States, a county is a political and geographic subdivision of a state. Of the 50 US states, 48 are divided into a total of 3,007 counties. Instead of counties, Louisiana is divided into 64 parishes, which are functionally identical to counties. Alaska is divided into 19 organized boroughs and a single Unorganized Borough. The United States Census Bureau has divided the Unorganized Borough of Alaska into 11 census areas for federal census and planning purposes. In addition to counties, the states of Virginia, Maryland, Missouri, and Nevada have 41 independent cities that are not part of any county. The Census Bureau and the Office of Management and Budget consider the 64 parishes, 19 organized boroughs, 11 census areas, 41 independent cities, and the District of Columbia, though not the Unorganized Borough of Alaska, to be equivalent to counties for statistical purposes. To sum up, in the United States, there are 3,142 counties and county equivalents.

6 The current NUTS 2013 classification, valid since 1 January 2015, lists 98 regions at the NUTS 1 level, 276 regions at NUTS 2, and 1,342 regions at the NUTS 3 level. The NUTS classification (Nomenclature of territorial units for statistics) is a hierarchical system for dividing the economic territory of the EU for the purpose of: (1) the collection, development and harmonisation of European regional statistics; (2) socio-economic analyses of regions (NUTS 1: major socio-economic regions; NUTS 2: basic regions for the application of regional policies; NUTS 3: small regions for specific diagnoses); (3) framing of EU regional policies.

Figure 1. 3130 US counties and 1252 EU-28 NUTS 3 regions (scale: 1 cm ≈ 270 km)

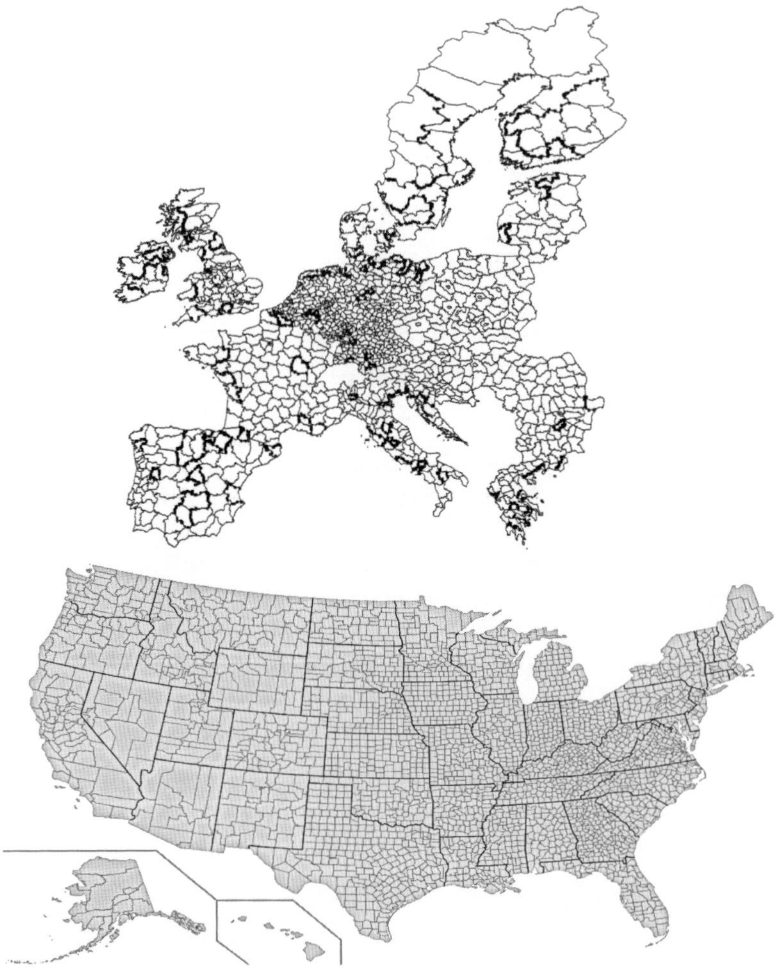

Source: own presentation; maps generated in R CRAN.

2. Estimation results

According to the estimation procedure (described in Section 1), I started with statistical tests examining the spatial dependencies between the US and EU regions (see Table 1). These tests confirmed the existence of spatial dependencies and pointed out that the spatial error model is better than the spatial lagged model to explain them. In the case of the United States, SEM is unequivocally better than SLM, but for the EU-28 there is a slight difference between the quality of SEM and SLM. Information criteria reveal that for the EU-28 regions, SLM is much better than SEM. Consequently, SEM estimation results for the United States and SLM estimation results for the European Union can be treated as the most adequate.

Table 1. Results of tests for spatial dependencies

	US	EU-28
Moran I test	0.1293308910***	0.3963877841***
LM test for SLM	135.8503***	434.7724***
LM test for SEM	143.393***	436.7111***
Robust LM test for SLM	0.0212	74.2054***
Robust LM test for SEM	7.5639**	76.1441***

***/** denotes statistical significance at level 0.001/0.01.
Source: own study based on estimation in R CRAN.

Next I estimated OLS models although they do not include spatial dependencies between regions (Table 2). As a result, the quality of these models is lacklustre (very low value of R^2). They confirm existence of absolute income beta-convergence and the speed of convergence is higher for EU-28 regions than for regions in the United States.

Table 2. Results of OLS models of absolute convergence

	US	EU-28
Intercept	0.2052541***	0.2485320***
$\ln y_0$	-0.0169098***	-0.0229645***
R^2	0.08379	0.01365
Adjusted R^2	0.0835	0.6618
F-statistic	286.1***	2449***
AIC	-18653	-7194.3

***/** denotes statistical significance at level 0.001/0.01.
Source: own study based on estimation in R CRAN.

Also SLM and SEM confirm absolute income beta-convergence for both the American and European regions (Tables 3 and 4). As mentioned above, the most proper comparison of convergence speed is to compare the annual speed of convergence stemming from SEM for US counties and from SLM for European NUTS 3 regions (grey column in Tables 3 and 4).

Table 3. Results of SLM of absolute convergence

	US	EU-28
Intercept	0.19232499***	0.1484877***
$ln\ y_0$	-0.01659583***	-0.0140344***
ρ	0.27912***	0.50173***
Wald-statistic	123.01***	503.68***
AIC	-18768	-7612.3
LogLik	9388.15	3810.135

***/** denotes statistical significance at level 0.001/0.01.
Source: own study based on estimation in R CRAN.

Convergence speed accounts for about 1.90 percent and 1.54 percent respectively. During the period 2000–2011, the average annual speed of convergence among US regions was faster than between regions of the EU-28. But EU-28 regions are characterized by stronger spatial dependencies than regions of the United States (see Rho-parameter values in the SLM comparison).

Table 4. Results of SEM of absolute convergence

	US	EU-28
Intercept	0.20579953***	0.20227444***
$ln\ y_0$	-0.01696100***	-0.01818721***
λ	0.29173***	0.63809***
Wald-statistic	127.94***	603.98***
AIC	-18774	-7570
LogLik	9390.773	3788.996

***/** denotes statistical significance at level 0.001/0.01.
Source: own study based on estimation in R CRAN.

Also, the estimation in the Durbin spatial models, combining the ideas of SLM and SEM brought similar results (Table 5). During the period between 2000 and 2011, the average annual speed of convergence among US regions was faster than between the regions of the EU-28 (1.90 percent and 1.78 percent per annum respectively). But, as noted earlier, the EU-28 regions are characterized by stronger spatial dependencies than regions of the United States (see Rho-parameter values).

Table 5. Results of Durbin spatial model of absolute convergence.

	US	EU-28
Intercept	0.14921261 ***	0.11717139***
$ln\ y_0$	-0.01695825 ***	-0.01599379***
lag $ln\ y_0$	0.00460232***	0.00498002***
ρ	0.29175 ***	0. 58479 ***
Wald-statistic	127.96***	440.78***
AIC	-18772	-7635.5
LogLik	9390.789	3822.746

***/** denotes statistical significance at level 0.001/0.01.
Source: own study based on estimation in R CRAN.

Growth in one region was related to about 34 percent of the pace of growth of surrounding areas in the case of the European NUTS 3 regions and to only about nine percent of growth in the US counties. It is likely that the number and size of the regions influence the results concerning spatial dependencies. However, the selection of regions was aimed at reducing as much as possible the power of this impact. Consequently, the European spatial dependencies appear to be stronger than the American ones. This fact is also confirmed by Moran's global statistics[7] (see Appendix).

Conclusions

To sum up, the SEM and Durbin spatial models are able to detect absolute income beta-convergence in regions of the US and EU-28 at the beginning of the 21st century. Between the years 2000 and 2011, the average annual speed of convergence among regions in the US was faster than between regions of the EU-28. Simultaneously, the EU-28 regions are characterized by stronger spatial dependencies than the regions of the United States. In this context, the forthcoming TTIP appears to be a positive impulse for the European Union to improve the speed of convergence among its regions.

7 Moran' s global statistics is a basic measure of spatial autocorrelation.

References

Baumol W., 1986, Productivity growth, convergence and welfare: what the long-run data show?, "American Economic Review", 76(5), 1072–1085.

BEA, http://bea.gov/, accessed 13 June 2015.

Eurostat, http://ec.europa.eu/eurostat, accessed 13 June 2015.

Genc I. H., J. R. Miller , A. Rupasingha, , 2011, Stochastic convergence tests for US regional per capita personal income; some further evidence: a research note, "The Annals of Regional Science", 46(2), pp. 369–377.

Higgins M. J., D. Levy, A. T. Young, 2006, Growth and convergence across the US: Evidence from county level data, "The Review of Economics and Statistics", 88(4), pp. 671–681.

Kopczewska K., 2006, Ekonometria i statystyka przestrzenna z wykorzystaniem programu R CRAN, Wydawnictwo CeDeWu, Warszawa.

Mikulić D., Ž. Lovrinčević, A. G. Nagyszombaty, 2013, Regional convergence in the European Union, new Member States and Croatia, "South East European Journal of Economics and Business", 8(1), p.p. 7–19.

Misiak T., Ł. Jabłoński, 2013, Realna konwergencja między regionami Unii Europejskiej w latach 1995–2008, "Studia Prawno-Ekonomiczne", 88, pp. 267–292.

Paas T., A. Kuusk, F. Schlitte, A. Võrk, 2007, Econometric analysis of income convergence in selected EU countries and their NUTS 3 level regions, University of Tartu – Faculty of Economics and Business Administration Working Paper Series, 60, pp. 1–56.

Rey S. J., B. D. Montouri 1999, US Regional Income Convergence: A Spatial Econometric Perspective, "Regional Studies", 33(2), pp. 143–156.

Supińska J., 2013, Does human factor matter for economic growth? Determinants of economic growth process in CEE countries in light of spatial theory, "Bank i Kredyt", 44(5), pp. 505–532.

Appendix

Plots illustrating Moran's global statistics for GDP *per capita* (in standardized values) in 2000 and 2011 (*y2000.std* and *y2011.std*)

EU-28, NUTS 3

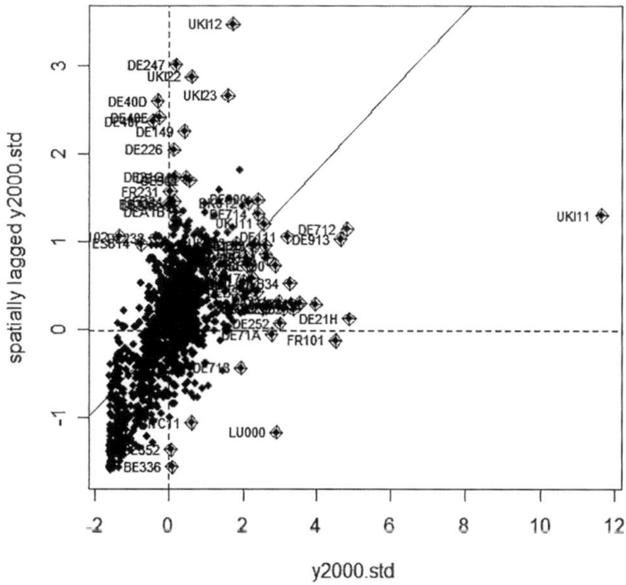
spatially lagged y2000.std
y2000.std
-2
0
2
4
6
8
10
12
-1
1
3
UKI12
DE247
UKI23
DE40D
DE149
DE226
FR231
DE712
DE913
UKI11
DE21H
DE252
FR101
LU000
BE336

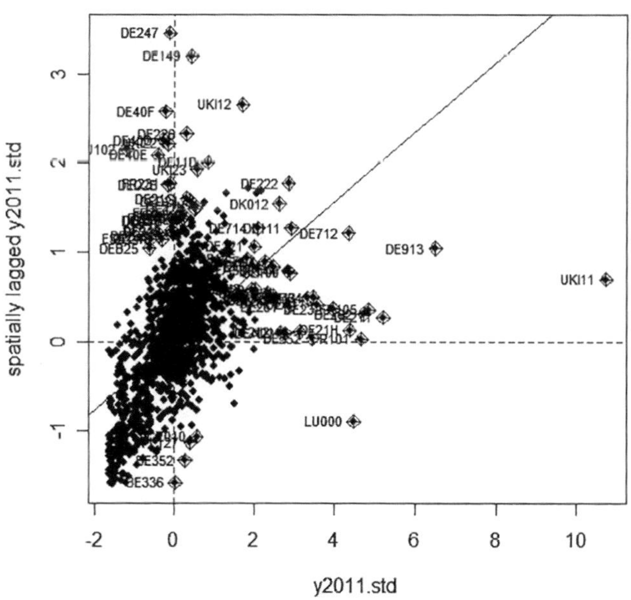
spatially lagged y2011.std
y2011.std
-2
0
2
4
6
8
10
-1
1
3
DE247
DE149
DE40F
UKI12
DE40E
UKI23
DE222
DK012
DE712
DE913
UKI11
DEB25
LU000
BE352
BE336

US, counties and their equivalents

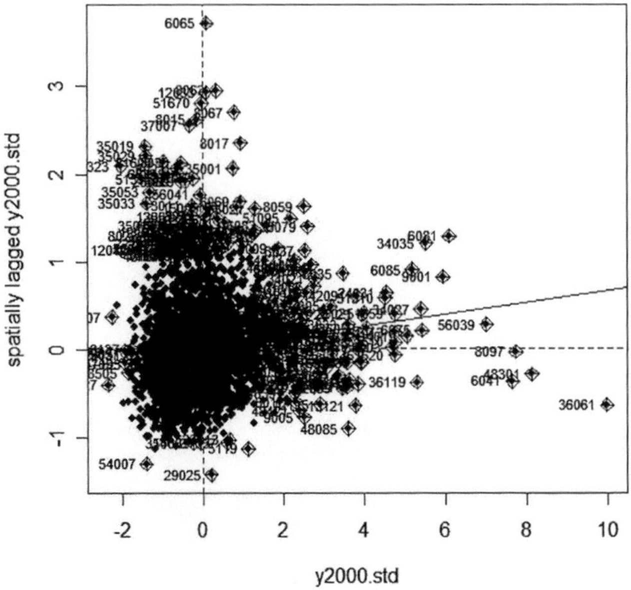

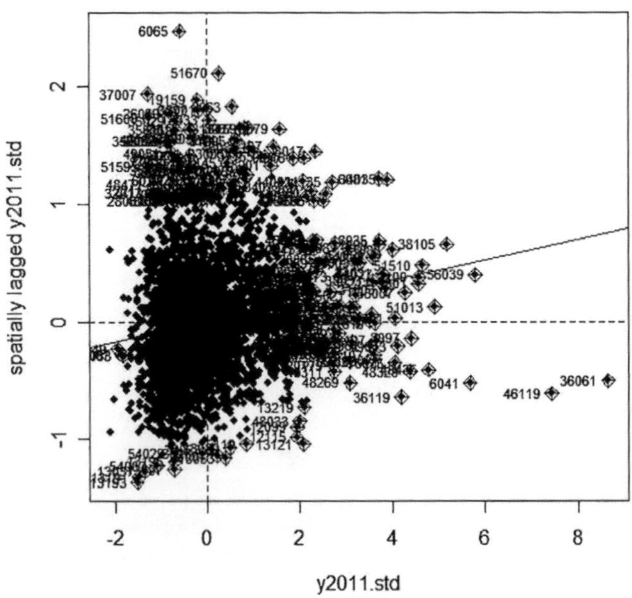

Bartosz Michalski (University of Wrocław)

Chapter 17. Trade Deals with the US. What Can We Learn from the Aussie Case?

The structure of the world economy from the beginning of the 21st century has been the subject of significant changes. Research on the nature of contemporary trade regionalism has to be anchored in the current institutional crisis of the World Trade Organisation (WTO).

An important dimension of proliferating regional trade agreements (RTAs) is their geopolitical meaning. They serve as vehicles that increase the level of representation of the Global South, boost economic integration in a more controlled way and compete for the position of an agenda-setter at fora of international economic organisations. Hence, political frustration resulting from the lack of substantial achievements by the WTO makes regional trade agreements more and more attractive and creates a new sphere of strategic rivalry for contemporary economic superpowers (United States, European Union, China) (see He, Sappideen 2013). Consequently, negotiated rules can sooner or later become a standard that others will have to follow. This seems to be the main purpose of the heatedly debated Trans-Pacific Partnership (TTP) and the Trans-Atlantic Trade and Investment Partnership (TTIP) which through their comprehensive character promote and reinforce the US approach to rules that lay out international trading regime (see Capling, Ravenhill 2013). By using the classical concept of free trade they impose new kinds of subtle obstacles or produce "unintended consequences" that result from harmonisation and standardisation of non-tariff measures whose main purpose seems to be aimed at benefiting multinational corporations (see more: Gagne 2014, van Tigerstrom 2013, Gleeson, Friel 2013, Ranald 2011, Searles 2009).

1. Structure and methodological remarks

The first section of this chapter provides an analysis of general long-term tendencies in trade relations between Australia and the US as well as focuses on identification of product clusters which are meant to be long-run winners and losers under the framework of AUSFTA.

For the purpose of the research, data of the International Trade Centre (Trade Map 2015) have been used. They cover detailed trade numbers between the US and Australia in 2001–2014 in particular sectors and product clusters on the 2-, 4- and 6-digit disaggregation level according to the Harmonised System (HS). In order to provide an extensive analysis of technological intensity of the Australian exports and imports to and from the US, the author converted the approach defined by UNCTAD (2012), which classifies particular groups of traded goods according to their production factor intensity (resource-intensive, labour-intensive, low-tech, mid-tech, high-tech and unclassified) based on the Standard International Trade Classification (SITC), into the one coherent with the Harmonised System.

Another research method applied was the calculation of the Grubel-Lloyd index (Grubel, Lloyd 1971) which is essential to identify the evolution of the US-Australian intra-industry trade (IIT) and its sub-categories (horizontal, vertical-high quality and vertical-low quality IIT).

The second section of the chapter discusses issues that tend to be neglected in *sensu stricto* economic analyses: political backdrop, social debate and international pressures that rationalise trade negotiations and interests in closing deals with strategic partners. That is why in the author's opinion the perspective of international political economy offers invaluable insights that can be treated as a lesson on how to avoid certain traps while attempting to negotiate new trade agreements and standardise non-tariff measures, which are considered to be the most devious tools hampering international trade.

2. General characteristics of the Australia-United States Free Trade Agreement (AUSFTA)

The analysed agreement was signed on 18 May 2004 and entered into force on 1 January 2005. It is worth emphasising that the accord was notified to the WTO just a few days earlier (22 December 2004), which from the perspective of contemporary knowledge and experiences may be meant just as a necessary fulfilment of a formal obligation of two WTO member states, even though the WTO Committee on Regional Trade Agreements was at that time supposed to examine – not only to consider as it is today – the notified deals.

From the very beginning both parties were striving towards a high quality, cutting-edge agreement which would pave the way for negotiations of the Doha Development Agenda and accelerate deeper economic integration in the Asia-Pacific region under the framework of APEC. Another vital aspect was also the enforcement of the US. Trade Representative Robert Zoellick's idea of competitive liberalisation. In the broader context, it was also an alternative through which the US has resisted the European Union model of linking trade accords with large-scale public resource transfers from richer to poorer countries and regions (Feinberg 2003). Officially, as the preamble puts it, both parties were aiming at reinforcing the long-standing ties of friendship, strengthening economic relations, further trade and investment liberalisation, encouraging a closer economic partnership, promoting transparent and consistent business environment, fostering innovation and promoting stronger links between dynamic sectors.

As a final result of the negotiation process the following areas were covered by legal provisions: competition, dispute settlement, environmental issues, government procurement, intellectual property rights, labour, rules of origin, safeguard measures, sanitary and phytosanitary measures, subsidies, tariff-rate quota, technical regulations, standards, technical barriers to trade, domestic regulation and mutual recognition (two latter in services) (see more: WTO 2015; Bennett 2005).

The period for full implementation was extended to 18 years (until 2023, mostly for politically sensitive products: diary, sugar, beef; cf. provisions of the Article XXIV GATT), which was criticised by the European Communities as a step backwards in terms of market openness (WTO 2005) and thus inconsistent with an ambitious public image of the agreement itself.

Interest groups supporting the deal were obviously corporate actors for whom it would create a platform for foreign investments (Australia as a safe harbour on the way to Asia-Pacific) and new cooperation networks, sustaining competitive potential and emphasising enforcement of the US approach to intellectual property rights, using at the same time experience of negotiations with Chile and Singapore (Stoler 2004; see also Ranald 2006).

3. Identification of long-term trade effects

While investigating data covering the US-Australian trade in the period 2001–2014 one can easily come to the conclusion that AUSFTA did not generate the expected results (see figure 1). The most striking fact is that despite constantly growing volume of bilateral trade the share of the US in Australian exports and imports was dropping. As far as the first one is concerned its growth was rather symbolic and was undergoing steady fluctuations, while the latter grew (45.9%) between 2005–2014, albeit it was still considerably lower than the growth of global imports (76.9%). Probably this may have been brought about by the trade expansion of both countries with dynamically growing South and East Asia, especially with China.

Figure 1. Australian exports and imports to and from the US (USD bn), 2001–2014

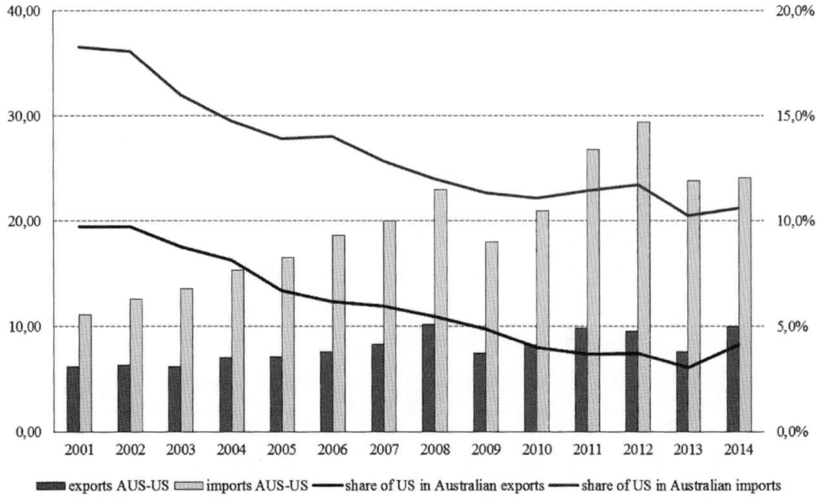

Source: author's calculations based on Trade Map 2015.

Australian deficit in trade with the US was mainly driven by a discrepancy in the technological intensity of bilateral trade flows (see figures 2 and 3). While Australian goods exported to the US were agricultural and mining products (unclassified in terms of technological intensity; the most significant Australian high-tech goods were wheat gluten, medicament mixtures, office machines, aircraft parts, mechanotherapy appliances), its counterpart was dominating in mid-tech (cars, trucks, parts and accessories of motor vehicles) and high-tech product clusters (medicament mixtures, automatic data processing machines, aircraft, electromedical apparatus). An obvious issue is also a huge discrepancy of their economic potentials: the largest economy in the world vs. the 12th one (Australian GDP being equivalent to 8.35% of the US).

Figure 2. Technological intensity of the Australian exports to the US, 2001–2014

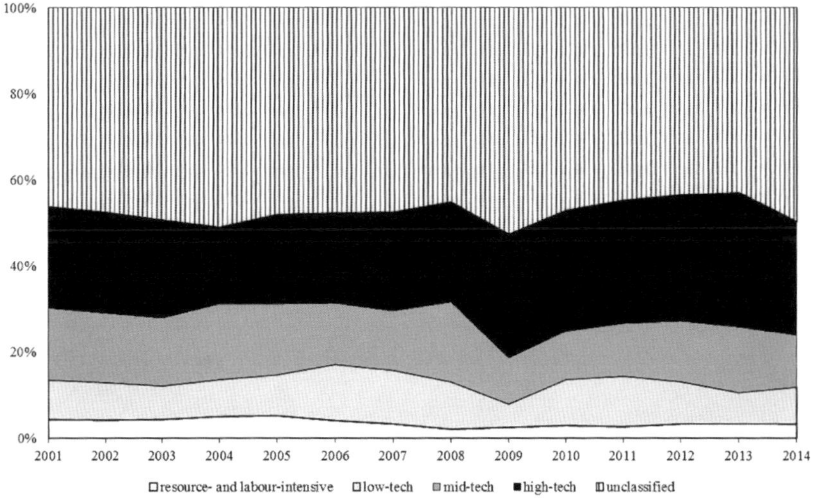

Source: author's calculations based on Trade Map 2015.

Figure 3. Technological intensity of the Australian imports from the US, 2001–2014

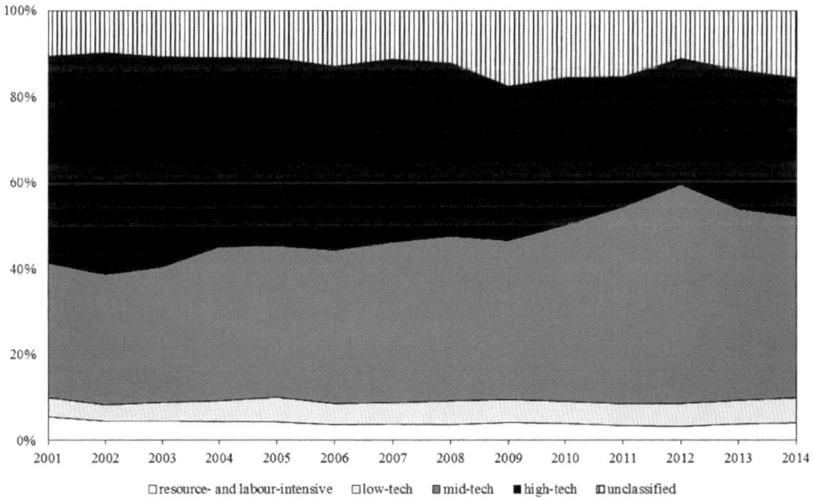

Source: author's calculations based on Trade Map 2015.

As far as intensity of intra-industry trade is concerned, the GL-index calculated for the trade relations between Australia and the US has been gradually dropping from the year 2001 (22.52 percent) reaching the value of 16.01 percent in 2014 (see figure 4). Therefore AUSFTA did not serve as a tool encouraging creation of more intensive cooperation networks, because competitive advantages of the Australian and US producers differ across sectors. Even if there are some stronger specific corporate linkages in industries like motor vehicles, aircraft or pharmaceuticals, their shares remain far too small to positively affect existing structure of bilateral trade.

Figure 4. Intensity of the Australian-US intra-industry trade (GL-index), 2001–2014

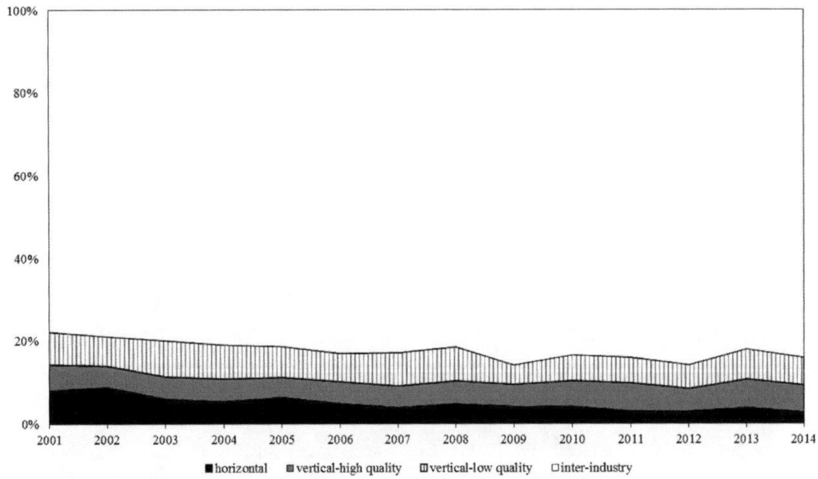

Source: author's calculations based on Trade Map 2015.

The general outlook presented here needs to be supplemented with a more detailed analysis of particular sectors (product clusters) which may be considered as long-term losers and winners after AUSFTA entered into force. Identification of the losers is based on the selection of clusters which had the share higher than one percent in 2005 in the Australian exports/imports to/from the US and which dropped more than 25 percent, so they lost their relative importance. Winners are these clusters which reached the share of over one percent in 2014 in the Australian exports/imports to/from the US while exceeding 100 percent growth rate between 2004–2015 (see tables 1 and 2).

What one can identify is that among the Australian companies which suffered the most from these new circumstances are both primary sectors (agriculture: mainly wine producers; mining: aluminium) as well as mid-tech and high-tech industries (respectively cars and pharmaceuticals). The Australian winners operate in agriculture (meat of bovine animals), mining (gold) and high-tech sectors only. As far as the US companies are concerned, the loser is the aircraft and spacecraft industry (high-tech sector), while the winners are car makers (mid-tech sector).

These results indicate clearly which industries have to be recognised as the most important stakeholders and which issues may have been raised and debated while assessing potential multifaceted impact of AUSFTA on the Australian economy, society and political life.

Table 1. Australian long-term losers and winners in trade with the US, 2005–2014

		Australian losers		
HS code	**product cluster**	**share in 2005 [%]**	**share in 2014 [%]**	**change 2005–2014 [%]***
2204	Wine of fresh grapes	9.79	4.07	-41.56
2709	Crude petroleum oils	3.08	0.60	-72.62
3004	Medicament mixtures (not 3002, 3005, 3006), put in dosage	2.49	1.20	-32.10
7601	Unwrought aluminium	1.61	0.67	-41.53
8703	Cars	3.97	0.91	-67.63
9504	Articles for funfair, table/ parlour games	1.51	0.15	-85.70
		Australian winners		
0201	Meat of bovine animals, fresh or chilled	1.90	5.38	297.98
0202	Meat of bovine animals, frozen	11.16	16.68	110.21
1109	Wheat gluten, dried and not dried	0.44	1.94	521.21
7108	Unwrought gold or in semi-manufactured forms	0.05	1.01	2490.95
8517	Electric appliance for line telephony	0.29	1.56	661.09
8803	Aircraft parts	2.61	6.68	259.51
9021	Orthopaedic appliance	0.97	1.92	177.32

* calculated as a change of trade value between respective years.
Source: author's calculations based on Trade Map 2015.

Table 2. US long-term losers and winners in trade with Australia, 2005–2014

US losers				
HS code	**product cluster**	**share in 2005 [%]**	**share in 2014 [%]**	**change 2005–2014 [%]***
2934	Heterocyclic compounds	1.90	0.02	-98.14
8473	Parts & accessories for computers & office machines	1.30	0.27	-70.07
8701	Tractors	2.12	0.97	-33.53
8802	Aircraft & spacecraft	4.49	0.06	-98.00
8803	Aircraft parts	2.73	0.35	-81.48
US winners				
4011	New pneumatic tires, rubber tires	0.58	1.34	238.37
7108	Unwrought gold or in semi-manufactured forms	0.19	1.42	960.04
8411	Turbo-jets, turbo--propellers and other gas turbines	1.22	2.29	174.24
8413	Pumps for liquids; liquid elevators	0.68	1.07	129.16
8431	Machinery parts	0.89	1.27	107.22
8481	Tap, cock, valve for pipe, tank etc.	0.92	1.46	132.27
8703	Cars	1.95	8.29	521.40

* calculated as a change of trade value between respective years.
Source: author's calculations based on Trade Map 2015.

4. Political context and controversies

Among the main reasons explaining and rationalising AUSFTA one has to be highlighted as it does not refer to purely economic reasoning. It is acknowledged that the strategic aim rooted in the political context of that time was to reward Australian support for the US during the war on terror (Stoler 2004; see more Beeson 2003). One of the greatest risks associated with this approach was that AUSFTA would enhance the perception amongst Asian neighbours that Australia's interests lie outside the region; the fact that would further marginalise Australia in regional initiatives, and possibly lead to retaliatory action from countries concerned about the trade-diverting impact of such an agreement (Garnaut 2002, Beeson 2003).

Analogically, it would then be highly desired to identify contemporary common global challenges shared by the EU and the US (i.e. rising China containment). This could help communicate more efficiently with numerous critics of the TTIP and evaluate potential economic and political costs of such policy, especially by exerting peer pressure on the WTO forum and simultaneously building an extensive network of regional trade agreements and strategic partnerships standardising trade with the loyal East and South Asian allies willing to enhance cooperation based on the norms determined by the EU-US leadership.

This in turn would prove one of the crucial arguments that many economic analyses deliberately overlook and which nowadays is an undeniable fact, that contemporary free trade agreements have very little to do with economic motives (see Capling 2005). Having said that, there is an alluring, but politically risky trade-off between issues of strategic trade policy aiming at increasing national welfare and security agenda being one of the most relevant factors of foreign policy making.

An additional intellectual challenge in terms of attempts aimed at identification of potential costs and benefits is that they remain immeasurable. Provided studies are founded on simplifications and unrealistic assumptions so that they are incapable of explaining potential impacts by using too broad a macroeconomic perspective, instead of putting a stronger emphasis on more focused, sector-oriented research. In other words, their credibility is substantially limited, especially as it comes to econometric modelling, which – as the Australian case shows – may not often pass the laugh test (see Stoler 2004, Capling 2005, Ranald 2006).

Doubts are also associated with the source of funding provided for such research. It is quite difficult to imagine that political bodies pushing for the deal would be interested in results weakening their position and beliefs on the positive nature of the negotiated agreement. The situation becomes even more complicated if political leaders try to make use of the trade deal as a tool for leveraging proposed reforms and rationalise them through the reference mainly to external expectations and image of a country and by highlighting the gravity of international ridicule: "Everyone will laugh at us if we refuse to notify the deal" (Weiss, Thurbon, Mathews 2004).

Another issue which needs to be emphasised are controversies over the US approach to the enforcement of intellectual property rights. These matters can affect important aspects of everyday life, as they cover access to cheaper medicine/generics (pricing policy and governmental subsidising under the framework of the Australian Pharmaceutical Benefit Scheme; see more PBS 2015), labelling of genetically modified food (full information provided for consumers vs. generating unnecessary fears on the quality and potential negative impact, especially when results of research are not available nor fully convincing) as well as pressure for change of specific sanitary and phytosanitary regulations (Australian quarantine). Certain controversies relate also to the period of legal protection of copyrights after the death of the author. This is why the US Copyright Term Extension Act was named the "Mickey Mouse Act," following the observation that the term of copyright is extended whenever the Disney copyright on Mickey is about to lapse (Quiggin 2015).

The Australian debate on the essence and nature of AUSFTA produced also a great deal of critical academic insights out of which one position – Weiss, Thurbon, Mathews (2004) – deserves particular attention, as it provides universal characteristics, if not a pattern for studies embarking on the multidimensional evaluation of potential consequences of contemporary trade agreements with the US. In general, any economic superpower may use its competence advantage in the negotiation process and firmly insist on enforcement of legal provisions favouring economic interest of its main stakeholders which in most cases are multinational corporations. This in turn often goes together with non-transparent negotiations and sparks further criticism on the impact of actors who are not democratically accountable for the final outcome. Paradoxically, on the one hand imperatives of civil society make officials inform everyone expressing their interests in the case, while on the other it may slow down the process of problem solving, reaching compromise, and limit best alternatives to a negotiated agreement.

The list mentioned above consists of the following warnings (Weiss, Thurbon, Mathews 2004):

1) Prepare a trade deal with the world's most powerful country, the one with the biggest track record of negotiating favourable FTAs: this idea suggests a misguided belief of a special relationship which should result in preferential treatment and/or mostly positive consequences of economic integration;
2) Take one of your most valuable sectors and undermine its key competitive advantage by dismantling safeguards against pests and diseases: the Australian quarantine system and strict regulations when entering this country are meant to be an effective measure protecting agriculture;
3) Make it impossible for the government to continue subsidising pharmaceuticals by making way for foreign drug companies to charge full monopoly prices

for their products. As explained above, this issue refers to the social security through economically affordable medicine which is confronted with private profits gained by multinational corporations;

4) Do away with a tried and true method of domestic industry promotion (public purchasing policy), making it harder for domestic firms to gain a foothold in the domestic or international market. In other words, it is about abandoning "buy Australian" norms in favour of "buy American" which clearly suggests that competitive advantages of particular sector may usually differ, so the decision on when and how to open them for international competition should be the subject of detailed case-by-case studies;
5) Substitute a world-class system of intellectual property protection and regulation for that of a foreign power. This would in turn stifle independent production of knowledge and culture in favour of American production;
6) Buy, bully or browbeat all those who would seek to challenge the damaging deal, closing off public scrutiny and debate and setting one sector against another. The old principle divide-and-conquer politics remains valid as an indirect, sometimes subtle measure which helps convince silent, but incompetent majority. However, if it does not work, just hammer your critics.

Conclusions

Experiences drawn from the case of the US trade agreements, especially the one with Australia, might be of great value, if the negotiators and various stakeholders were able to agree what their common strategic goals were. This approach should be deeply rooted in a strategic culture which would require an ongoing debate on long-term consequences and a wide democratic participation. The situation when business interests are more preferred, simply because international trade and related issues are their everyday practice, cannot be accepted, mainly because it raises doubts why and for what reason trade talks are kept secret.

Developing strategic culture would also be beneficial for the quality of further, more in-depth studies which would in turn provide additional competence pressure on political decision makers—lest we forget the limited credibility of econometric modelling for the reason that numbers may be tortured as long as they confess to everything.

As far as external pressure is concerned, it is worth emphasising that contemporary trade agreements can be treated increasingly as solutions complementary to former military treaties and are being used to securitise new types of threats emerging today. Trade issues merely provide the decorum which serves the purpose of a far more important non-economic agenda.

If this is the case, the question arises whether we will feel safer and economically stronger with the US companies being present with their products and investing in our country. This relatively new kind of strategic dilemma, posed by the possible trade-offs between issues of foreign and security policy and more down-to-earth problems, needs to be addressed properly.

References

Beeson M., 2003, Australia's relationship with the United States: the case for greater independence, "Australian Journal of Political Science", Vol. 38, Issue 3, November.

Bennett A., 2005, 'Guide to the Australia-United States Free Trade Agreement', CCH Australia Ltd., Sydney.

Capling A., 2005, All the way with the USA, UNSW Press, Sydney.

Capling A., J. Ravenhill, 2013, Symposium: Australia-US Economic Relations and the Regional Balance of Power Australia, the United States and the Trans-Pacific Partnership: Diverging Interests and Unintended Consequences, "Australian Journal of Political Science", Vol. 48, Issue 2, June.

Feinberg R. E., 2003, The Political Economy of United States' Free Trade Arrangements, "The World Economy", Vol. 26, Issue 7, July.

Gagne G., 2014, Free Trade, Cultural Policies and Digital Revolution: Evidence from the US FTAs with Australia and South Korea, "Asian Journal of WTO and International Health and Law Policy", Vol. 9, Issue 1, March.

Garnaut R., 2002, An Australia-United States free trade agreement, "Australian Journal of International Affairs", Vol. 56, Issue 1.

Gleeson D., S. Friel, 2013, Emerging threats to public health from regional trade agreements, "The Lancet", Vol. 381, Issue 9876, April.

Grubel H. G., P. J. Lloyd, 1971, The Empirical Measurement of Intra-Industry Trade, " Economic Record", Vol. 47, Issue 4, December.

He L. L., R. Sappideen, 2013, Free Trade Agreements and the US-China-Australia Relationship in the Asia-Pacific Region, "Asia Pacific Law Review", Vol. 21, Issue 1.

PBS, 2015, http://www.pbs.gov.au/info/about-the-pbs, accessed 15 November 2015.

Quiggin J., 2015, A completely misleading description, http://evatt.org.au/papers/completely-misleading-description.html, accessed 15 November 2015.

Ranald P., 2006, The Australia-US Free Trade Agreement: A Contest of Interests, "Journal of Australian Political Economy", No. 57, June.

Ranald P., 2011, The Trans-Pacific Partnership Agreement: Contradictions in Australia and in the Asia Pacific Region, "Economic and Labour Relations Review", Vol. 22, Issue 1, May.

Searles A., 2009, The PBS in a globalised world: free trade and reference pricing, "Australian Health Review", Vol. 33, Issue 2, May.

Stoler A. L., 2004, Australia-US Free Trade: Benefits and Costs of an Agreement, in: Schott, J. J. (ed.), Free Trade Agreements: US Strategies and Priorities, Institute for International Economics, Washington DC.

Trade Map, 2015, http://www.trademap.org/SelectionMenu.aspx, accessed 9 November 2015.

UNCTAD, 2012, http://unctadstat.unctad.org/UnctadStatMetadata/Classifications/Methodology&Classifications.html, accessed 26 October 2012.

Van Tigerstrom B., 2013, How Do International Trade Obligations Affect Policy Options for Obesity Prevention? Lessons from Recent Developments in Trade and Tobacco Control, "Canadian Journal of Diabetes", Vol. 37, Issue 3, June.

Weiss L., E. Thurbon, J. Mathews, 2004, How to kill a country. Australia's devastating trade deal with the United States, Allen&Unwin, Crows Nest.

WTO, 2007, Consideration of the Free Trade Agreement between the United States and Australia, Goods and Services. Note of the Meeting of 13 September 2007, WT/REG184/M/1.

WTO, 2015, http://rtais.wto.org/UI/PublicShowRTAIDCard.aspx?rtaid=41, accessed 9 November 2015.

Julianna Pontet, Beata Udvari[1]
(University of Szeged, University of Szeged)

Chapter 18. The TTIP and Banana Trade from the Aspect of Policy Coherence for Development

The European Union aims at development to ensure economic and social development in developing countries. In order to achieve this objective, the EU seeks to harmonize different policies and tools of international development cooperation (Policy Coherence for Development, PCD). PCD aims to avoid different policies undercutting the objectives of development cooperation and poverty reduction in developing countries, and PCD aims to achieve that various policies and the policy of international development cooperation support each other. In line with these objectives, the EU supports international agreements which are consistent with these principles.

There is no doubt that a future free trade agreement between the EU and the US (TTIP) may affect not only the participants but also third countries including developing countries, our research is therefore focusing on developing countries. Since the EU has a contractual relationship with African, Caribbean and Pacific (ACP) countries, namely the Cotonou Partnership Agreement, in this study we are focusing on these countries. Our aim is to analyze whether the TTIP is a risk for ACP countries or not, and how it may affect the principles of PCD. We strive to answer the research question with analyzing the trends of banana trade because it is a crucial issue in EU-US trade relations (decades old banana dispute), on the one hand, and the largest banana traders are ACP and Latin-American countries, on the other hand. Although the banana war between the EU and the USA was concluded in 2009, the fear that ACP countries are unable to integrate sufficiently into the world economy still exists. In this chapter we highlight with statistical analysis of banana trade how the TTIP and principles of development cooperation can be related to each other and how the TTIP affects the banana trade of ACP countries.

This chapter is structured as follows. The first section describes the policy coherence for development introducing general information and investigating

1 Corresponding author: udvari.beata@eco.u-szeged.hu

its trade aspects. Then we detail the TTIP and provide insights into its potential effects on developing countries. As a case study, we analyze how the TTIP may influence banana trade and whether ACP countries may lose market or not due to the agreement. The chapter ends with the conclusions.

1. Policy Coherence for Development

The EU pays close attention to the underdeveloped situation of developing countries and tries to help them in the framework of its international development cooperation policy. In the last few years, the European Union became one of the largest donors in the world, but the EU provides not only aid to developing countries but also tries to reintegrate developing countries into world trade (Udvari 2013). As a result, trade as a development tool appears in its international development cooperation policy. In order to achieve the aims of the international development cooperation policy, the EU tries to harmonize its policies to avoid any counter effects. This is under the principles of Policy Coherence for Development (hereafter PCD).

The PCD has become crucial in order to improve aid effectiveness. Nevertheless, policies other than the international development cooperation policy may influence the possible results (see Figure 1). Education, trade, taxation and investment policies and practices have a strong influence on aid effectiveness, therefore it is a must to analyze their effects on development policy.

Figure 1. The basic logic of policy coherence for development

Source: own construction

1.1. The role of PCD in the EU

Although we are speaking about the EU's practice, the PCD is not a European notion – it was accepted in the OECD. The OECD defines it as follows (OECD 2012, p. 3): 'Policy coherence means different policy communities working together in ways that result in more powerful tools and products for all concerned. It means looking for synergies and complementarities and filling gaps among different policy areas so as to meet common and shared objectives.' The OECD raises some questions which help in understanding this initiative: 'Do our trade policies reinforce our development co-operation policies, or do they work at cross purposes?' 'Do our migration policies, such as in the health care sector, potentially undermine prospects to achieve health-related MDGs in sending countries?' or 'How can we promote economic growth at the same time as environmental sustainability in the developing world?'

In the European Union, several official documents mention that PCD must be taken into consideration. The first important document titled *Policy Coherence for Development Accelerating progress towards attaining the Millennium Development Goals* was published by the European Commission in 2005. This document claims that 'When exploring ways to accelerate progress towards achieving MDGs, the EU is committed to look beyond the frontiers of development cooperation, and consider the challenge of how non-aid policies can assist developing countries in attaining the MDGs' (EC 2005, pp. 3–4). The document emphasizes trade aspects, too (EC 2005, p. 5): 'The EU is strongly committed to ensuring a development-friendly and sustainable outcome of the Doha Development Agenda and EU-ACP Economic Partnership Agreements (EPAs). The EU will further improve its Generalised System of Preferences, with a view to effectively enhancing developing countries' exports to the EU. The EU will continue to work towards integrating trade into development strategies and will assist developing countries in carrying out domestic reforms where necessary'. The European Consensus on Development – issued also in 2005 – states that development policy goals must be analyzed taking other policies into consideration as well (EC 2006).

The next official document titled '*Increasing the impact of EU Development Policy: an Agenda for Change*' was published in 2011. The Agenda for Change lays down the need for change in international development cooperation and PCD also appears in it as an important principle (EC 2011, p. 11): 'The EU is at the forefront of the Policy Coherence for Development (PCD) agenda and will continue to evaluate the impact of its policies on development objectives. It will strengthen its country-level dialogue on PCD and continue to promote PCD in global fora to help shape an environment that supports the poorest countries' efforts'.

PCD is so important in the EU's practice that the EU publishes annual reports on the achievements of PCD. Furthermore, the EU accepted the Sustainable Development Goals (Post-2015 development goals) in 2015 and among them we can find a reference to the importance for PCD. Goal 17 contains the following sub-goal: Enhance policy coherence for sustainable development[2].

1.2. Trade in the EU's development cooperation

The EU has been playing a great role in promoting development in less developed countries. To achieve this aim, the EU grants not only financial assistance but also trade preferences to the developing countries within the framework of its international development cooperation policy (Udvari 2013). The EU has established relationships with almost all developing countries, but the preferences the EU provides them are different. ACP countries receive the greatest preferences and the most support from the European Union (Persson, Wilhelmsson 2006), meaning these countries are the main beneficiaries of the EU's development policy. The EU-ACP relationship is based on contracts which ensure a high level of security for the contracting parties. The preferences granted by the contracts cover a wide range of products and there are only few restrictions and exemptions (Persson, Wilhelmsson 2006). Currently 79 countries belong to the ACP-group, out of which 48 are situated in Africa[3]. The framework of the EU-ACP relationship started with the Lomé Conventions, but currently the Cotonou Partnership Agreement and its Economic Partnership Agreements are decisive. The main aim of these agreements is to achieve economic development and poverty reduction in the beneficiary developing countries, and to help them participate in world trade. The Cotonou Partnership Agreement lays down that the two pillars of development cooperation remains trade and aid (EC 2000).

To sum up, the European Union emphasizes and supports trade in its international development cooperation policy. Regarding policy coherence for development, it is crucial to analyze whether a trade agreement between the EU and other (developed) partners may influence the trade with developing countries (determined by a multilateral agreement such as the Cotonou Partnership Agreement) or not. From this point of view, our study has a big relevance because it seeks to answer how the TTIP may influence the position of ACP countries in the international market and how the TTIP may affect the principles of PCD. To

2 https://sustainabledevelopment.un.org/focussdgs.html

3 http://europa.eu/legislation_summaries/development/african_caribbean_pacifi c_states/index_en.htm

answer these questions, in the next section we analyze the relationship between the TTIP and banana trade.

2. The TTIP and banana trade

Bananas, just like coffee, sugar, tea and cocoa, are among the most important traded agricultural goods produced by developing or least developed countries—developing countries are the source of the majority of banana production (98 percent), but bananas are consumed by developed states (Kacsirek 2010). The banana sector plays a major role in several developing countries, especially in banana exporting states: in most cases, the export of bananas is the sole export revenue in these countries. Furthermore, this sector also has a dominant role in employment or different policies primarily through the presence of multinational corporations (MNCs). The main actors of international banana trade are ACP and Latin American countries on the producer side and the European Union and the US on the consumer side, thus, possible effects of the TTIP would be a crucial point in developing countries heavily dependent on banana export. Therefore, characteristics of the banana sector and possible effects of the TTIP are analyzed in this section.

2.1. Characteristics of the banana sector

Banana production is a very dynamic sector. Both world production and international trade have increased rapidly in the past few decades: global banana production more than doubled between 1990 and 2013 (from around 47 million tons to 107 million tons) and banana trade shows a similar growth, increasing from 9 million tons to 20 million tons (Anania 2015). The sector is regionally segmented which is true for both the export and import of bananas: international banana trade is highly concentrated between exporter and importer countries or regions (Dodo 2014). The most important banana producer countries are India, Brazil and China but these countries are also consumers. The main exporters are Latin American countries (60 percent of total import) – especially Ecuador, Costa Rica, Colombia, Philippines and Guatemala – and the ACP countries, mainly Cameroon, Ivory Coast, Belize, Dominican Republic (20 percent of total import) (Kacsirek 2010). ACP banana suppliers mainly export bananas to the EU member countries in contrast to Latin American banana exporters who supply the EU as well as the US or Canadian markets (Dodo 2014). In the case of imports, market concentration is even higher than for exports: the two largest banana importers are the European Union (25% of the world market followed by the US with 22%) and other important importers are Japan, Russia and Canada (Anania 2015).

The two largest importers, the EU and the US have different banana import policies. While the US has open and liberal banana import regimes, the EU has tariff-rates quota policy and applies preferential trade treatments (GSP, EPAs) which are based on the Bananas Protocol of the Lomé IV and the Cotonou Partnership Agreement (Dodo 2014). Banana supply in the US comes from Central and South America, so the main banana suppliers of the US are Latin American countries. In contrast, banana supply in the EU comes from three main sources: domestic production, ACP countries and third countries which include primarily Latin American countries (see Figure 2). The EU's import regime for bananas has been protecting firstly domestic and ACP producers from Latin American imports (Anania 2015).

Figure 2. Banana supply in the European Union, 2006–2014

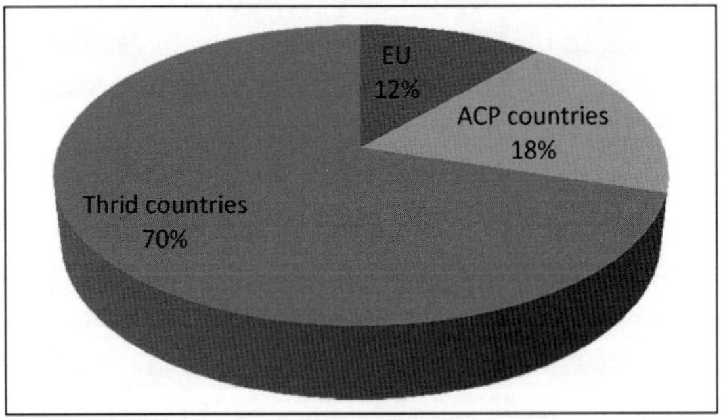

Source: European Commission 2015

International banana market has an oligopolistic nature. Only five multinational companies[4] play a major role in this sector which implies that these MNCs can enforce their will at most levels of the supply chain (Kacsirek 2010). But the influence of these companies has changed over the past decade: market shares of all five companies have declined between 2002 and 2013 (see Figure 3), nowadays other companies account for half of all exports (FAO 2014).

4 These companies are three US firms namely Del Monte, Chiquita and Dole, one European company, the Fyffes in Ireland, and the Noboa from Ecuador.

Figure 3. Market shares of selected companies in global banana export, by volume

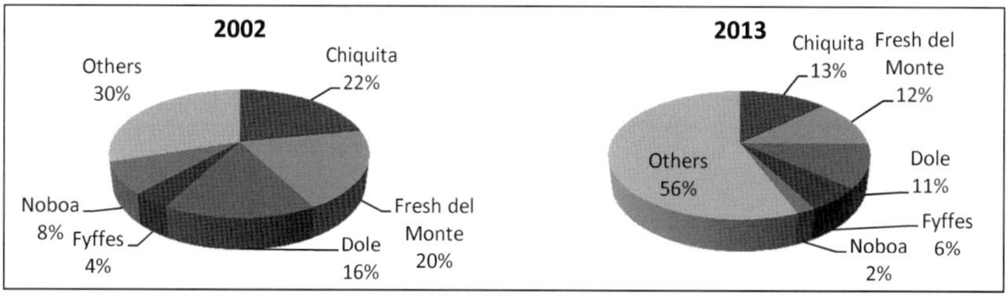

Source: FAO 2014, p. 1

These vertically integrated companies have played a major role in international banana trade, exerting significant market power especially on the purchasing side (FAO 2014). Due to their size and relative importance in the banana market, these companies have considerable power particularly in producer countries. This means that these MNCs can influence employment, tax policy, environmental regulations or wage policy in producer developing countries (Kacsirek 2010). One of the most important problems in connection with MNCs is that benefits of the banana sector are not generated in developing countries and in their companies but they are generated at multinational companies in developed countries (Kacsirek 2010).

2.2. Effects of the TTIP on developing countries and banana trade

The TTIP aims to primarily foster the European and US economies with reducing trade barriers but there is no doubt that the TTIP may affect not only the direct participants but also third countries including developing countries. These possible effects on developing countries could be positive or negative, on the one hand, and direct or indirect, on the other hand (Manrique Gil-Lerch 2015). Potential benefits and dangers are unclear and opinions are largely divided on possible effects of the TTIP in developing countries: while one group of these opinions – including the European Union – permanently emphasizes the advantages of the TTIP, others highlight a set of adverse effects of the TTIP for developing countries.

The implementation of the TTIP may have a significant effect expressly on trade with ACP countries – these effects depend on the existing levels of trade and the structure of trade between ACP members and the EU/US (Draper et al. 2014). In most cases, researchers mention trade diversion and preference erosion as negative impacts of the TTIP on developing countries including ACP members. Many opinions (e.g. Draper et al. 2014, Manrique Gil-Lerch 2015) claimed that mega trade deals such as the TTIP might endanger the current preferential access of developing countries to EU markets and cause trade diversion. Preference erosion takes place when two trading partners (EU and US) agree on lowering their tariffs (or abolishing their tariffs) between each other reducing the advantage that developing countries previously enjoyed through different trade preferences (Manrique Gil-Lerch 2015). In the case of trade diversion, lower import barriers replace imports from third countries, including developing countries, thus trade is diverted from a more efficient exporter towards a less efficient one, namely toward the EU or the US (Fair Politics 2015).

According to Draper et al. (2014), preference erosion would be relevant in both the EU and the US market in the case of low-income countries which export textiles, clothing or specific agricultural produce such as fish, bananas and sugar. Furthermore, as a result of trade diversion, some ACP countries must face significantly higher export competition in existing markets; it is particularly true where the structure of ACP members exports are similar to exports between the two parties of the TTIP, the EU and the US (Draper et al. 2014).

Contrary to what the critics say, others emphasize the advantages and a set of positive spill-over effects of the TTIP which can offset the negative effects of trade diversion and preference erosion. Among others, the European Union emphasizes the positive effects of the TTIP on developing countries. According to European Union, trade diversion from the TTIP should be relatively small for developing countries because these countries export different types of produce to the EU and US, so developing countries do not compete against either European or American producers. Furthermore, as a positive spill-over effect, reducing transatlantic regulatory divergences can improve market access for developing countries (EC 2015). Finally, EU studies found that low-income countries would gain from the TTIP thanks to increasing liberalization of transatlantic trade which results in an increase of GDP in the rest of the world, including developing countries (Draper et al. 2014).

Conclusions

As a conclusion, it can be stated that the banana sector has a crucial role in developing countries. For many developing countries the export of bananas is the sole export revenue. Furthermore, the role of MNCs should also be noted as they have a significant influence on banana exporting countries. Therefore, possible effects of the TTIP would be a crucial point in development policy. Nevertheless, the effects of the TTIP in developing countries are rather unclear and controversial. The TTIP may have both beneficial and harmful effects on third countries including developing countries or emerging economies. In the case of banana trade and

ACP countries, preference erosion seems to be the largest danger on both the EU and the US market. To achieve the goals of Policy Coherence for Development, the TTIP and its future effects should play a crucial role in the development policy of the EU. The EU should encourage making the TTIP development friendly because it seems that the TTIP may endanger interests of ACP countries primarily through preference erosion. Thus, the EU should pay special attention to their preferential trade agreements with ACP countries. However, the TTIP would also be beneficial for developing countries and it would be an effective and important tool for fostering economic development in less developed countries if the two parties , the EU and the US, paid enough attention to the interests of third countries. Finally, the TTIP should be a great tool for achieving developmental goals, because market access and trade liberalization would be a better route for developing countries than aid dependence.

References

Anania M., 2015, The role of trade policies, multinationals, shipping modes and product differentiation in global value chains for bananas. The case of Cameroon, International Conference of Agricultural Economists, Universitá Degli Studi Di Milano.

Dodo M. K., 2014, Multinational Companies in Global Banana Trade Policies, J Food Process Technol, 5: 351.

Draper P., S. Lacey, Y. Ramkolowan, 2014, Mega-Regional Trade Agreements: Implications for the African, Caribbean, and Pacific Countries, Occasional Paper, 2, European Centre for International Political Economy, Brussels.

EC, 2000, Partnership agreement between the members of the African, Caribbean and Pacific Group of States of the one part, and the European Community and its Member States, of the other part, signed in Cotonou on 23 June 2000, „Official Journal of the European Union", L 317.

EC, 2005, Policy Coherence for Development Accelerating progress towards attaining the Millennium Development Goals, COM(2005) 134 final, Brussels.

EC, 2006, The European Consensus on Development, „Official Journal of the European Union", C 46/1.

EC, 2011, Increasing the impact of EU Development Policy: an Agenda for Change, COM(2011) 637 final, Brussels.

EC, 2015, Policy Coherence for Development, SWD(2015) 159 final, Brussels.

European Commission, 2015, Banana supply in the EU, http://ec.europa.eu/agriculture/fruit-and-vegetables/product reports/bananas/statistics/supply_en.pdf.

Fair Politics, 2015, The Trans-Atlantic Trade and Investment Partnership. What about the impact on developing countries?, http://www.fairpolitics.eu/doc/TTIP%20case%20Fair%20Politics%20Update%20DEF.pdf.

FAO, 2014, The Changing Role of Multinational Companies in the Global Banana Trade, Market and Policy Analyses of Raw Materials, Horticulture and Tropical (RAMHOT) Products Team, Food and Agriculture Organization of the United Nations, Rome.

Hagemejer J., 2015, Liberalization of trade flows Under TTIP form a small country perspective. The case of Poland, Working Papers 17/2015 (165), University of Warsaw.

Kacsirek L., 2010, Az EU-USA-banánvita és ami mögötte van, "Fordulat", 3,8, pp. 106–136.

Manrique Gil M., M. Lerch, 2015, The TTIP's potential impact on developing countries: A review of existing literature and selected issues, In-Depth Analyses, Policy Department, Directorate-General for External Policies, European Parliament.

OECD, 2012, Policy framework for policy coherence for development, Working Paper, 1, OECD, Paris.

Persson M., F. Wilhelmsson, 2006, Assessing the effects of EU trade preferences for developing countries, Working Paper, 4, Lund University, Department of Economics.

Seshadri V.S., 2013, Transatlantic Trade and Investment Partnership, Discussion Paper, Research and Information System for Developing Countries, India.

Udvari B. 2013, Az Európai Unió nemzetközi fejlesztéspolitikája: a kereskedelem-politikai eszközök eredményessége, JATEPress, Szeged.

Elżbieta Czarny, Andżelika Kuźnar, Jerzy Menkes

Instead of conclusions

This book examines various aspects of the TTIP, so it is very difficult to construct a unified summary of them. Instead, since all of the authors have included a specific one in each of their analyses, we present a list of the main pros and cons of the TTIP.

PROS:

1. Cheaper American goods for EU consumers (and investment goods for producers). This is true especially in the case of manufactured goods (no tariffs, lower NTMs). In the longer run, perhaps EU goods will become cheaper as well as a result of tougher competition and increased efficiency. An additional source of efficiency would be the removal of redundant duplication of inspections by authorities from both sides.
2. The American market as an alternative source of energy and, more broadly, raw materials for the EU. This. The possibility to gain independence from Russian oil and gas exists. It is important economically and priceless politically. It is even more important since Russia, through Gazprom, to a great extent under state ownership, behaves like a price discriminating monopolist on the natural gas market.
3. A possible boom in Polish agriculture and in the production of intermediate goods. If the other EU members concentrate on the production of manufactured goods for the newly opened US market, Poland can win because of its complementary economic structure in relation to the other EU states (and complementary export structure).
4. Working out of RTA standards. This can be important for the future of regionalism as well as for WTO negotiations on the non-discriminatory liberalisation of economic cooperation.
5. One of the first effective reactions of the developed countries to the economic expansion of developing countries and an attempt to overcome the decline in political and economic position in the world.
6. A possible source of economic growth in Europe (through specialisation and, consequently, the creation of new jobs and regaining efficiency).
7. A potential to open some closed sectors in the US (services, government procurement).

8. The TTIP's role in education of society: negotiations made many people interested in economic cooperation. The public on both sides of the Atlantic has started to look for information and explanations of economic mechanisms. This may pay off in the future through more conscious voting and decision-making.

CONS:

1. Fear of Polish producers that EU members will replace Polish goods with American substitutes (this view is not only held by food and tobacco producers but also by firms in manufacturing industries).
2. Tougher competition for producers on both sides of the Atlantic expected (especially in the manufacture of goods). EU producers fear most that the Americans will win more often than the Europeans, forgetting that the TTIP is not a zero-sum game.
3. Expectations of more expensive energy imports to the EU from the US than from Russia (because of higher transportations costs and more complicated technology of transfer, such as LPG).
4. The use of RTAs as the institutionalisation of discriminatory liberalisation of economic cooperation regarded as the second-best solution after intensification of WTO non-discriminatory liberalisation.
5. The TTIP as a tool for the developed world against the development of the poorer countries. It can work against global stability and worsen the development opportunity for these countries.

Polish Studies in Economics

Edited by Ryszard Kokoszczyński

Volume 1 Wojciech Grabowski: Employee Stock Options, Payout Policy, and Stock Returns. Shareholders and Option Holders in Large U.S. Technology Corporations. 2012.

Volume 2 Jan Jakub Michałek / Michał Brzozowski / Andrzej Cieślik (eds.): The Relationship between Human Development, Exports and Foreign Direct Investments in Emerging Europe. 2013.

Volume 3 Tomasz Żylicz: The Economics of International Environmental Cooperation. 2015.

Volume 4 Juliusz Jabłecki / Ryszard Kokoszczynski / Paweł Sakowski / Robert Ślepaczuk / Piotr Wójcik: Volatility as an Asset Class. Obvious Benefits and Hidden Risks. 2015.

Volume 5 Janusz Kudła / Konrad Walczyk / Robert Kruszewski / Katarzyna Kopczewska / Agata Kocia: Modeling Fiscal Policy in the European Union. 2015.

Volume 6 Andrzej Cieślik / Jan Jakub Michałek (eds.): Liberalization of Transportation Services in the EU: the Polish Perspective. 2015.

Volume 7 Katarzyna Metelska-Szaniawska: Economic Effects of Post-Socialist Constitutions 25 Years from the Outset of Transition. The Constitutional Political Economy Approach. 2016.

Volume 8 Elżbieta Czarny / Andżelika Kuźnar / Jerzy Menkes (eds.): The Impact of the Transatlantic Trade and Investment Partnership on International Cooperation. 2017.

www.peterlang.com